P9-DFA-970

67-31541   (12-1-68)

THE WORLD OF PAT CHUNG

by

Patrick Wilkinson Chung

MERKLE PRESS INC.
WASHINGTON, D.C.

WINGATE COLLEGE LIBRARY
WINGATE, N. C.

DEDICATION

To My Wife

Beatrice May Chung

37532

Copyright © 1967
by
PATRICK WILKINSON CHUNG
Printed In U.S.A.
Library of Congress Catalog Card No. 67–31541

Printed by Merkle Press Inc.
810 Rhode Island Avenue N.E.
Washington, D.C. 20018

17 17

Table of Contents

I
CREDO

I AM NO LATINIST, and make no pretences of being one, and yet I feel that the Latin word "Credo" is the best available for heading this, the opening section, of my book. This is the first of many apparent anomalies which will be diffused among these pages.

I make no apologies. What has been granted to me in this life in the way of material and spiritual success has been granted because I have dared to be different, and to think and act differently when the occasion demanded.

But, this book is in no way an autobiography; it is, rather, an attempt to pay a debt of gratitude I owe to the human race. In my sixty years and more upon this earth I have travelled much, learned much, and in my way, thought much, and I feel the least I can do, now that I have reached retirement, is to transmit to those who will follow, some of the ideas I have formulated in my years of travail.

First let me introduce myself. My name (and this is in itself an apparent anomaly) is Patrick Wilkinson Chung. I am totally Chinese in heritage, a Jamaican by nationality, a capitalist by vocation, a sportsman by avocation.

I was born in British Guiana, in 1906. My grandparents emigrated to that unlikely spot from China, in 1850. They became Christians, and assumed the names of "Paul" and "Rose". A circumstance which explains my own rather startling combination of names.

They were poor but they were great. They reared me just as if I were their own son. Grandfather was the chief person of our Chinese community and I remember, as a youngster, that once a week, on Fridays, the Chinese immigrants in the neighbourhood would come from as far as thirty miles away and sit at grandfather's feet and listen to the wisdom that poured from his lips. They would come to him with their problems, with their hopes, their fears, their dreams. He would preside over these gatherings with wonderful dignity and compassion. No one challenged his authority or doubted his right to precedence in our community.

I adored my grandparents. I knew them much better than I knew my own parents and, frankly, felt much closer to them.

I might say that it is extremely difficult for a Chinese to prosper, or even to make ends meet, in the Occidental world. The language barrier is hideous. Europeans (with the exception of the Finns, Hungarians and Basques) who come to America can rely upon the relationships existing within the Indo-Germanic family of languages to establish a familiarity with English. With an Oriental (particularly one of humble birth, and we, like almost all Chinese immigrants, came from the most humble social strata of the Chinese social structure and had no advantages of formal education) there is no such accessible crutch to help him on his way to linguistic proficiency. Not only is the alphabet different, but the whole *concept* of language is different. To an untutored Chinese landing in an English speaking country, the language problem is similar to that which will face those astronauts who will land for the first time on another planet inhabited by intelligent beings. But, the astronauts will be trained and educated persons; the Chinese immigrants were not.

And, of course, in the early part of the 20th Century, there was, also, in most English speaking countries, a prejudice barrier. This was an artificial, but intensely human, complication which made progress doubly hard for a Chinese. I think it speaks highly of the capability and the tenacity of the Chinese that we have done as well as we have in those areas to which our forefathers emigrated. I am just as proud of my Chinese inheritance as any transplanted Irishman is of his. (It was not for nothing that I was named Patrick.)

But, I digress. Up until my early teens I lived in the cocoon of an impoverished but secure Chinese society. Then it all came to an end. My grandparents died and I was forced to make my own way in the world.

Fortunately, I had an uncle in business in a small way, and he had (or made) an opening for a young clerk. I worked as a clerk and went to school at nights, concentrating on English, mathematics and accountancy. Once one learns the Arabic figures, the language of arithmetic is universal, and we Chinese have an almost instinctive aptitude in this area. I applied myself with almost fanatical zeal.

The zeal paid dividends rather quickly. I found myself a succession of jobs in British Guiana, each one better than its predecessor: clerk, cashier, pay roll clerk, distribution clerk, inventory clerk, ration stores manager, and finally accountant.

By this time I was 24 years old. I decided to go into business for myself. I taught myself the life insurance business and became an underwriter, travelling through the Guianas and the West Indies. Eventually, I became agency manager, for Jamaica, for the Crown Life Insurance Company and the North American Life Insurance Company, both of Toronto, Canada. I moved to Kingston, the capital of Jamaica. For two terms, beginning in 1940, I served as President of the Crown Life Insurance Company (Underwriters), the first Jamaican, and indeed, the first person who was not from the United States or Canada, to serve in that capacity. This gave me, and still gives me, enormous satisfaction. I think it is understandable, and allowable, for a man who started life under such difficulties, to take pride in the fact that, while still in his mid-thirties, he was granted the acknowledgment of leadership by his colleagues in a difficult and highly-exacting profession.

To round off the story swiftly (since this, as I have said, is not an autobiography) I entered the real estate development business in Jamaica in 1945, dealing in everything from residences

3

and office buildings to entire townships. I expanded into cocoa, sugar, citrus, coconuts and cattle. And, more for pleasure than for profit, into the fascinating enterprise of breeding thoroughbred horses. At the latest count, I have 150 horses in my stables and derive more pleasure from them than I do from all my other interests. I feel an instinctive kinship with horse-lovers (and horse-players!) the world over, and I find our brotherhood warm, entertaining, varied and, above all, full of surprises.

To complete the background, I am married, most happily, to the former Beatrice May Chin and have seven sons and three daughters, of whom I am inordinately fond. And, finally, I am a Protestant but, as will become apparent in these pages, a somewhat different type of Protestant.

This, you may say, is all very well, but why write a book?

It's a good question and I hope I have a good answer.

In my travels, and through my experience with peoples of many lands, many colours, many backgrounds, have been almost obsessed by the idea that human beings are almost entirely preoccupied with learning all the things that do not matter.

"What a piece of work is a man", says Hamlet. And, indeed, he has done wondrous things. He has learned to weigh the sun, and measure the moon, and predict with certainty what time high tide will occur on the beaches of San Francisco 10,000 years from now,—and how to teach a flea to dance. But he has obstinately refused to learn the lessons which will prolong his reign on earth and, presumably, will provide for him a better life in the world to come. He would rather die, it seems, than learn the relative unimportance of the colour of his brother's skin, or the shape of his nose, or the way he pronounces his vowels. He has forgotten how to perform the miracle of love. And yet, only when and if he does re-learn the art of that miracle, in its fullest sense, will the divine curse be lifted from the barren tree. The alternative to this education is an incinerated death. We were not put upon this earth to perpetrate a nullity. Man has, in short, done very little to insure that there will *be* 10,000 more years of life on earth.

4

My thesis, simply stated, is that there is something good in every man, and, therefore, in every race and every culture and every civilization, and every religious and political system. We are all inclined to be absolutists when we consider those who differ from ourselves. Each country not only believes its own particular kind of Government is the best, but that all other types of government are wrong and dangerous. The first conclusion is allowable, the second is disastrous.

The same goes for religion. Millions of human beings have died in the most painful manner in defense of beliefs they barely understood. Who, except the professionals, know about the Albigensian heresy, the Lollards, Arianism, the doctrine of Transubstantiation, Jansenism? Who really understood them when they were (quite literally) burning issues? Not, certainly, the infantry soldiers in the front lines who were being eviscerated by other ignorant men who knew as little about these mysteries as their victims. Not, certainly, the peasants and merchants whose homes were razed and whose daughters were ravaged for the greater glory of a Christ who was crucified for the love of humankind!

Over the centuries men have been tortured, mutilated, burned and flayed by the millions just because their ideas of religious salvation differed slightly from that of their oppressors. Worse still, most of them suffered because the religious beliefs of their *masters* differed from those of the masters of the soldiers who overcame them.

It seems ridiculous to us now that men should have been subjected to fire and dungeon and sword for comparatively piddling theological differences and have so bull-headedly sought to "prove their doctrine orthodox by apostolic blows and knocks."

Even the names of the principal heresies have a pompous and almost ridiculous sound to them: Monothelites, Nestorians, Bogomils, Cathars, Waldenses, and so forth. It never occurred to anyone in authority, until well into the 18th Century, that human beings could work out their own salvation in their own way according to their own ideas, and should be permitted to do so.

In fact, in some countries of the world it *still* has not occurred to those in authority. The words of Jesus Christ, "in my father's house there are many mansions", seem to have no meaning at all.

In our so-called enlightened society of the 20th Century we scoff at the idea of men fighting to the death over theological abstractions. But, was it any worse then than it is today when we obliterate people in wholesale lots because of *political* abstractions? Have we not substituted the State for God and made a kind of synthetic patriotism our religion? Mankind has merely shifted the direction of his compulsive, almost manic intolerance.

Men used to slaughter other men over the question of how many angels could reasonably stand upon the head of a pin. Today we slaughter other men over the question of how many nations should be represented in the United Nations, or how many, and which, nations should be permitted to enrich themselves at the expense of populations which we are pleased to call backward.

Civilization and learning are wonderful. They have turned the world topsy-turvy. In the days of Prester John and Genghis Khan, the "civilized" nations dreaded the brutality of the "savage" hordes. After six hundred years of progress, the savages live in dread of the brutality of the "civilized" people.

The tragic difference is that the weapons of today are universal. There is no such thing as a small war. There is no such thing as a distant country. A border incident between Israel and Syria can start men marching five thousand miles away, and start missiles flying towards areas far removed from the seat of the original problem. A bomber strikes the wrong target in Viet Nam, and Albanian mobs demand that the Peiping Government explode an atomic device on Washington. A sentry in Korea shoots another sentry stationed on the other side of a disputed border and nervous fingers over the world start itching to press the button that will reduce the earth to a meaningless heap of cinders.

6

The prototype of modern man is not Adam and it is not Jesus, it is Samson, blindly stretching out his arms for the pillars, seeking to bring down the roof that will destroy not only his enemies but himself.

All this sounds enormously depressing and, of course, it is. But it isn't necessarily fatal. Not necessarily. I happen to be an optimist. Indeed, considering the conditions of my birth and the odds against my survival, let alone the chances of my making anything whatever of myself, I had to be an optimist to keep going at all. But, I am not an unreasonable optimist. I believe mankind has a chance—an outside chance, perhaps, but still a chance—to survive its own perverse inventiveness.

I feel a moral compulsion to set my reasons for this belief down for others to read. I do not in the least claim that I have all the answers, or even all the questions. But, perhaps out of my own ideas and experience a grain of ultimate truth can be gleaned, and perhaps that grain of truth, added to others produced by men more learned than I can be developed into a storehouse of common sense, and common sense is what eventually will save us from dissolution—common sense gathered from many sources and universally applied.

No one in his right mind would call me a learned man. My formal education was earnest but sporadic. I believe I have improved on it since my youth. But I have found that learned men are inclined to write and talk only for other learned men. They are rarely understood, or even heeded, by the masses of the unlearned. But the unlearned are the dominant majority. If one can reach and instruct and convince the unlearned of every land, then one reaches to the heart of the problem. It is therefore to the unlearned that I write—in my own way and in my own style—in the hope that I can reach their hearts, and their minds, and their understanding.

To put it crassly and directly: God knows I have sold enough insurance in my time, and enough real estate, and enough of other things; now I feel the time has come for me to try to sell more intangible and more important commodities, such as hu-

7

man love and understanding and common sense, and, perhaps, an idea or two.

I believe, in short, that men have concentrated for too many centuries on their differences, and not on their similarities. I believe that men have gloried in the real or supposed deficiencies of their brethren rather than in their manifest and manifold virtues. Like the Pharisee in the temple, they have thanked God that they were not like other men, instead of seeking a brotherhood with those who were superficially different from themselves.

I also believe that the still continuing religious prejudices which are expressed more politely these days than they were in previous times, are as frivolous as they are dangerous.

What in hell (and I use the word advisedly) does it matter whether a man believes true baptism consists of total submersion, semi-submersion or a symbolic sprinkle? Can any reasonable person believe that an innocent babe is forever condemned because his parents thought it necessary only to submit certain parts of his anatomy to cold water, rather than all his anatomy?

The Catholics have become vastly more ecumenical since that great and good man, Pope John, dragged them into the twentieth century, and yet they still cling to at least a superficial belief in indulgences, which conjures up a picture of God, to non-Catholics, as the great big C.P.A. in the sky, totting up ridiculous quarantines on a celestial computer.

The Protestants who look down their noses at the Catholics, have just as little (and just as much) upon which to congratulate themselves. The Episcopalians, worthy as they are, cannot really deny that their religion came into being because of the glandular disorder of an English King. The Methodists and Baptists came into being because of fundamental intolerances which would have caused Christ to retch with disgust.

For the greater love of Jesus, Cromwell slaughtered the women and children of Drogheda so the blood ran down the streets ankle-deep, and the Catholics of France, in the same blessed name, perpetrated such horrors on St. Bartholomew's

8

Day in 1572, that the nostrils of civilized men still twitch at the memory.

One of the blandest lies of all concerns the Puritans who, it is repeatedly and solemnly said, came to America in search of religious liberty. They did nothing of the sort. They were searching only for the liberty to persecute others according to their desires. And their desires were pretty insatiable.

Of course, everyone, in his time, has persecuted the Jews. They were an easily recognizable minority and an easy target for Christian (or Moslem or pagan) majorities to attack with impunity. But, sad to relate, the Jews, when they are in the majority, are not inculpable. The Arab States and their inhabitants have some reason to doubt that the Jews are immune to the curse of intolerance.

I was born into a religious sect called the Brethren. They are worthy people, no doubt, as the majority of the communicants or adherents of all religions are, for the most part, worthy, but their doctrine is so limited and so harsh upon those who do not believe exactly as they believe, that I feel that no intelligent man could subscribe *in toto* to their version of the road to salvation. Like many other sects they insist upon a literal acceptance of the Old Testament (which is, really, the least literal of all books). The odd thing is that so many fundamentalist sects quarrel about what the Bible actually means! The animosity between the Fundamentalist Baptists and the ordinary, workaday Baptists seems so much more virulent than does the old, traditional animosity between the Baptists and the Catholics.

I imagine that by this time I have managed to irritate everyone who has read this far in this book. I have done this purposely, in order to make people think a little beyond the artificial boundaries imposed upon them by their prejudices. The point is: it is all so silly! Why should it bother any man what any other man believes or thinks, as long as the other person doesn't try to forcibly impose his beliefs on others?

We hear from all sides today that Christianity has been a failure. I cannot for the life of me see how anyone can condemn

Christianity until a sufficient number of people have decided to *practise* it.

Certainly, if we look objectively at the number of human lives and the vast sums of money and effort that have been spent in the past 2,000 years to spread the influence of Christianity, we must admit that it has been, in a material way, a failure. After 2,000 years of trying and spending, most of the world's people are still pagans and have every intention of remaining so. Hundreds of millions of the world's population have never even heard of the Christian God, and hundreds of millions of others who have heard of Him, couldn't care less. Even in countries that are statistically Christian, such as those of Latin America, the ancient pagan rites and beliefs exist side-by-side with the superimposed Christian rites and beliefs. The natives may go to Mass on Sunday (at least, the female natives do), but they will stop along the way home to make an offering to the pagan gods of fertility, the harvest, or whatnot, just to make sure.

And if this lack of real conviction seems naive, let's take a look at ourselves. Many a man in our own society who attends Church regularly, takes up the collection and acts as a vestryman or a deacon, would not think of walking under a ladder, or of lighting three cigarettes on one match, or of embarking on a serious project without first consulting the astrology chart in his daily newspaper. We all have our own compromises with our atavistic gods, and each compromise represents, unconsciously, a degree of disbelief or unbelief in our professed religion.

After all, if we really, sincerely and thoroughly believed in the tenets of Christianity, we would all be out beating the bushes in our attempt to save souls. If we *really* believed in the indescribable joys of Paradise, we would account this world as worthless, and the goods thereof as dross. We would be willing to put up with any amount of suffering, hardship and ignominy—indeed we would welcome them—if we *really* believed that by enduring these things patiently we were creating for ourselves a permanent state of bliss in Paradise.

10

Really, we involve ourselves in the workaday, materialistic activities of the world in inverse proportion to our belief in the teachings of Jesus Christ, the founder of the religions which most of us claim to profess.

And, of course, if we all believed what we *say* we believe, there would be very little suffering on this earth. If we *really* believed in the Sermon on the Mount, and its Beatitudes, we would be making it our business to see that the naked were clothed, the hungry were fed, the sick were comforted, and so forth. We do nothing of the sort. We keep scurrying around storing up the good things of the earth and then salve our consciences by making occasional donations to charitable institutions which (it is piously believed) will perform the good works for us without subjecting us to the nasty necessity of doing the actual work ourselves.

This is indeed: "Charity, scrimped and iced; in the name of a cautious, statistical Christ."

And yet—and here is where the "Credo" comes in—the only hope for mankind is to adopt, far more seriously and more universally, the principles which Christ taught us.

Of course, the first step would be to convert the Christian Churches to Christianity. If the Christian Churches would spend the money they now dissipate on magnificent edifices, on vestments and sacred vessels, on propagandizing their specialized beliefs, and on competing with and fighting against other Christian Churches, on the conquest of disease, poverty and ignorance, they could cure most of the ills which are tearing the world asunder today.

If they taught real Christianity, then war would be an impossibility. If all the peoples of the world turned over to useful purposes all the money they now spend on making armaments and supporting massive military forces—*for just one year*—most of the human miseries of the world would be so substantially eliminated that this earth would indeed be an imitation of the Paradise to come.

11

This, of course, is too much to ask, but it is a consummation devoutly to be wished. But we must start somewhere, and in the succeeding pages I intend to examine certain other nations, (and other cultures and civilizations) with which I am intimately acquainted, and try to set forth, in my own untutored way, what I feel to be their weaknesses and strengths, morally, culturally, politically.

If we examine these strengths and weaknesses we may perhaps, in our own minds and hearts, develop a compassion for and an understanding of those who differ from ourselves. We may even learn enough to emulate what is desirable in others, and avoid what is undesirable.

I am particularly interested in reaching the hearts and the minds of the young. In the United States, and in other western nations (and even in Communist China) the young are asserting themselves and imposing themselves on the patterns of their cultures, much more than they have in the past. They are doing this in most cases through sheer force of greater numbers and through their own superior aggressiveness, as opposed to the accelerated weariness and defeatism of their elders. But the revolt of the young has been undisciplined and non-directed and can never accomplish good unless it *is* motivated by essential goodness.

As one example, many of our young radicals wear badges screaming: "Make Love, Not War"—an excellent idea, in many ways. But when they say "Make Love", they are talking about a very specialized and private (even selfish) type of "love" which, in this limited sense, is very little better in its effects than is war itself. But, if the meaning of "Make Love" were extended beyond the bed, the pad, the field or the back seat of an automobile, and made to include the whole wide world, and everyone in it—if *love* were given its original Christian meaning with all its connotations—if, in short, the slogan referred less to *eros* and more to *agape*, then this, indeed would be a movement to sweep the earth, and one that would deserve the constant and complete support of every thinking human being.

12

If *love* were to involve the heart and the mind, instead of merely the organs of production—if it were truly sentient instead of being merely sensual—then the movement would have universal meaning and every Pope, Patriarch, Bishop, clergyman and Christian worker in the world would be morally obliged to wear the slogan as a badge of honor, and as a profession of Christian faith.

My generation is finished. It has been a failure and most of us are so disillusioned and so weary of our own disillusionment, that we have become almost useless in the important business of arranging and settling the world's affairs. Our world is jaded and beyond recuperative power. But the young—that is different. It is their fate to shape the world of the future and they can, perhaps, be guided somewhat in this endeavour by studying the pitfalls as well as the achievements of their elders, the vices as well as the virtues.

And, since youth seems today to be so pragmatic, they will perhaps have the courage and the objectivity to examine what is good and what is bad in each culture, and choose wisely among them—disregarding the labels that our generation has placed upon them (such as: "Communist", "Socialist", "Democratic", "Christian", "Oriental", "Occidental", and so forth.)

And perhaps the power of youth will be so great and so intelligent that their wishes will make it necessary for such a body as the United Nations to take heed and set up powerful guidelines for the future governance of the nations of the world so that all men everywhere can live in harmony and love.

I know this sounds grandiose. I suppose it is. But something very like this must be attempted and achieved if we are to survive and prosper as a race. A start must be made somewhere and, in my own particular way, I am trying in this book to make such a start.

13

WINGATE COLLEGE LIBRARY
WINGATE, N. C.

II
CHINA

We are all inclined to think of other peoples and other races in stereotypical terms. This is obviously absurd, but it is convenient. It relieves most of us of the trouble of using our brains at all whenever we indulge in human relationships.

It is convenient, but it is also dangerous. It has hardened our personal prejudices into national and international attitudes, which, in turn, have made mutual understanding much harder than it should be.

Mention "China" to the average Occidental and he instinctively dredges up in his mind some cliché like "mysterious East". When he thinks of the Chinese as individuals at all, he usually conjures up a picture of some impossibly elegant and impossibly sinister character like Fu Manchu, or he thinks in terms of comic Chinese laundrymen, or of hopelessly deprayed opium addicts.

This last stereotype is particularly irritating. After all, it was the rugged, honest, upstanding, brave, Protestant English (another stereotype) who forced the importation of opium on China through two brutal wars, in 1840 and 1855. The Chinese fought against the intrusion of the international drug merchants, by law, by moral strictures, and by force of arms, for almost 60 years before being forced to succumb to the persuasion of the Christians of the western world! The average Chinese is no more "mysterious" or "inscrutable" than is the average Californian. (Perhaps less so.) He is simply different. If one were to throw a net over an indiscriminate gathering of Chinese one would catch just about the same percentage of scholars and morons, scamps and saints, strong characters and weak characters, as one would if he cast his net at Picadilly Circus.

I have no idea whether it was good for the West to force the opening of China in the past century, or whether it would have been wiser to let China develop on her own and then seek out the rest of the world. Historians of the future can quarrel over this. But the West has the problem now of living with a hostile China which is growing stronger year by year. We cannot solve the problem by ignoring it. We must realize that its solution is the major task of the twentieth century, or the twenty-first century, if there is going to be such a century.

In this troubled world far more important than trying to reach the moon is to try to reach the minds of those who hate you.

At the moment, the West knows very little of what is going on in China. We know only the surface opinions. In a way it is as if some sea-monsters were engaged in a death struggle in the depths of the Philippine Trench. We see the bubbles rise to the surface, and we observe the waves, but we don't really know what is going on beneath the surface. And too few people in the West really care.

Yet, we must care. China has the bomb, and in ten years she will have more bombs. She must be taught, somehow, that she is the principal cause of the world's disorder and that this is unnecessary, since the opportunity is there for her to live in brotherhood with the rest of the world, if she so desires.

Naturally, we cannot teach her such things by ignoring her, keeping her in quarantine, refusing to recognize her or trade with her, and not permitting her to join with us in our international deliberations.

The most tragic error we could make would be to underestimate the potential for development in China. (This springs from the old comic laundryman syndrome.) Everything the West has done, China can do. Obviously the culture that invented gunpowder (for ceremonial reasons, however; it took the western world to pervert the invention), who gave us the 365-day calen-

16

dar, the art of printing, the art of making pottery and a million other benefactions which we take for granted, cannot safely or sensibly be underestimated as hopelessly backward or primitive.

We made the mistake of underrating the potential of Soviet Russia, until Sputnik I shocked us out of our complacency. All we need do to shed our complacency about Red China is to consider how swiftly she has learned and adapted our technology since the end of World War II. She has leaped from the oxcart to the cyclotron in just twenty years. Where her next leap will lead is, of course, the question of our time. It is incumbent upon the West to participate, as much as possible, in the determination of the direction which the leap will take. We cannot do this by remaining aloof.

The land mass of China is approximately four million square miles, or about one-fifteenth of the land area of the entire world. I refer to what is now known as "Red China". The Republic of China (as opposed to the People's Republic of China) is located on Taiwan (formerly Formosa), an island of only 13,885 square miles. The population of Red China is 735,000,000, or almost one quarter of the population of the entire world. (The population on Taiwan is about 13 million.)

These are formidable statistics. It is obvious that the west cannot continue to ignore a land or a people who take up so much of the world's area and represent such a large percentage of the world's population.

China was a national entity long before the recorded history of most other nations began, and she has every intention of remaining one forever. She is, in short, here to stay. She will not disappear just because we choose to ignore her.

The history of China is almost incredibly confusing and includes innumerable periods of almost unimaginable brutality and cruelty. The Chinese have a saying, intended as a curse, which, roughly translated, is: "May you live in interesting times!". When times are interesting in China the people suffer. In her long history she has endured every conceivable kind of rule: imperialism, feudalism, anarchy, communism and democ-

17

racy. She has suffered from tyrants and prospered under benign rulers. She has been ravaged by invading hordes and she, herself, has invaded her neighbours with equal brutality. But, through it all, the people have endured, and multiplied, and, at times, even flourished.

Perhaps the key to her endurance has been her philosophy which was organized by that remarkable genius, Confucius, who lived five hundred years before the Christian era. Confucius has had a profound effect on the thought of the Chinese *literati* for almost 2,500 years and, to this day, there are hundreds of thousands of educated Chinese, in and out of China, who can repeat every word in his classical books. In the simplest possible terms, Confucius insisted that good relations must be maintained between sovereign and minister, among brothers, between father and sons, between wife and husband, and among friends. Just before he died, (478 B.C.) he said: "The great mountain must crumble, the strong beam must break, the wise man must wither away like a plant." The Chinese people, who have endured so much and survived so much have traditionally taken strength from the knowledge that, no matter how bad affairs may be at the moment, these things, too, will pass away. It is, if you will, a cold comfort, but it is something to which a desperate man, and a desperate people, can cling.

The beginnings of Chinese history, of course, are hidden in myth and conjecture. Certainly there is archeological evidence that a superior and orderly culture existed in China 5,000 years before the Christian era.

Hereditary kingship was introduced by the Hsia Dynasty, to which are ascribed the doubtful dates of 2205 to 1766 B.C. This was the period in which Stonehenge was being built by a Druidical culture in England, when the Sumerian civilization was at its height in West Asia, when definable civilizations were coming into their own in the Indus Valley. It is noteworthy that the Hsia dynasty ended through the overthrow of an intolerable tyrant, Chieh Kuei. It was succeeded by the Shang (or Yin) Dynasty, which lasted until 1122 B.C.

The significant point of the overthrow of the Hsia dynasty is that the contemporary chronicles state that it came as the result of "popular demand". The leader of the revolt, in a proclamation to his soldiers, said:" Heaven sees and hears through the eyes and ears of the people." This was a remarkable statement for a war lord to make at that particular juncture in history, since there is very little evidence that any ruler, in China or elsewhere, cared anything at all about what the ordinary people heard, saw or thought. It has been cited as an example of democratic thought in China at that time. This is perhaps rating it too highly, but it was an extraordinary admission for its time of the potential power of the people, and the strength of its massed opinion.

Ironically, the Yin Dynasty was overthrown because of the misdeeds of another tyrant, Chou Hsin, who was dominated by a depraved concubine named Ta Chi. (This was not to be the last time that the combination of a weak emperor and a strong concubine brought desolation to the people of China.)

The Chou Dynasty, which followed, was the longest-lived dynasty in China's history, lasting almost 900 years, until 249 B.C.

The dynasty is so-called because its leaders came from the principality of Chou, on the western frontier of China. Its leaders may have, originally, been foreigners, but when they came to power, they were known for their learning and their beneficence. Before the successful uprising against the Yin, one of the rulers of Chou, Wen Wang, was imprisoned for protesting against the cruelties of the Emperor Chou and while incarcerated, wrote the *I Ching* (or *"Canon of Changes"*) which was eventually incorporated into the Confucian Canon and has had a profound influence on subsequent Chinese thought. His son, Wu Wang, effected the coalition of princes which led to the overthrow of the ruling despotism.

The nine hundred years of the Chou Dynasty saw many important developments, including the vast expansion of the empire, to the Yangtze River in the South and to the eastern borders of the Szechwan. The peoples who were conquered by the armies of the empire, apparently were assimilated into the Chinese cultural pattern.

However, the rulers of the Chou dynasty, after the death of the founders, were far from outstanding. They were much more interested in fostering Chinese culture than they were in fostering the national aims of the empire. This created a power vacuum into which the feudal lords moved. China was eventually broken up, to all intents and purposes into warring semi-independent States which paid scant attention to the ruling authority. This brought about a condition similar to the later feudalism of Europe.

It was during the Chou dynasty that the famous Chinese philosophers flourished, notably Confucius, Lao Tzu and "Mencius" (the latter being the Latinized version of Mang-tsze). The philosophies developed during these years were humanist, emphasizing ethical relationships and the dignity of man. ("Mencius", for example, set down as the essentials of good government, care for the welfare of all the people, a light system of taxation, the performance of such public improvements as drainage and irrigation; liberty of commerce and total accessibility to education. He even advocated abolition of all game laws, so the people could eat decently. "Benevolence," he said, "is the path of duty." And again: "When one by force subdues men, they do not submit to him in the heart. When he subdues them by virtue, in their heart's core they are pleased, and sincerely submit.")

It can truthfully be said that during the latter years of the Chou Dynasty, the Chinese thinkers anticipated almost every generally accepted type of philosophy, political and otherwise, which we have experienced in the western world in the twentieth century. Lao Tzu, the founder of the Taoist school, for example, had very much in common with twentieth-century Gandhi in his insistence on non-violence and passive resistance to tyranny.

Certainly, despite constant internecine strife within China, civilization developed in many interesting and essential ways, during the Chou Dynasty. The idea of a standard of weights, measures and currency came about. The "Nine Chapter Legal

Code" was at least as impressive as the code which Solon produced in Greece. Architecture developed to an astounding degree. And, of course, the arts of sculpture, painting and ceramics grew, in their own way, to a point just about equal to that at which the arts of Classical Greece arrived.

Of course, there is no need to extol the cultural contribution China has made to itself and to the rest of the world. But, at this time, there was also the talent for assimilation. (The Chinese still retain this ability, as witness their amazing ability to grasp and adapt the mysteries of western technology.) The Chinese, in the years before the Christian era, found their way to Persia, and, through the Persians, established contact with the Roman world. This also led to a tremendous influence running in the opposite direction; the best of Persian and Indian art had a profound effect upon the art of China. (The famous stone carvings at Tunkang and at Lungmen, in Honana, attest to this influence at its best.) And, of course, one of the principal "imports" of this period was Buddhism, which was introduced into China by missionaries about two centuries before the beginning of what the western world calls the "Christian" era.

But, for the modern world the greatest lesson to be learned from the China of this era is the enormous durability and productivity of the people. The Chinese, heaven knows, have always had a talent for reproduction! They have always been numerous and, as a race, and as labourers, they have been more than usually productive, without receiving the ordinary recompenses for their labour which were common even by the brutal standards of the western world. The Great Wall of China, for instance, was built entirely by hand, and so was the even more remarkable Grand Canal, which opened up commerce effectively from north to south through the empire. Both these achievements (like the building of the pyramids in Egypt or, on a minor scale, the erection of Stonehenge in England) seem impossible to modern man, accustomed as he is to reliance on sophisticated tools for his earth-moving endeavours. (The Chinese brought this same talent to the United States in the 19th Century, when the time came to build the transcontinental railroad from the West Coast across the Sierra Nevada and Rocky Mountain ranges. They performed prodigious feats of road building during World War II, and are still capable of such feats today.)

The last 250 years of the Chou Dynasty were so marked by internal strife that the period has been called the time of the Warring States. Order was finally restored, about 249 B.C. by the rulers of the province of Ch'in, on the northwest border. They had a strong infusion of non-Chinese blood and were possessed of a genius for organization, and for rule. The Ch'in ruler who ascended the throne in 246 B.C., Shih Huang Ti, was indeed the "first emperor" of China, in the modern sense. He abolished the old, unwieldy system of government by hereditary, autonomous princes, and divided China into 36 provinces, over which he set officials who were appointed by himself and who were responsible only to himself. He established a uniform set of laws, and of weights and measures. He completed and strengthened the Great Wall, and greatly extended the borders of his empire by making massive forays against the barbarians.

But, with all his virtues, Shih Huang Ti was a totalitarian whose actions parallel peculiarly the aims and activities of the present day "Red Guard" of Communist Mao Tse Tung. He ordered all the old books to be burned so the people would forget the past and concentrate on the present and the future. He forbade the scholars even to discuss the past and ordered numerous executions just to make his point clear. The only books he exempted were those that dealt with agriculture, pharmacy, medicine and fortune telling.

Although innumerable and priceless treasures were destroyed by the flames, the Chinese *literati* courageously hid their books when and where they could and preserved a surprising amount of the old culture.

Like so many strong rulers, Ch'in Shih Huang Ti left a vacuum behind him when he died, in 210 B.C. His successor was a weakling and was murdered soon after he assumed the throne. War lords started fighting for imperial power and, at last, Liu

Pang, in 202 B.C. emerged as the victor and established the Han Dynasty.

The new Emperor built on the structure erected by Ch'in Shih Huang Ti, and bettered it. He encouraged and developed the idea of a national Civil Service, based on merit, and regulated by examination.

Although Liu Pang did not rescind the order of Ch'in Shih Huang Ti against the old books, his successor did, and the manuscripts which had escaped the flames were brought out of hiding.

Although the Han Dynasty was not as remarkable for the development of philosophical thought as the Chou Dynasty had been, many remarkable achievements in the arts came about during the 422 years of its ascendancy. Poetry was revived, and literature and religion both were greatly expanded by the constant contact with the outer world. (Those countries which the Han did not conquer, they allied themselves with through the exchange of Ambassadors.) It was during this period that paper was invented (circa 150 A.D.) and, with it, a vast increase in the development of literature.

During the period of the Ch'in and the Han, China for the first time became a truly great State, dominant in the East and spreading its influence throughout much of the world.

The Han line degenerated in the latter years of the dynasty and by 220 A.D. it was finished. There followed a period of disunity which lasted for almost four centuries. China was broken up into three kingdoms and was plagued by almost constant warfare, both domestic and imported.

The Tatars, the Hsiung Nu and the Tibetans all invaded China. Each brought something of their own culture, and each, in turn, became totally assimilated into the Chinese whole. It was during this period that the foreign cult of Buddhism became dominant in China. The invaders brought the religion with them and the adherents of Confucianism were no longer strong enough to resist, as they had been under the Han.

Once again China proved her vitality and out of the chaos a

new order arose in the Sui Dynasty (589-618 A.D.) and, particularly, the Dynasty of the T'ang (618-907 A.D.) During this latter period China once again became the strongest and largest empire on earth. Its governmental bureaucracy was extraordinarily efficient and incorruptible, for its time.

China attracted thinkers, explorers and evangelists from all over the eastern world, even representatives of certain "heretical" sects of the Eastern Christian Church, such as the Nestorians. The Manichaeans, an ascetic cult with Babylonian and Zoroastrian overtones (and with an idealism very like that of the early Christians) also had a significant effect on Chinese thought at this, and subsequent, periods.

Certainly during the T'ang years there was more freedom of thought, religion and person than China had ever known previously. Occasionally during this period there was almost a foreshadowing of democracy in some areas of China, so much were talented representatives of the common people permitted to emerge and participate in the governance of the land.

But, like all dynasties, the T'ang petered out. As the quality of the emperors declined, the power of the palace eunuchs increased, and rebellions and invasions multiplied.

Eventually the Sung Dynasty emerged to rule, from 960 to 1280 A.D., but their rule was disastrous to China. An ill-advised attempt to conquer the K'itan Tatars, who ruled the Liaotung peninsula, brought about vigorous reprisals. The reprisals proved so successful that further invasions were invited, and in the early part of the 13th century the great and ruthless general, Genghis Khan (Temuchin) led his Mongol hordes into the troubled land and eventually possessed all the territory north of the Yellow River. After the death of Genghis (1227) an attempt was made to create peace between the Mongols and the Sung but the alliance fell through and the Mongols eventually seized the rest of China.

In 1280 the last of the Sung emperors cast himself into the sea and Khublai Khan (immortalized in Coleridge's famous fragmentary poem) became the first Mongol emperor of China.

24

Despite the weakness of the Sung, notable cultural advances were made during their 320 years of ascendancy. Painting (due to the strong Buddhist influences) enjoyed its greatest period. Philosophical schools flourished and literature and history experienced a golden age.

The era also saw one of the boldest political experiments in the first Christian millennium. Wang An-shih, who served as Prime Minister of China for 18 years in the eleventh century, may well have been the world's first practising Socialist. He sought to make the State responsible for providing the masses with the opportunity of earning and providing for the necessities of life. At his direction the State took over the management of agriculture, commerce and industry, regulated wages and prices, distributed seed. He even arranged for State-supported loans at small interest for farmers and shifted the burden of taxation onto the shoulders of the rich. In many ways he would have been perfectly at home in the New Deal administration of United States President Franklin Delano Roosevelt. He was eventually driven out of office by the nobles and the old patterns of oppression were restored.

The Mongol rule, officially called the Yuan Dynasty, lasted only until 1368, but it had its periods of great brilliance, particularly under Khublai Khan. From his capital (Khanbaliq, on the present site of Peiping) he ruled not only over China, but the Mongol empire as well, his domain stretching as far as Mesopotamia and Eastern Europe.

Under the Mongols, China became cosmopolitan to an unprecedented degree. European missionaries (notably the Franciscans) brought Christianity to the western fringes of the Empire. One Franciscan, John of Montecorvino, made his way to the capital city itself and stayed there thirty years, building up a Christian community of several thousand communicants. He was made a Bishop, and his progress was considered so significant that the Pope sent to China a diplomatic envoy, John of Marignolli.

25

The missionaries were able to penetrate into China because of the brilliant aggressiveness of the Venetian merchants, Nicolo and Maffeo Polo, and Nicolo's son, Marco. In search of commerce, the Polos found their way (about 1260) to the court of Khublai Khan. They were the first Europeans the Khan had ever seen, and he was delighted with them. Khublai sent them back to the Pope (Clement IV) with a request that a corps of educated men be sent to him to instruct his people in Christianity, and the liberal arts.

Unfortunately, Pope Clement IV died before the mission could be accomplished and an interregnum of more than two years before the accession of Gregory X caused this magnificent opportunity to be lost. This episode did pave the way for subsequent missionaries, however, and the Polos grew rich in China. Marco entered the service of Khublai and rose rapidly in esteem and honor. The Polos remained in China until 1295, and returned to Europe despite the protest of the great Khan.

No other Mongol ruler approached the genius of Khublai, and the Yuan regime gradually withered and collapsed. When a former Buddhist monk, Chu Yuan-chang led a successful revolt in 1368 there was surprisingly little opposition to his movement. He founded the wholly-Chinese Ming dynasty, which lasted until 1644.

With the disintegration of Mongol rule an anti-foreign reaction set in and the Christian missionaries and the European merchants were suppressed. The trade routes disappeared and communication with the western world once again closed down.

The Ming Dynasty was not particularly notable for its brilliance, but it did unify China after the disruptions caused by the revolt against the Mongols.

In the earlier years of Ming Rule, the emperors were great builders and maintained a lively interest in the rest of the world. Many of the temples which make Peiping the magnificent capital it is were built, in the early 15th Century, by the third Ming emperor, Yung Lo. Expeditions were sent to Ceylon and Java. Korea was invaded and the Mongols were kept at bay.

As the Dynasty degenerated, however, the old routine of invasion and pillage was re-enacted. Japan seized Korea and Japanese pirates ravaged the coast. The governance of the land became oppressive and, for the first time, Chinese began to flee their own land and to institute their own colonies on foreign soils, particularly in what we now call the South Sea Islands. They exist to this day, and still maintain their distinctive Chinese quality.

During the Ming period the Europeans returned to China, with differing results. The Portuguese arrived in China about 1514 and established footholds in several ports. However, they behaved with such arrogance and cruelty that they were soon driven out or massacred. They did maintain a base at Macao and were permitted to remain there.

The Jesuits came also. St. Francis Xavier was the dominant spirit of the missionary attempt and did wonderful work until his death, on the island of Shang-chuan in 1552. However, his mission was continued and a very able man, Father Matthew Ricci, S.J., not only reached Peiping but became the head of the Government's bureau of astronomy and mathematics (1601). This was considerably less of a cultural exchange than Kublai Khan had envisaged three centuries previously, but it did bring to the Chinese people a knowledge of geography and of certain branches of mathematics, which was not previously available to them.

All dynasties deteriorate, and the Ming regime was no exception. It fell in 1644 before an invasion from Manchuria, from the northeast. The Ming did not capitulate without a bloody fight but, eventually they were subdued.

For the first 150 years the Manchu Dynasty provided excellent, if rather oppressive, rulers. Although they adopted Chinese culture, the Manchus ruled as foreign conquerors. They maintained garrisons throughout China and prohibited any Chinese from holding office in his native province, thus giving them an opportunity to shuffle the officials around so they could not become too powerful or too popular in any one area. They perpetuated Chinese law, nonetheless, and made accessible to eligible and qualified Chinese all the ladders to the top governmental positions.

During the first part of the Manchu dynasty, European interests in China, both religious and commercial, flourished. The Emperor K'ang Hsi, in 1692, issued an edict of religious tolerance, and the Catholic missionary fathers founded Christian communities in every province and built up a flock of approximately 300,000 communicants.

But, once again, the Church flubbed its opportunity. First of all, the Vatican issued an unnecessarily legalistic order concerning the attitude which Chinese Christians must take toward Confucius, and toward the traditional Chinese reverence toward their ancestors. This annoyed K'ang Hsi, since it proved that the foreign sect had no intention of being as tolerant toward Chinese beliefs as he had been toward theirs! (It must be remembered that the Chinese considered all other races inferior, and accepted them only on sufferance. Intolerance *toward* them was insupportable!) The imperial irritation was manifested by persecutions throughout China. Then the Pope (Clement XIII) dissolved the Society of Jesus. The Jesuits were far and away the most able and the most energetic of missionaries, and no one could effectively take their place. Finally, the French Revolution deprived the French orders working in China of support and this all but ended missionary activity there. The Christian community dwindled away.

During the two centuries in which they were most active the missionaries had a considerable effect upon China's religious and ethical thought. They served to acquaint the Chinese with European customs and European science. On the other hand, in their home countries, through their own writings, they were able to acquaint Europe with China to a degree that was otherwise impossible.

The merchants continued to do business in China but, as time wore on, the Manchus became more and more isolationist, and the conduct of commerce became all but impossible. It was forbidden to teach a foreigner the Chinese language. Business could be conducted only through a selected group of Chinese merchants. Tariff charges became prohibitive. Finally, by the close of the 18th century, Canton was the only port open to foreign commerce.

The misunderstanding between the two cultures was deep and wide. The Chinese refused to deal with Europeans as equals. The Europeans, accustomed to think of other peoples, especially these of darker skins, as inferior breeds without the law, were galled by this condescending and uncooperative attitude. China's isolationism from the outer world became almost absolute. She knew little of what was going on in Europe, and cared less. The Europeans could not find out what was going on in China. An artificial curtain of ignorance and darkness, for the first time, descended between the two worlds.

This program of isolation could not last. The Industrial Revolution forced the most powerful western countries to seek new markets and to find raw materials for their new factories. It was intolerable (in their eyes) to have a potential market covering more than 6 percent of the world's land surface, and including one-quarter of the world's population, shut off from them.

The British were marking time, doing the best they could in the restricted area of the only port accessible to them, Canton. When the Manchus decided to crack down on the illegal opium trade in 1839, seizing and destroying illicit stores of the noxious drug, hostilities broke out. After two wicked and shameless wars China was forced to capitulate. Through a series of treaties (1842-44, 1858-60), regulations for trade were developed, foreigners were permitted to travel in the interior, foreign merchant vessels were permitted on the Yangtze and several additional ports were opened to foreign commerce. Ironically, freedom to practise Christianity and freedom to import opium were also promised, in the same treaty. This would have amused Karl Marx (if he had any sense of humor, which he hadn't), since he had always claimed that religion was the opium of the masses.

29

In addition, the Chinese were made to pay indemnities! The British took Hongkong and the Kowloon promontory opposite. The Russians took territory south of the Amur and east of the Ussuri, a very long and useful coastline which now includes Vladivostok. The French and Americans gained their own concessions, though they were more modest in nature.

The treaties weakened Chinese sovereignty. They built up in official Chinese minds a hatred and distrust of the west, dragon's teeth which are being harvested to this day. The two Opium Wars of the middle nineteenth century marked the low point of morals in the international relationships between the West and the East in the nineteenth century, and their deleterious effects have been durable.

The loss of the Opium Wars created great dissatisfaction among the Chinese people with their Manchu rulers, and constant uprisings threatened the sovereignty of the royal house. Then, in 1900, a serious uprising by patriotic Chinese groups, called the "Boxers" (a jocular translation of "I Ho Ch'uan", or "Righteous Harmony Fists") broke out against the "foreign devils". The Boxer motto was "Protect the Country, destroy the foreigner" and they attacked with equal viciousness foreigners and Chinese Christians. Scores of western missionaries and thousands of Chinese Christians were slaughtered, often in a disgusting fashion. An international force from eight western powers put down the rebellion and China was disarmed, humiliated in many ways and forced to pay a huge indemnity to many European nations. Russia, which had occupied Manchuria, refused to withdraw, a circumstance which led to the Japanese-Russian War of 1904. When the Japanese surprised and alarmed the Western world by winning this conflict, they took control of Korea and rights and interests in South Manchuria, leaving North Manchuria in Russian hands. This led to subsequent difficulties between Russia and Japan.

All this, naturally, disillusioned the Chinese people with their rulers. When the wicked, but able, old Empress Dowager Tzu Hsi died in 1908, revolt was inevitable. In 1912 the Revolution began, the royal troops mutinied and, finally, the great Dr. Sun Yat Sen emerged as the leader of the Chinese Republic. A young general, Chiang Kai Shek also came into prominence in this successful revolution.

Unfortunately, history kept repeating itself. The fall of every dynasty in the past had created civil strife, with military chieftains fighting for ultimate power. This happened again when the Republic was formed.

Also, the new leaders of China, imbued with Western ideas, were inclined to experiment with the machinery of government too enthusiastically, causing considerable chaos and inefficiency, despite the idealism of Sun Yat Sen who wanted to create a State based on democracy and the well-being of all strata of society. And as the government showed its weakness, foreign influences began to cause great trouble. The Russian Communists, from 1922 on, made determined efforts to create in China the same kind of revolution they had managed in their own country. Japan, feeling she needed the markets and the resources of China to survive, began to exert considerable influence in Chinese affairs.

These two developments have had a profound and tragic effect on the subsequent history of China.

Chiang Kai Shek, a brave and able man, a fine soldier but a poor administrator (as so many soldiers are) became the leader of the Chinese nation. He over-reacted, as so many soldiers are likely to do, against the Communist incursion and attacked the Communists and their sympathizers with such brutality that he not only aroused the hostility of Russia, but also caused serious misgivings among humanitarians in the western world. Photographs of impromptu, curb-side beheadings as well as of even more barbaric tortures were circulated in America and elsewhere and turned not only many stomachs, but many minds, against the leaders of the new Republic. Chiang was ineffective in his attempts to stamp out Communism. The belief blossomed under persecution, much as the Christian belief, in older times, flourished not only in spite of, but because of the barbarous over-reaction of the Roman emperors. The mismanagement of the government in this crucial period split the nation badly and laid the groundwork for the dissolution that was to come.

The Japanese invasion, beginning with the Marco Polo Bridge incident in 1931, was inspired by the interior weakness of China.

The Chinese people fought bravely against Japan and, at times, they presented a united front. But their effort was constantly hindered by internecine struggles for power and the comparative primitiveness of the Chinese arms.

Japan was finally driven from the borders of China but more as a by-product of her involvement in World War II than for any other reason. The allies fought Japan wherever her soldiers were arrayed and, of course, this included occupied China.

Russia's role in the liberation of China has been scandalously exaggerated by Communist propaganda. She did not declare war on Japan until the day after the United States dropped the atomic bomb on Hiroshima and made further resistance by the Japanese nation demonstrably impossible. Furthermore, the United States, after the recapture of the Philippines by the great General Douglas A. MacArthur, sent 75 shiploads of armaments to Vladivostock for Russian use against Japan. The Japanese surrendered a few weeks after the armaments arrived and the armaments, ironically, were subsequently used to assist the Communists to drive Chiang Kai Shek and his adherents off the mainland into the Formosan exile.

It is not difficult to explain the Communist success in China after 1945. The people were exhausted, and so were the resources of the country. China had been at war since 1931, and the fighting had taken place at every level and among many factions. The widespread and pernicious corruption of the Chiang Kai Shek regime disgusted the ordinary people, particularly since the regime was capable of performing very little toward the alleviation of their sufferings.

The Russians are masters of propaganda. They helped the Chinese in driving the Japanese out of Kalgan and made great political capital out of their efforts. (While withholding the information, of course, that they were fighting with American weapons.)

It was during these years that the United States of America committed the greatest blunder in the history of her relations with foreign nations. She became disgusted with the corruption and the inefficiency of the Chiang administration. Certainly there was cause for dissatisfaction, but the Communist propagandists magnified the deficiencies of the leadership of the Republic out of all proportion. Also, a small but powerful element within the U.S. State Department became convinced that the Chinese communists were merely idealistic "agrarian reformers" and were therefore a progressive element in a backward country. As a result of this propaganda and its naive acceptance by the leaders of the United States, America withdrew her support from Chiang at the most crucial moment in China's history. This virtually assured the success of the Communist revolution.

As I say, this was the greatest blunder in America's history. Its effect on the Chinese people has been profound and lasting.

The Chinese had grown to regard the United States of America as a friend; certainly her best and least selfish friend in the West. She knew that the United States had no territorial aims in the Orient. She was deeply impressed that the United States, after the ugly business of the Boxer Rebellion, had used her indemnity funds to provide scholarships for Chinese students to attend colleges in the States. She had protected China against the aggression of more cynical nations and had imposed economic sanctions against Japan during the cold-blooded invasion of Manchuria. Thus, when America withdrew her support at this crucial time, millions of Chinese began to believe there was something incurably wrong with the Chiang Kai Shek government, and either accepted, or favored, the Communist side.

When the Chiang Kai Shek government was driven off the mainland, they took with them most of those Chinese who knew the long history of American idealism in China, and even these were somewhat embittered by U.S. defection at the time of their greatest need. The Communists, of course, made certain that the entire history of Chinese-American relations would be perverted in the minds of those who remained on the mainland. America was painted as the arch-villain of the world, the ruthless aggressor. A new generation of Chinese has been taught from birth to hate America with all their being and, as of now, there is no way to reach their minds and convince them otherwise. America's aloofness from Communist China only helps to encourage this dangerous condition.

Chiang was ineffectual and his government was corrupt and too weak to control the traditional internal struggling that has always plagued China, but his administration was infinitely better than that which dominates Red China today.

China is now a split nation and, if unification is to come at all, it can come only from the mainland. It cannot come from Taiwan.

The United Nations refuses to admit Red China within its precinct, while permitting the Nationalist Government of Taiwan to participate in its deliberations. This state of affairs has been brought about almost entirely because of the adamant position of the United States against admitting Red China.

I do not intend to argue the moral rights and wrongs of this position of intransigence.

I would like to point out, however, that by excluding 800 million human beings from the counsels of peace, we are doing nothing to help their ultimate conversion to some form of global co-operation. We are encouraging the Chinese to consider the entire non-Chinese world as their mortal enemy. We are forcing China back into the position of isolationism which caused such trouble to the world in the past.

I might also point out that the attitude of the United States is inconsistent. She is unalterably opposed to communism and every other form of totalitarianism, but she sits down at the conference table with Russia and all her satellite nations which are just as Communist as is Red China. She has no hesitation about dealing on friendly terms with countries that are dominated by totalitarian despotisms of the far right. She has even extended a substantial amount of financial and technical aid to countries that are communist as well as to nations that are essentially fascists.

Why draw the line at China, and at China only?

As I pointed out at the outset of this book, I am a capitalist by vocation, and politically I am on the conservative side. (I like to think of myself as being slightly to the right of centre, albeit I find the position hard to maintain because the location of "centre" seems to shift without warning from year to year. Sometimes, from month to month.)

Certainly, I am unalterably opposed to Communism and all it stands for. I find the communist philosophy repulsive and degrading. But, nonetheless, I believe it is essentially illogical and self-destructive to refuse to "recognize" a nation which includes about 25 percent of the total population of the world, and about 6 percent of the world's land mass. I believe that the only road to peace lies through reason and discussion, and that there is no hope for peace in a policy that shuts the door on reason and makes discussion impossible.

The west has misunderstood and underestimated China in the past. As I write these words, it is becoming more and more apparent that Russia has done the same thing. Russia made it possible for Communist China to survive, succeed and grow, not for any eleemosynary reasons, but because she planned for China to remain a subservient satellite which would present to the world a unified and irresistible Russian-dominated communist force across the entire eastern world.

It is obvious now that Mao Tse Tung and the other Chinese communist leaders have no intention of being subservient satellites at all. The tensions between Russia and China have grown so great that at this moment (Summer, 1967) a complete break in diplomatic relations seems inevitable and a war between the two greatest communist nations seems at least a possibility.

But once again, because of our lack of channels of information, we know very little of what is actually going on. As I have said, we are in the position of trying to judge the struggle between sea monsters thousands of feet below the surface of the ocean. We see the bubbles and the waves, but we know very little of what is actually occurring. And yet, we *must* find out what is actually occurring if we hope to preserve the peace of the world. There can be no cure unless we know the cause of the disease.

We of the west are still underestimating China, and we underestimate the accomplishments of the communist regime. Our journalists are inclined to tell us what we want to hear, and often this is not accurate. They emphasize the poverty and the starvation conditions of the Chinese. Certainly these exist, but they have existed in China for years, under many different types of government, and the condition of the ordinary peasant (if he is politically reliable) is certainly a little better today than it has ever been. They play up the ideological foolishness, the excesses, the mismanagement of certain aspects of the educational program, the distrust of scholars and *literati,* but they do not stress the fact that despite these administrative idiocies, education is far more universally applied and far more practical than it has ever been in China's history.

The Communist regime has made vast strides in the areas of agriculture and industrialization. The strides have exacted a terrible toll in human life and in human misery, but it would be unrealistic to deny that they *are* strides.

Perhaps, most significantly, they have changed the thinking of the Chinese people. Confucianism, while most commendable in many ways, did encourage the people in adopting a fatalistic philosophy of life. The theory of "why worry about death when one knows so little of life" has its virtues, particularly when it comes to keeping the lower classes docile, but it is impractical when applied to a nation bent upon progress and the development of human capabilities. The Chinese people, under the Communist atheism, no longer accept natural disasters as unavoidable and inescapable phenomena. They have learned to control floods, to irrigate parched lands, to provide, to a certain

36

degree, against crop failures. In ignoring (or worse still, seeking to destroy) the past, they have lost much. But by concentrating on the present and the future, they have gained much, too. Red China today is far from the Utopia that the Communists predicted, but in certain materialistic ways, it has shown more progress in the past twenty years than it had shown in the previous twenty centuries.

As I have said, I detest Communism and I abominate the cold blooded exploitation of human life which the Communist leaders of China have exhibited in their administration of the nation's affairs, but I am forced to salute them for having achieved certain results which the scornful west had deemed impossible.

And, if the Red Chinese leaders would only agree to join the family of nations (and if the family nations would be willing to receive them), who knows what wonders they could perform! If they would concentrate their very great capabilities on improving the state of humankind, rather than on destroying it! If only they could understand what madness it is to spend their money and talent on the development of dreadful nuclear devices rather than on the development of means for raising the standard of living of their people! Most of all, the leaders of Red China should be persuaded that it is insanity for them to seek to acquire and dominate more real estate when they cannot provide a decent way of life within the huge borders which they now rule!

There is no limit to what the Chinese people could perform for their own betterment and the betterment of the entire human race, if only they were encouraged and permitted to do so.

It is hard for us to credit, but the Chinese leadership actually believes that if they do not maintain a warlike, minatory stance their western "enemies" will support Chiang Kai Shek and conduct him under arms back to power on the mainland. And yet, if they were to abandon their hostility and be more conciliatory in their attitudes toward the west, their revolution would eventually be accepted as a *fait accompli* and the Nationalist Government on Taiwan would cease being even a potential threat to them. But, as long as the United Nations "recognizes" Nationalist China as the true representative of the entire Chinese people (which, in all frankness, it is not), and forbids Red China to put its feet under the same council table with the other nations of the world, the Chinese attitude will remain. And as long as Red China threatens the peace so belligerently, the rest of the world is going to think of the Chiang Kai Shek government as a possible alternative, if for no other reason, for considerations of self-defense. But, the fact remains, there is no way to reason with the Chinese leaders unless we find a way of communicating with them.

In arguing my point, I may seem to have down-graded Chiang Kai Shek somewhat. If so, it has been unintentional. He has proved to be a far greater peace-time leader on Taiwan than he ever was on the mainland. The Nationalist Government has performed miracles on the island in the areas of agriculture, industry and education. The Nationalist Chinese nation is small but it is probably more genuinely prosperous and progressive than any other segment of the Chinese nation has ever been. He has exhibited a talent and an enthusiasm for democracy that never before was apparent in his performance. Nationalist China is, by western standards, a modern State and a surprisingly successful one, despite its smallness and incapacity for growth.

Can a reconciliation between the two factions of China take place? Certainly not while Chiang and Mao still live. They are old and bitter adversaries and their antagonism is to the death. But they are old men. Death must one day soon conquer them both. What then?

There are those that say that Communism and democracy cannot exist together in nature. I feel this is extremist talk. On a smaller scale they exist together within the framework of many European nations. However, they do not exist together in any nation that is Communist *dominated* because the totalitarian mind, as of now, does not brook any opposition.

But who is to say that just because it has never worked before, it can never work in the future? The Chinese are a remarkably homogeneous people. They have assimilated their conquerors over the centuries. The Chinese on the mainland are the same basically as the Chinese on Taiwan (and the same, basically, as I, who am totally Chinese in heritage). If given the means of co-operating, there is no reason why they should not find ways to do so and eventually become a unified nation again. And failing this, there is no real reason why they should not work out a viable method of living side by side in amity, following differing philosophies of government, agreeing to disagree but not interfering with each other.

There is no international enmity that is irreconcilable. After the horror of World War II, Britain and Germany found a way toward friendship; so did Japan and the United States; Italy is a friend of everybody, and all prosper, in varying degrees. France, because of the peculiar personality of its leader, gets along better with its former enemies than it does with its natural allies. Even as I write these words, Maoist leaders in Red China are denouncing Soviet Russia and her "imperialist ally", the United States!

If I may call to the attention of an atheistic society a Biblical text, I would like to cite to the leaders of the People's Republic of China the admonition: "Where there is no vision, the people perish." China has suffered over the millennia from a lack of vision. She has always been introspective and complacent, refusing to acknowledge that younger cultures were worthy of her attention. All those who had intercourse with her were treated as vassal states, fit to bring tribute, but worthy of no other consideration. This tendency still exists among the leaders of Red China today. There is a national mental block against admitting that any other civilization has anything of value to offer her, except in the field of industrial development. (The attitude, of course, has been intensified by the refusal of the western world to have dealings with her.)

China does not realize, and does not wish to realize, that the other countries of the world have grown great because they *have* recognized the values in other cultures and have chosen and adopted what they thought was best for them. The United States of America, with its great assemblage of ethnic groups, is perhaps the outstanding example of this in the world but, right next door to China, Japan, ever since she was opened up to the world, has herself profited by opening up the world in return, to her own advantage.

It is said that shortly after the Russian Revolution, the American writer, Lincoln Steffens returned from Moscow and exclaimed, in exultation, "I have seen the future, and it works!" He was somewhat premature. I think, also, he was wrong. I do not think that classic Communism works, or ever will work. The Russian experiment has been brilliant in spots, but I am hidebound enough to believe that the spots that have been most successful have been those in which compromises with capitalistic methods and procedures have been introduced. Certainly, before he was deposed, Nikita Khrushchev was talking about economic matters like a middle-of-the-road liberal member of the Democratic Party of the United States. His principal successor, Kosygin sometimes looks and sounds like a rather colourless Republican. I believe, in other words, that the most sophisticated and the most able Communist leaders recognize that their philosophy does *not* work unless it is diluted by healthy injections of capitalism. If they could do so without losing too much face with the people and the more doctrinaire Party members they would lean even further to the right. They are going about as far as they can go.

The Chinese leaders, who are totally doctrinaire, have resented this, and they now call the Russians traitors to Communism. This is a typical Chinese reaction, an almost complete unwillingness to study or try to understand the problems and the mental processes of others.

I do not say that China should contemplate becoming a capitalistic nation overnight. I am not even certain that the western brand of capitalism is proper for the governance of the Chinese people. But I do say that the Chinese leaders should open their minds to the ideas of the western world, and should strive to profit by the successes and the failures of nations other than their own.

Certainly, constant exposure to other ideologies and other governmental techniques through participation in some such international body as the United Nations would be a giant step toward accomplishing this end.

China has so much to offer the rest of the world. The rest of the world has so much to offer her.

Any semblance of a free exchange of ideas and philosophies would be of benefit to all humankind and could lead to the permanent peace of the world. But both the east and the west have dropped their almost impenetrable curtains which make the free exchange of ideas, and even of news, almost impossible. This is stalemate and there is no conceivable way of making peace until the stalemate is broken.

As a Chinese I find this heartbreaking. My grandparents were Chinese emigrants. I find myself a Chinese exile,—an ideological exile who cannot even return to visit the land of his forefathers because of the impenetrable walls of doctrinaire stubbornness which separate the two worlds.

China is Brunnhilde on the fire-girt island but she is determined to destroy any Siegfried who attempts to rescue her.

III

ISRAEL AND THE JEWS

ISRAEL A ZIONIST REPUBLIC, artificially created in the Middle East, occupies 7,992 square miles of what was originally called Canaan, or the land flowing with milk and honey to which Moses led the Jews across the desert from Egypt. The population of Israel is about 2.7 million, ninety percent of whom are Jewish. The non-Jewish population is mostly Arab.

Israel was formally declared an independent State on May 14, 1948 after years of agitation and bitterness. For generations Zionist leaders among the Jews had been striving to achieve a homeland of their own in the Palestine area. During World War I, one of the principal Zionists, the great and good Chaim Weizmann, an eminent scientist, made what was probably the greatest single contribution by any civilian to the British War effort. He tamed cordite and thus made British munitions far more manageable and predictable.

In return, a grateful English government, in effect, offered him anything within its power to grant. He scorned all personal rewards and had but one request: "Palestine". The government, through the Balfour Declaration, promised him that the way would be cleared to create a Jewish independent state in that area.

Unfortunately, in another part of the political jungle, the famous T. E. Lawrence, who had led the Arab tribes to such romantic and spectacular desert victories over the Turks, exacted a promise from the Government that the Arabs would control Palestine.

This stalemate continued for thirty years, but Weizmann persisted in his claim of a debt of honour. Finally, after World War II, and the dreadful savagery of the Fascists against the Jews in Germany and elsewhere in Europe, Great Britain was at last compelled morally to meet its debt of honour. Israel was established and populated mostly by survivors of the German concentration camps, and other refugees from German bestiality.

The experiment has been almost incredibly successful. However, Israel's neighbors, Syria, Lebanon, Jordan, Egypt and the rest of the Arab world have bitterly resented the creation of a Jewish state on land they think of as their own. There has been constant warfare on a small scale and the tensions of the Middle East are probably greater than they are anywhere else in the world. Both sides have exhibited almost total intolerance and an almost total disinclination to compromise on even the smallest points. The patterns of hostility are ancient and, so far, have shown no signs of diminishment in their durability.

The history of the Jews, as we all know, has been one of persecution and sadness. The tendency of the human race to persecute a recognizable minority is apparently not eradicable.

During the Middle Ages, and indeed up until the 17th Century, European rulers found in the Jews a convenient scapegoat upon which to blame all their woes. Sovereigns like Elizabeth I, of England, or Ferdinand and Isabella, of Spain, when they found the Treasury growing bare, would seek to solve their financial troubles by banishing the Jews from their lands, and confiscating their property, much to their own enrichment. Then, of course, when the Treasury once again became empty, the Jews were quietly permitted to return so they could lend money to support the luxuries of the court. When the task of repaying the loans became burdensome, the crown would once again banish them and confiscate everything it could lay its greedy hands upon.

44

It is ironic that during the early 20th Century, and all during the 19th Century, it was the fashion, in Europe especially, to blame the Jews because they had little taste for agriculture. In the glory days of the "landed gentry", Jews were scorned because they lived almost exclusively in the cities. The truth is, of course, that whatever taste for the soil they might originally have had was pretty thoroughly discouraged by this repetitive habit of confiscating their possessions. In many nations, at many times, the Jews were forbidden by law to own land. It is not surprising that they, with their wonderful and courageous talent for survival, should have developed their commercial and mercantile abilities to such a remarkable degree. These were the only abilities they *could* develop if they were to survive in a hostile society which despised them and still needed them; and the more Gentiles needed them, the more they hated them.

Of course, once they got their own land, Israel, the pastoral tradition of Biblical times reasserted itself with remarkable vigor. The Jews, when given the opportunity, proved themselves to be brilliant agriculturists, just as they have shown a native brilliance in almost every other field of human endeavour. The agricultural progress of Israel, achieved in desert soil, has been one of the greatest glories of the land.

Anti-semitism over the centuries has been one of the most hideous and recurrent vices the human race has exhibited. And yet it has its ironic side. There was something bitterly amusing, for instance, in the magnanimous gesture of the Vatican Council in "forgiving" the Jews for the execution of Christ. The Italian cardinals had been the strongest in their opposition to this decision. Why? Well, if the Jews didn't kill Christ, then the only other persons who could be blamed are the Italians themselves! The soldiers on Calvary were all Romans. The Romans were not in the habit of permitting subservient peoples to bear arms. The Jews may have performed the carpentry work of the crucifixion, but the power and the strength behind the atrocity were Roman.

It is significant that when Jesus, in his agony on the Cross, cried out: *"Eli, Eli, lama sabachthani?"* those who were standing there . . . said: "He is calling Elias." If they had been Jews they would not have made such an error. The Italian, or Roman, soldiers didn't understand much Hebrew. (See Matthew XXVII/ 46, 47.)

The soldiers who threw dice for the garments at the foot of the cross were Italian soldiers, not Jews. There were no Jewish soldiers in Jerusalem in the time of Caesar Augustus, nor for many years afterwards. And when there were, in the time of Titus and Hadrian, the soldiers were guerillas (and very effective and troublesome they were, too.)

It was one of the most effective "public relations" programs, on a global scale, in all history for the Italians eventually to confiscate and control the religion which Jesus founded and to turn around and blame and persecute the Jews for committing a crime of which they were at least equally guilty!

It really was an act of amusing effrontery for the Council, 1900 years after the event, to solemnly debate whether or not they should forgive the Jews for committing an Italian atrocity. It is not surprising that world Jewry did not prostrate itself in humble thanksgiving for this act of magnanimity.

It was quite common for the Italian Fascists before and during World War II to excuse their anti-semitism on the grounds that the Jews were Christ killers. The history of the crucifixion added a very special little touch of indecency to their brand of anti-semitism.

The German brand of anti-semitism was something else again. It was on a much larger scale and it was both more efficient and more brutal. The Italians amused themselves with dirty little attacks of bullying and the shipping of a few carloads of unfortunates off to the Nazi slaughter pens. The Germans killed off approximately (no one knows how accurate any figures are) 8 million Jews during the Nazi ascendancy.

Like so many nations before them (the English, the Spanish, the Portuguese, the Russians, to name a few) the Germans made a good thing out of anti-semitism. Because the Jews were recognizable and, somehow, "different", as well as because they were

46

a minority, they made a most useful whipping boy. It was easy and convenient to cover up the blunders of the ruling administration by blaming the Jews for all the world's woes, and it was financially satisfactory to use this as an excuse for confiscating Jewish property and Jewish goods. In every century it worked out very well for everybody, except, of course, for the Jews.

The Germans are big in virtues and big in vice. They do things on a Wagnerian scale, and they nauseated the rest of the world by their brutality and sadism in trying to exterminate the entire race of Jews. I have doubts that the Nazi leaders had even the excuse of sincerity. I cannot think that they actually believed the lies they broadcast through their propaganda mills. Their sin was much greater. They cold-bloodedly played upon the German tendency toward mass hysteria and sought, and achieved a peculiar type of national unity by concentrating public hatred against a distinguishable and defenseless minority.

There is no doubt that the Jews have managed to create envy among Gentile peoples over the centuries. They are, as a race, remarkably resilient. Forbidden to own land, they became, by necessity, merchants, and dealers in money and ideas. Generally speaking, they were willing to work much harder to achieve success in any given field than the average Gentile was willing to work.

In the universities of the world, in the 19th and into the 20th centuries, the less industrious Gentile students excused their failure to do as well in their studies by deriding the Jewish "drudge", the stereotype with thick glasses who permitted himself no relaxation but worked incessantly at the tasks before him. Of course, it was inconvenient to recollect that, for many of the Jewish students, a proficiency in academic work was the only passport available out of the ghettos and near-ghettos of the big, steaming cities and into the world of culture and achievement, where stupid prejudices are rare and comparatively unimportant. The university was not a playground for the Jewish student; it was the gateway to liberation.

And, of course, it was more than inconvenient for Gentile students and teachers to acknowledge that the Jews are basically the most talented of the white races. Carlyle was only partly right in his aphorism about genius being the transcendent capacity for taking trouble. And Edison was only partly right when he said that genius was 90% perspiration and only 10% inspiration. Hard work is, of course, essential if genius is to amount to anything worthwhile, but hard work *alone* cannot begin to explain the ascendancy of Jewish genius in (to name a few categories) music, the arts, the theatre, philosophy, finance, the mercantile world, science, publishing and certain fields of literature.

It is a tiresome and dangerous *canard* to say that the Jews dominate these areas of achievement, but their influence and control is far greater proportionately than one would expect from their share of the world's population. If one were to name quickly the ten most famous names in each of the categories I have listed, more than half of them would be Jewish.

Since there are only 13 million Jews in the entire world, out of a total population of more than three thousand million, this concentration of talent at the top of so many fields of useful human endeavour is remarkable. It should excite, not our envy, but our wonder, and our desire to do as well.

The intellectuality of the Jewish race is, of course, renowned throughout the thinking world. It has sometimes led to enormous benefits for the human race. Sometimes it has taken a wrong turning and has produced misery.

Communism, for instance, is one of the most unfortunate and most formidable products of Jewish intellectuality. Although Communism (under various names) had been advocated and even sporadically practised in many areas of Europe over the ages, it took Karl Marx, that peculiar and repellent German-Jewish *provocateur,* to organize the belief into some kind of a political system.

Marx, of course, turned against his own people. He became so violently anti-Semitic that his language at times would have given pause, in later days, to a Storm Trooper. (He was also anti-Russian, and indeed, anti-almost everything else. Above all, through his own letters and writings, he proves himself to have been anti-*people*.) Nonetheless, the leaders of the Russian revolution were, for the most part, Jewish: Lenin, Trotzky, many others. It is ironic, therefore, that the revolution which the Jews created has now turned against them. The Russian Communist government is officially anti-Semitic and Jews are widely suppressed and persecuted throughout the Union of Soviet Republics.

This history of constant, continuing antagonism against the Jews as a race is a strange and tragic phenomenon and it must be faced up to. Why? What has caused it? Why is it so recurrent?

I have suggested that it has been convenient. The Jews are distinguishable from the Gentiles and they are a minority. Therefore they make easily accessible scape-goats. But, really, that is not sufficient in itself to explain it.

It isn't sufficient, either, to lay all the blame on envy. Certainly the Jews, through talent and hard work, have gained ascendancy in many fields of the arts and in business, but not to the exclusion of Gentiles. Certainly, the Jews have proved to be most adept at making money but, as a whole, they are no richer than the Gentile community. The greatest fortunes in the world are in the hands of Gentiles. The poor Jews in certain areas of New York, for instance, are just as poor as the poor Gentiles of, let us say, West Virginia, though one has the feeling that the poor Jew has a better chance of breaking the bonds of his poverty, becase he has within him a greater talent for discontent and a greater ambition to make something of himself.

The Jews, also, have been accused of excessive clannishness. It is charged that in those fields of endeavour in which the Jews are dominant it is very difficult for a non-Jew to succeed. Certainly, I, a Chinese, have not found this to be true. I feel this is a falsehood that unsuccessful Gentiles make up to excuse their own lack of capacity and drive. Certainly, Jews help each other out whenever they can. But so do Irish Catholics, Masons,

49

Poles, Italians, Germans and Orientals. This is a normal attitude in any group and, on the whole, a rather admirable one. It's just that the Jews do it better than anyone else.

What *is* it then, that turns people against the Jews? It may be partly because the Jew usually is not only different, but insists upon his right to be different. He remains partly an Oriental in a western world. He rejoices in one of the oldest and most honorable cultures known to man, and sees no reason to abandon elements of that culture in order to integrate with a culture he considers jejune, immature, illogically-based and even sinful. By maintaining this aloofness from the ways and beliefs of the predominantly Gentile world he offends those who see virtue only in a kind of bland homogeneity.

The Jews have shown a disinclination not only to integrate with other races and cultures, but also among themselves. The fact that someone calls himself a Jew does not mean that he will be received with open arms in Israel. On the contrary. One has to be a certain kind of Jew, from a certain environment.

It was first thought that the Army and the principle of "mixed *kibbutzim*" would unite all the people of Israel into a homogenized group. This has not worked out. The *kibbutz* collective farm system has managed to segregate the Jews in Israel on a straight ethnic or national basis: European Jews, Moroccan Jews, Iraqi Jews, Tunisian Jews and so forth. American and English Jews who go to Israel inspired with romantic Zionist ideas of Hebraic "togetherness" are rudely disillusioned once they arrive. They are not accepted, and they live in ghettos of their own, remote from the mainstream of Israeli life.

The Hebrew University in Jerusalem has recognized the problem and has conducted seminars of economists, psychologists and sociologists in the hope of coming up with some kind of solution. The results of the seminars were discouraging. It was generally agreed that the differences between the Oriental Jews and the European Jews was widening, not narrowing, and that it would take generations of hard work and thought to reverse the trend.

Today, as Israel faces serious economic difficulties, after a brilliant beginning, this segregationist tendency within her own borders creates real problems for the future. Just to give one example: the Oriental Jews are used to a far lower standard of living than are the European Jews, and are willing to work for a far lower wage. This causes internal dissension on a very basic level.

It should be remembered that European Jews, despite their dominance in many aspects of Israeli life, make up only 35 percent of the population. The other 65 percent is made up of Oriental, African and Middle Eastern Jews, who are the low men on the totem pole, socially, politically and economically.

Unfortunately, Israel is a legal entity but it has not matured as a political entity. It is not yet a complete and solid nation.

Over the centuries, Jews have been blamed because, despite all their talents, they have no talent for assimilation.

But even when, in the Western world, they try to slip unobserved into the Gentile culture, they are blamed just as much as are those who refuse to yield an inch.

Hundreds of thousands of Jews have given up the struggle against the forces of anti-semitism and have changed their names, joined fashionable Protestant Churches, and after several generations have successfully passed as White Anglo-Saxon Protestants. But those that do this have earned the contempt of their fellow Jews and the somewhat amused condescension of the Gentiles.

This is a characteristic in which the Jews differ greatly from other persecuted peoples. The Irish, for instance, met with unremitting hostility when they first emigrated to the United States. In Boston, in the mid-nineteenth century, it was common for potential employers to hang out a sign, "No Irish Need Apply", to discourage any applicants but White Anglo-Saxon Protestants. Elsewhere in New England, the Irish Catholics were denied the vote and were not permitted to hold public office. Yet there is no evidence of any number of Irish changing their name from O'Brien to something like Jones or of forsaking the faith of

51

their fathers in order to gain greater social and economic acceptance. Instead, they stood their ground, fought back and eventually out-numbered their former oppressors.

Somehow, the situation is reminiscent of the old story of the two rabbits being chased by a pack of hounds. One of them turned to the other and said, "Shall we keep running, or shall we stay here and outnumber them?" The Irish chose the latter course and in many instances, in Boston particularly, they ended up by controlling the community and even electing one of their own as President of the United States.

Although there is some evidence that the Jews have been able to accomplish something like this in New York City, it can, I think, be fairly said that this is not typically the Jewish way. The Jewish community in New York City did not become aggressive or a dominant element there until they had established an irresistible numerical position. Not that it matters, but the Jews in New York City have not yet elected a Mayor of their own race.

One characteristic of the relationship of the Jewish community, particularly in the United States, is its sensitivity to criticism and its aggressiveness against even its most well-meaning critics.

The Nazis made everyone, Jewish and Gentile alike, almost excessively conscious of every manifestation, no matter how slight, of anti-Semitism.

Anti-Semitism was transformed in a short while from a nasty little vice practised on a private scale, to a major catastrophe practised on a genocidal scale. Suddenly, even a minor criticism of anything or anybody Jewish exposed the critic to the danger of being branded as some kind of a Fascist monster.

At one point immediately after World War II it was practically *verboten* in the United States for a comedian to tell Jewish dialect stories, which once were one of the principal staples of the vaudeville and night club stages. It was permissible to tell Irish dialect stories, or Chinese, or German or anything else, but not Jewish stories. Even Jewish comedians were excoriated by certain bleeding hearts, like the Columnist Walter Winchell, if they told stories, no matter how gentle and kindly, about, and

52

with the accents of, their own people. Fortunately, this phase passed rather quickly. (Now, of course, it is *verboten* to tell stories in a negro dialect.)

Charles Augustus Lindbergh, who had been one of America's greatest heroes, irretrievably tarnished his reputation when, in his sincere if misguided campaign to keep the United States out of World War II, he criticized the Jewish community for insisting upon an immediate declaration of war against Germany. For making an unwise but rather mild remark, which was at least more than half true, Lindbergh was pilloried as being practically a Nazi agent!

The same is true today. If a public figure is bold enough to state that there is some value in the resentment of the Arab States against the establishment of Israel in their midst, he is immediately branded as an anti-Semite. Some ten years ago the Arab States were shopping around in America to find a top-flight public relations firm which would present their side of the case to the public and to the Congress. Although the fees offered were princely, there were no takers. It was felt that any firm accepting such a commission would be ruined forever after. Not only would it be almost impossible to get the Arab side of the story any effective coverage in communications media that are to a great extent controlled by Jewish executives, but any attempt to do so would cause the firm making the attempt to be boycotted.

And yet, may I say (very *sotto voce*) that if there are not two sides to the Israel-Arab controversy, there is at least a side and a half and, in fairness, the Arabs should have had the right to try to present their version of the controversy to the American people.

Perhaps the most ridiculous manifestation of this hysteria was the attempt, in New York City some years ago, to get Shakespeare's "Merchant of Venice" banned from the schools and even the public libraries as an anti-Semitic play.

This was not only silly, it was illiterate. It shows a vast misunderstanding of William Shakespeare and of what he was trying to do.

The "Merchant of Venice" was, for its period, a very courageous play. The England of Elizabeth I was just about as anti-Semitic as the Germany of Adolf Hitler. It was dangerous to write anything at all sympathetic to the Jews.

In "The Merchant of Venice", Shakespeare makes a real villain out of Antonio and, by contrast, Shylock, the Jew, is a far more admirable character. Although certain anti-Semitic elements had to be thrown into the play to appease the groundlings, it took enormous courage, in the society of England of 1594, to write such lines as: "I am a Jew. Hath not a Jew eyes? hath not a Jew hands, organs, dimensions, senses, affections, passions? fed with the same food, hurt with the same weapons, subject to the same diseases, healed by the same means, warmed and cooled by the same winter and summer as a Christian is? If you prick us, do we not bleed? if you tickle us, do we not laugh? if you poison us, do we not die? and if you wrong us, do we not revenge? if we are like you in the rest, we will resemble you in that. If a Jew wrong a Christian, what is his humility? Revenge. If a Christian wrong a Jew, what should his sufferance be by Christian example? Why, revenge. The villainy you teach me, I will execute. . ."

Courageous words, these, for 1594. And, to point up the fact that there are different kinds of Jews, as well as different kinds of Christians, Shakespeare even introduced the unattractive Tubal to make the contrast with Shylock clear.

This may not be enough to appease the B'nai Brith in 1968, but it went a whole lot further in 1594 than any other Gentile writer in England dared to go.

If the agitators had to choose a play to ban, they might at least have hit upon something like Webster's "Jew of Malta". Now there is a really anti-Semitic play of almost overpowering indecency. And, of course, there were scores of other lesser plays produced on the Elizabethan stage which are far more worthy of condemnation. The trouble is that "The Merchant of

Venice" is the only Elizabethan play about Jews the agitators ever heard about and they never even read that!

Perhaps the most damaging prejudice the Gentiles hold against the Jews lies in the belief that the Hebrew religion supports the Mosaic law of "an eye for an eye and a tooth for a tooth" rather than the more gentle "other cheek" approach of the Christian faiths. It is true, as Shylock points out so bitterly in the passage quoted above, that Christians generally do not practise the admirable laws of their Founder, yet there is a disturbing belief among non-Jews that the Jews operate under a different, and more ruthless set of ground rules.

This belief is, for the most part, due to ignorance and superstition. The Christian religions are based upon the Hebrew religion and except for the basic point of the divinity of Jesus, are similar in their ethics and their fundamental approaches to morality. (After all, we all operate, or are supposed to operate, under the same Ten Commandments.)

Yet, the Jews (in my opinion) have done nothing to allay Gentile fears concerning their inbred thirst for revenge. The Nuremberg Trials, for instance, which were insisted upon by Jewish opinion throughout the world, were based upon a very dubious *post facto* interpretation of international law. The nations of the world had not anticipated the emergence of such monsters as those who perpetrated the Nazi atrocities against the Jews and therefore had made no laws to deal with such sins against humanity. This was unfortunate. No one in his right mind could feel the least bit of sympathy for the degenerates who were convicted by the court at Nuremberg, but the proceedings set a very dangerous precedent in that they condemned people to die for crimes that were not specified as crimes at the time of their commission. (Significantly, when a great and courageous United States Senator, Robert A. Taft, of Ohio, expressed his disapproval of the trials, he was libellously and predictably labelled as being anti-Semitic and a secret sympathizer with Fascism!)

The Eichmann Case was even worse. The man was a certifiable ogre. He deserves no tears. But the fact remains that the world kept silent while Israel broke every international law by brazenly kidnaping Eichmann from the Argentine, spiriting him away to Tel Aviv, and then trying him in a totally Jewish Court under the laws of a land that did not even officially exist when the crimes were committed. This was not an act of law, it was an act of vengeance.

The world is a better and a cleaner place for not having Eichmann in it, but the ends do not justify the means. It would have been morally indefensible for Israeli agents to have assassinated Eichmann in the Argentine in retribution for his crimes against the Jews, but it would have been more honourable than what actually happened, which was a disgusting attempt to dress up a political murder in the trappings of a phoney justice. The Nazis, it will be remembered, were very meticulous about trying to dress up even their most hideous atrocities in the habiliments of a meretricious "legality". It did Israel no credit, and the Jews no good, to imitate the practices of their German persecutors.

To many of us who are Christians, Jerusalem is the womb. It is an endlessly interesting city, a city of countless living religions. It is a city inhabited by people who have forgotten more than they ever knew.

The famous Biblical sites are disappointing because they have no real authenticity. The *Via Dolorosa,* Calvary, the Mount of Olives, Gethsemane, the Manger are all objects of veneration, but also of skepticism. The world-moving events of Christian belief *could* have happened in these precise localities, but there is really no reason to believe that they did. The sites may be those of the Biblical story, but, after centuries of destruction and rebuilding, the sights are not.

The Roman Emperor Hadrian, in the second century after the birth of Christ, said: "I was anxious . . . to make Jerusalem a city like the others, where several races and several beliefs could live in peace; but I was wrong to forget that in any combat between fanaticism and common sense the latter has rarely the upper hand."

This was very Roman in its point of view and, like many Roman opinions, universally correct.

Certainly, the differences between Israel and Jordan (and the rest of the Arab world) could be ironed out by an application of common sense on the part of all the involved governments. Jordan and Israel are both modern States with enormous potentials, and these potentials will never be realized if they insist on keeping their hands at each other's throats instead of upon the plough (or the computer, as the case might be).

There should be no more waving of the bloody *kaffiyeh*.

No other part of the world needs more international understanding and more international co-operation than does that portion of the Middle East in which Israel and the Arab States reside, and no portion is blessed with less.

Perhaps the Jews, so accustomed to being stateless and "international" in their thinking, are having difficulty in adjusting to the rather sudden exigencies of nationalism. Knowing their actions are backed by an international community of Jews influential in every important nation in the world, they have behaved with totally inappropriate aggressiveness against their neighbors. The Arab States, on the other hand, have been impossibly hostile and have retaliated with almost manic anti-Semitism. There is no tolerance, no understanding, no compassion. Both sides have behaved like gangs of angry children, not States.

And yet, despite all the financial aid from the Jewish and non-Jewish peoples of the world, Israel must do a great deal better than she has been doing, externally and internally, if she is truly to succeed in the comity of nations.

Between 1956 and 1966 the population leaped from 1.8 million to 2.7 million, and the economy expanded at an astounding rate of 10 percent a year, the highest sustained rate in the world. But, in 1966, concurrent with the renewed troubles with the Arab world, the Israel economy nosedived. In 1966, the economic growth rate increased only 3 percent and unemployment has become, for the first time, a serious problem. The financing of the Israeli debt now costs 17 percent of the entire national budget. This is more than is paid out for either education or development. These are ominous signs in a small nation which hopes to attract twenty to thirty thousand new immigrants each year.

Internally, Israel is suffering from a dearth of pre-planning concerning her economy. She needs development in heavy industry and in such specialized areas as printing, medical, surgical and optical equipment, textiles, agricultural equipment, and so on.

Externally, she needs considerable applications of coolness. Like so many infant states, Israel burst out of her egg like a baby crocodile, snarling and snapping at all her neighbours. (Much of the snarling and snapping, it must be stated, was in self-defense, but not all.)

Her original successes against Egypt surprised the world and fed Israel's ego. Then came the Suez Canal war in 1956, when her adversary, Egypt, proved herself to be a bloated and empty political bladder capable of almost indiscriminate puncture.

The Israeli Army dashed across the Sinai desert and seized the Mediterranean Coast, as well as the Gaza Strip and the nation found itself embarrassed by its own conquests. Israel suddenly found itself faced with the impossible prospect of feeding and caring for a third of a million underfed and undertrained Arabs whom they didn't want, and whom they fundamentally despised. (Red China, as we shall see in a subsequent Chapter, encountered the same phenomenon when she invaded India in 1962.) Israel learned from this that the sudden ingestion of real estate must inevitably mean also the sudden ingestion of hungry Arab bodies, and that this would upset, not only the economy, but the ethnic balance of the nation. The Jewish nation, which had shown many of the alarming characteristics of ancient Sparta up to that time, has lost a great deal of its hunger for conquest as a result of this experience.

And yet, Israel is inclined to over-react to Arab hostility. When Syria, in 1966, committed some particularly stupid acts of sabotage along and inside the Israel border. Israeli troops retaliated by moving in and deliberately and methodically blowing up every building in a village, not in Syria, but in *Jordan!* (It happened to be easier and cheaper to invade Jordan at that particular time.)

This was enough to unify the hatred of all the Arab world, once again, against the Jews. Arab firebrands used the incident to point up the supposition that the Israelis hated all Arabs indiscriminately—a supposition that could have a seriously detrimental effect since a unification of the Arab nations against the Israelite interests could be most damaging. The best thing that Israel has going for her during these difficult times is that the Arabs nations are too busy warring among themselves to unite in a concentrated and effective effort against her.

No one suggests that Israel should accept senseless acts of petty aggression from her neighbors without reprisal. But she must learn to defend her national honor with more dignity and discretion. She must try to work out some way of living at peace with her neighbors, even though those neighbors are maddeningly provocative. Her economy cannot support an armed camp *in perpetuo* and the world is growing weary of the dreary alarums and excursions which so constantly desecrate her borders.

The world looks to Israel to exert moral leadership in the Middle East. There is no trick in constantly fighting battles with borrowed arms. The trick is to keep the peace. This is something the Jews, apparently, have not yet learned.

There are times when I feel that the Jews do not exhibit the same tolerance toward non-Jews that they expect and demand toward themselves. This is manifested not only at the international and national level, but also in their personal relationships.

This is not only a pity, it is a mistake.

Fortunately (perhaps because of the giant strides toward ecumenism that the Roman Catholic Church has taken in recent years) co-operation between Jewish and Christian groups in

59

working toward common goals has increased. There should be and must be a great deal more of this, on a much higher level than the occasional fellowship luncheon or the once-a-year interfaith "get together".

There has been too much of a tendency within the Jewish community to take care of their own and to exclude non-Jewish causes from their philanthropies. This has led to a spiritual inbreeding which has sapped the vigor of their spiritual life. (Someone once said that the Jews are very generous to their own poor and to the Christian rich.)

It may seem almost impossibly naive to say this in this modern agnostic world, but I happen to believe devoutly, sincerely and totally in God. I believe in God as the father of us all and I believe that every man and woman placed upon this earth was made, somehow, in His image and is equally entitled to His love and His mercy.

What a glorious thing it would be if the Jews would join with the many Christian sects in the effort to bring an awareness and knowledge of God to all the people of the world who have never heard of Him!

I am not talking about the propagation of the beliefs and rituals of any particular sect or cult, I am talking only about God Himself and the principles which all those who believe in Him share together.

I am convinced that most of the great troubles which contort the world today spring from the ignorance of, or the rejection of, God Almighty. The godlessness of the Communist States, the paganism of so much of the African continent and of a great part of the Arab world has made even basic communication between the two blocs almost impossible. There is literally no common ground on which to hold discussions, no basic *ethos* on which to build a structure of understanding.

If the Jews would direct part of their enormous talent, and their enormous energy as well as part of their wealth to a common effort with Christians in spreading the knowledge of God into every corner of the earth, there is no telling what we all could accomplish together in the way of creating a durable peace.

Since Biblical times, the Jews have not exerted, as a race or as a religion, any moral leadership on the world, nor have they tried to do so. There have been great individual Jewish moralists, and great individual Jewish religious leaders, but their efforts have been individualistic. There is no such thing as a Jewish missionary, nor have the Jews ever sought to proselytize among the unbelievers. They have accepted the belief complacently that they are the chosen people and have had little concern for those whom they believe not to be so fortunately situated.

I feel it is time that the Jewish community throughout the world should reassess their position and try, as do the Christian religions, to exert a moral influence on the rest of the world, not only in regard to the relationships among Jews, or between Jews and Gentiles, but between Gentiles and Gentiles also, and between Gentiles and pagans.

And, in doing so, the Jews would necessarily shed some of their exclusiveness which keeps them, as a community, apart from the Gentile community. And the Gentiles would, in turn, have the privilege of knowing and understanding Jews better than they do now.

Unfamiliarity breeds fear and distrust. (Our English language has plenty of examples to prove this point. The word "uncouth", for instance, merely meant, in Anglo-Saxon, "unknown". The word "barbarian" came into being because the Greeks thought the speech of stranger tribes sounded like the "baaing" of sheep!) Much of the anti-Catholic bigotry of past years arose from the fact that non-Catholics were distrustful of practices they considered mysterious being carried on in a language they could not understand. Much of the anti-Semitic bigotry springs from the same cause. Gentiles know nothing of the Jewish beliefs, even though they parallel their own in most important fundamentals. (How many Christians, for instance, know what Jews believe about the hereafter?) They have never been inside a synagogue. They have, for the most part, never conducted a conversation with a Jew on a level more serious than a transaction over a store counter, or at a desk in a bank.

This is wrong on both sides, and it is dangerous. We can no longer afford these expensive luxuries such as prejudice and bigotry. All people who know and love and fear God should forget their differences and concentrate on their similarities, and then join in a common effort to make some substantial and significant sacrifices to spread the knowledge of Jehovah to the bleak meridians where men know Him not.

This, if it were done, would create a truly meaningful brotherhood of man. It would divert both the Jewish and the Christian communities from their sterile preoccupation with materialism. It would go a long way not only toward creating peace among nations, but it would also create peace within nations.

IV

THE ARAB WORLD

THERE IS A STORY popular in Lebanon which concerns a scorpion that wished to cross a river. He asked a turtle to ferry him across. The turtle demurred. "Why should I do that?" he asked. "Half way across you would sting me and kill me."

"That's silly," the scorpion replied. "If I did that I would drown with you."

The turtle was convinced by this reasoning and finally agreed to ferry the scorpion across the water. Half way across, the scorpion could not resist his murderous urge and he stung the turtle viciously in the neck.

As the dying turtle started to sink he cried out in anguish, "Why? Why?" The scorpion, who was himself going under for the third time, merely shrugged his shoulders. "Because," he said, "this is the Middle East."

This story tells, in capsule form, what is tragically wrong, and what has been traditionally tragically wrong, with the Arab world, almost since the beginning of recorded history.

The ancient history of what we know as the Arab World was more distinguished by far than its most recent or its present history. While the Chinese may be said to have forgotten what they once knew, the Arabs have forgotten more than they ever knew.

Certainly, the past was glorious. During the Dark Ages it was the Arabs who kept the lamps of knowledge burning in the Middle East, much as did the monastic scholars in Ireland. Both areas were out of the reach of the barbarians and could provide sanctuary for the preservers of science and the humanities.

The Arab contribution to the scientific world was basic. Although they borrowed the system of numbering we know as "Arabic" from India, it was the Arabs who popularized the system and earned for it precedence over the cumbersome Roman system throughout Europe.

The Arabs learned from the Greeks the art of navigating by the stars, and they preserved that knowledge for the purpose of guiding their caravans across the almost trackless desert. Of the 57 stars selected by international agreement for navigational purposes, 38 have names of Arabic origin. Some of the most familiar words we use in navigation today were derived from the Arabic: zenith, azimuth, nadir, alidade, almanac.

There are many other English words borrowed from the Arabs. To name just a few: algebra, alcohol, alcove, zero, cork, magazine, orange. Few people know that when they part company with each other with the breezy phrase "So long!", they are acknowledging a debt to Arabia. The expression is derived from the Islamic "Salaam!", or "Peace!"

The Arab civilization (excluding that of Egypt, which is even older) goes back at least as far as 1500 B.C., and almost certainly further. The Arab lands were divided and warlike, not only against intruders, but against each other as well. However, inspired by the belief in Mohammed (who died in 632 A.D.) the Arabs effected a certain degree of unification and taking advantage of the weakness of European civilization at that period, pressed their arms through Spain and well into France, as well as into the Balkan lands. The tide in Western Europe was stemmed at the Battle of Tours(732 A.D.), when the Frankish King, Charles Martel decisively and surprisingly defeated the armies of Abd-ar-Rahman. Although the Arabs remained in Spain for 750 more years, they never again threatened to advance their crescent and star farther north.

The fact is generally forgotten or conveniently ignored by western historians, but at the Battle of Tours it was the Arabs who more closely represented the forces of civilization and culture, and the Franks who more closely resembled the barbarians. Abd-ar-Rahman undoubtedly thought of his antagonist, Charles, with much the same kind of condescension as that with which Julius Caesar had considered Vercingetorix, 700 years previously. A gallant soldier in his crude way, no doubt, but illiterate, superstitious and dirty. Hardly the sort of person one would invite to dinner, or, the Prophet forbid!, permit to marry one's sister.

The Arabs were constantly victimized by their inability to get along with each other, a failing that plagues them to this day. Internecine wars prevented them from keeping together and from moulding their empire, except for short periods, into a cohesive mass, or even to consolidate their gains.

The failure at Tours is a classic example of this. Although Christian historians, particularly in the 18th and 19th centuries, were inclined to exult about the victory as proof of the superiority of Christian virtue over Moslem barbarism, the fact remains that the Arabs turned back just as much because of a serious revolt at home among the Berbers as because of the Frankish triumph. The Arab lines were too far extended and they could not push farther into Europe, and still spare the troops to put down uprisings at home.

During World War I most of the Arab World came apart at the seams and soon degenerated into a conglomeration of dependencies and protectorates. Most of the nations which now comprise the Arab World (Saudi Arabia, Muscat, Yemen, Kuwait, Qatar, Bahrein, the Federation of South Arabia, the Trucial States, Jordan, Lebanon, Libya, Morocco, Sudan, Tunisia, Egypt, Iraq and Syria) are quite recent political entities. Archeologically they are old as the hills, and historically as old as man, but politically most of them date from the post World War II era.

The Arab World as we now know it has a population of about 80 million, with Egypt (30 million) being by far the dominant nation.

In 1945, the Arab nations banded together in the Arab League, with headquarters in Cairo, with the purpose of establishing and co-ordinating ties among Arab States, co-ordinating their political activities, preserving their political integrity and ensuring closer co-operation in political, cultural, health, economic and legal areas. The real reason, of course, was to create a united front against Israel. In 1965 the nations formed an "Arab Common Market" which was meant to step up the boycott of Israel and exert economic pressure on European nations which do business with Israel. The Arab League, thus far, has fallen far short of success because of the squabbling among its members, and the Common Market has been a dismal failure.

The anti-Semitism of the Arab nations has been both childish and virulent. (Ironic, too, in that the Arabs are, by definition, a Semitic race.) As soon as Israel was created an independent State (May 14, 1948), Egypt declared war on her and tried to overrun her. To the surprise of the rest of the world (and particularly of the Arab nations), Egypt was soundly trounced and was forced to sign a humiliating armistice nine months later.

The Arab nations try to boycott corporations and industries that do business in Israel. (Coca-Cola was recently banned in some of the nations because it granted a bottling franchise in Israel to an Israeli businessman.) Motion pictures with Jewish actors in them are often prohibited. Perhaps the nadir of silliness came about when Egypt banned a Walt Disney film because the leading character's horse was given the Biblical name of Samson!

Another touch of the absurd, on a more elevated level, came a short while ago when the Arab League withdrew diplomatic contacts with West Germany (a nation with a fairly redolent record of anti-Semitism itself) because she had extended diplomatic recognition to Israel.

Fanaticism, once the greatest strength of the Moslems, has become their greatest weakness. They have irreparably hurt their image with the rest of the world by their unceasing and nonsensical attacks upon Israel. And they have hurt themselves almost as badly by the fanatical hatreds among themselves. Recently, when great international trouble was threatened because of border incidents between Israel and her neighbours the crisis was averted, almost by default, when the neighbours, instead of fighting against Israel, started attacking each other!

The crisis among the Arab nations is as permanent as it is dreary. Here is the sort of thing that goes on. President Nasser, of Egypt, recently, with no discernible profit to his country, went out of his way to offend King Faisal of Saudi Arabia by providing lavish sanctuary in Cairo for the deposed King (Faisal's brother), old Ibn Saud, along with Saud's enormous complement of wives, slaves, concubines and advisors. This, naturally, intensified the running feud between Egypt and Saudi Arabia.

Meanwhile, Nasser is maintaining an Army of 50,000 Russian-equipped soldiers in the Yemen, carrying on a desultory and hopeless war with that country, but really waiting for the English to pull out of Aden and southern Arabia so he can move in. This, naturally, arouses resentment and apprehension among other Arab nations, most of whom do not like Egypt very much anyway.

Syria, the most difficult of all the states in recent years, keeps beating her breast about pushing the Israelis into the sea, but directs its warlike actions toward a harassment of Jordan. In a moment of almost total economic irresponsibility, Syria decided to nationalize the Iraq Petroleum Company's trans-Syrian pipeline. She wanted a larger cut from the revenues deriving from the oil that flowed through the line. As a result, no oil is moving through the line at all. This has cut off revenues not only from Syria, but from Iraq as well. Since Iraq had no part in the impulsive decision to nationalize the pipeline, she is understandably furious at the hardships that have been so arbitrarily forced upon her.

And so it goes, endlessly, maddeningly and dangerously.

There are great potentials in the Arab world; economic, social and cultural. They will never be realized until the Arab nations face up to the fact that the State of Israel is a *fait accompli* and is there to stay. They may not like it, but there is nothing, really, they can do about it. The strength of the Jewish community throughout the western world is such that any potentially successful aggression against Israel would almost certainly be met with reprisals, and would be foredoomed to failure. The only sensible reaction to a situation such as this is to accept it and learn to live with it. If the Arab nations would forget their hostilities toward the Jews and toward each other, and concentrate on peaceful co-operation, their future could be almost unlimited.

The dominant economic fact in the Arab world is oil.

The industrial world of the 20th Century runs on petroleum. In many more accessible places the reserves are running low, and almost everywhere the demand is multiplying. The greatest, relatively untapped known reserves are in the Arab world. (It is estimated that Saudi Arabia and tiny Kuwait have half the known oil reserves in the world under their soil.) It is desperately important to the free world that those reserves remain available and not fall into the hands of the Communist world. For this reason, every tremor of aggression in this area creates spasms of worry throughout the rest of the free world. The stakes are too high, and every minor incident has major implications on the broadest international scale.

Egypt, as the dominant nation in the Arab world, has proved to be a vast disappointment. In 1952 an Army revolt, headed nominally by General Mohammed Naguib, but organized by Lieutenant Colonel Gamel Abdel Nasser, overthrew the administration of the porcine King Farouk I and drove him from the country. Naguib became President, and Nasser Vice-President. There followed a power struggle between the two soldiers, which Nasser won in 1954, gaining absolute control over the nation. In 1956, Nasser was "elected" President, being the only candidate on the ballot. He has maintained absolute control ever since.

Nasser, an impossibly vain and unpredictable leader, has managed over the years to betray most of his friends, antagonize most of his allies, and to fail in his sporadic courtship of certain elements of the Communist world. He has created such a personal rule that he, and his thinking of the moment, represent his nation. For very good reasons he is not trusted and his country, (as well as the rest of the Arab world) has suffered thereby.

Most notably, he has chosen to forget history. For demagogic purposes he had delighted in twisting the tail of the British lion and has treated England generally like an enemy. This is both unfair and ungrateful. The British protectorate over Egypt (1914-1922) and her influence after that, were remarkably benign and economic conditions under her guidance were far better than they have been under Nasser. England saved Egypt (although for selfish reasons) from being overrun in two World Wars and, if it had not been for British intervention, Egypt would have twice-over been a slave State.

One of Nasser's first acts as President in 1956 was to seize the Suez Canal, the lifeline of commerce in the Middle East, which had been built on Egyptian soil, mostly by English money, between 1859 and 1869. The nationalization of the Canal caused immediate trouble. Israel, which was threatened with economic strangulation by the act, mounted a serious invasion of Egypt in order to protect her future existence. This brought about military intervention on the part of Great Britain and France. Russia issued a stern ultimatum and the United States, unwilling to provoke the U.S.S.R. adopted a wishy-washy, hands-off policy that helped nothing. Finally, a cease fire was ordered. Israel withdrew her troops from the areas she had conquered (the Gaza Strip and the country around the Gulf of Aqaba).

The original concession of the Suez Canal was to last 99 years, and was due to expire in 1968. By nationalizing the waterway 12 years early, Nasser brought about an international crisis which could easily have worsened into something disastrous.

The management of the Canal since that time has done little to improve matters. Nasser still considers himself at war with Israel and, from time to time, he reminds the world of this fact by seizing or delaying cargoes to that country, thereby capriciously necessitating United Nations intervention and negotiation. He is more interested in creating trouble than in preventing it.

Like so many dictators, Nasser is far more intrigued by power politics than he is in the welfare of his people. His purchases of arms from the Soviet Union and his fruitless and stupid insistence on carrying on a war with Yemen have kept the economy unstable. Men and women starve in Egypt, despite the fact that the nation is the most industrialized in the Arab world. And despite enormous monetary and economic assistance from both the United States and Soviet Russia, the health standards are primitive and inadequate and the people are afflicted with epidemic diseases which have long ago been conquered almost everywhere else.

Only 4 percent of Egypt's land is arable, and it is all in the Valley of the Nile. When the Aswan High Dam is completed (through Soviet aid) about 2,000,000 more acres will be capable of cultivation and the nation's electric power capacity will be trebled. This will undoubtedly benefit the nation very much, but the future of Egypt ultimately will depend upon the emergence of national leadership which values butter over guns, human values over doctrinaire posturing.

Social awareness is spotty in the Arab States. In a vast and wealthy nation like Saudi Arabia, for instance, it scarcely exists at all. The enormous profits from the oil concessions in this country go to the Royal Family and its friends, while the common people try to scratch out a bare existence from raising camels, sheep and goats. In a nation covering 870,000 square miles, and with a population of 6,750,000, there are only 495 doctors, and only 1,500 students in institutions of higher learning. The royal family spends its money recklessly (mostly outside of the country) and, apparently, feels no responsibility to take care of the ordinary citizens whom they are supposed to govern.

The most heart-warming story in the Arab World, on the other hand, is that of little Kuwait, which awoke one morning to find itself the richest nation, *per capita,* in the world. For centuries, other Arab nations have been nibbling away at Kuwait, cold-bloodedly seizing territory right and left. They took all the scenery and most of the coastline, and left Kuwait only 6,178 square miles of the greatest oil field ever discovered by man!

The ruling family of Kuwait is enlightened and generous. With an annual income of $1.5 billion (population 475,000), they have turned the nation into a kind of Utopian welfare State. Education is free, from kindergarten through university, and clever students are sent at the Government's expense to study abroad. School uniforms, hot lunches, books, stationery and transportation are all free. Health service and hospitalization are free to everyone, including strangers within the borders, and the facilities are excellent. Half the population is employed by the Government and free public housing abounds.

The Government has invested a major portion of its vast holdings abroad and has even instituted something unique in the Arab world, the "Kuwait Fund for the Economic Development of the Arab Countries", with capital resources of almost a billion dollars, to make loans to the other Arab States.

Kuwait is a Moslem State, with only 5 percent of the population being Christian. It has suffered much from its Moslem neighbours, especially Saudi Arabia and Iraq, but it has responded to its enormous, new-found wealth in a way that we would consider ideal in a Christian State.

The money, incidentally, is so abundant that there is serious talk about air-conditioning the entire capital city of Kuwait (population 97,000). Not air-conditioning the *buildings,* of the city—that's been done. Air-conditioning *the city itself* under some gigantic version of the Astrodome! Even Texas hasn't thought *that* big!

Another bright spot in the Arab world is little Jordan which contains within its borders most of what the Christian world calls the Holy Land.

Jordan has only 37,737 square miles, and 2,000,000 people, and (as yet) no oil. But, in a constitutional monarchy with an enlightened King, Hussein, Jordan has done very well with what it has. With foreign aid, the Government is developing irrigation and hydro-electric projects which will make up in great part for the aridity of the land. Imaginative economic development has led to considerable industrial expansion. Phosphate is a major export and potash plants are being developed. The Gross National Product of Jordan has increased by 10 percent in the past ten years, and seems to be growing in vigor.

In short, Jordan, located in one of the oldest seed-beds of man's civilization, in an area considered sacred to three of man's greatest religions, is showing most encouraging signs of modernity and progress.

She has her troubles with the Jews, of course, and many of these (but by no means all) are her own fault. She finds it necessary to maintain an armed force of 36,000 men and to buy supersonic fighter planes from the United States, a luxury she can ill afford. But she manages a far higher health standard than does Egypt, for instance, and she maintains a literacy average of about one-third, which is far better than average throughout this part of the world.

But, despite these occasional flashes of hope, the Arab lands remain a disappointment and a trouble to the rest of the world. They still stand with one foot tentatively poised in the twentieth century, and the other firmly implanted in the dark ages. Their rulers and their people seem incapable of forgetting or forgiving blood feuds, no matter how ancient. If they refuse to ignore border disputes stretching back over 1,000 years, how can they accept the imposition of Israel in their midst in the middle of the twentieth century?

The Arab World will remain just as much a threat to the peace of the world as did the Balkans in the years before World War I as long as they look backward instead of forward. Any nation like Saudi Arabia, which permits the ruling family to hoard all the wealth, and distributes none to the common people of the land, is practically sitting up and asking for a Communist takeover from within or without. As long as the Arab countries

72

prefer to feud among themselves instead of joining together under their common bond of the star and crescent, and working for their united self-interest, they are doomed to remaining hopelessly backward in the family of nations.

And as long as they expend their energies on hating Israel, instead of trying to work out some kind of a *modus vivendi* with her, they are going to be in many ways outcasts except among those countries which intend to use them for their own selfish ends.

In short, the Arab World luxuriates in racial and national hatreds that were made risky centuries ago by the invention of the percussion artillery shell, and which have become outrageously dangerous with the advent of the long-range bomber and the nuclear devices of today. For the peace of the world they must learn something of the give-and-take of international life. They must learn that concessions in the name of peace are a strength, and not a weakness. They must also learn that certain kinds of pride are too expensive to be nurtured in this period of the world's development in which there is no longer any such thing as a small international dispute.

All these things they must learn if their world is to survive. But who will teach them these things? And who among them are willing to learn?

V

INDIA

I HAVE SAID, somewhat superficially, that the Chinese have forgotten almost everything they once knew and that the Arabs have forgotten more than they ever knew. In contrast, the Indians have perhaps not forgotten enough.

India's stuttering plunge into modernity, during its 20 years of independence, has been greatly hampered by the persistence of old beliefs, outmoded religious observances, ancient prejudices and hatreds. There is also, among her leaders, a curious complacency based upon the awareness of the extreme antiquity of Indian culture, which makes them almost incapable of searching and constructive self-criticism. In some areas, India's progress has been dazzling; in some others, it has been lethargic.

The size of India is staggering. It covers almost 1,230,000 square miles, or about one-fifteenth of the entire land mass of the world. Into this area, almost 500 million people are crammed, or about one-sixth of the entire human race. Unfortunately, the population continues to increase at a dizzying pace, a factor which seriously, and perhaps fatally, inhibits India's chances for real and lasting progress.

Certainly India's culture and civilization are among the oldest, and perhaps the very oldest, on earth. Archeologists have found in the Indus Valley indisputable traces of a highly advanced urban culture dating back 4,000 years before the Christian era. These earliest Indians were creating arts and crafts when most other races were painting themselves blue and scratching out a precarious living by grubbing for roots.

Around 1500 B.C., the Aryans poured into India and destroyed or absorbed the original culture, settling in the Punjab and the upper Ganges regions. This was the first of many painful attempts at racial unification which India was destined to go through during her history. The Aryans developed the pattern of village life which has characterized India ever since, and brought with them the rigid and stultifying caste system, which has proved to be one of her greatest moral, social and economic burdens. (Even in modern post-colonial India remnants of the caste system exist, despite the Government's efforts to eliminate it.) It was in the Aryan kingdom of Magadha, when Bimbisara was king (542-490 B.C.) that Indians first heard the teachings of Jainism and Buddhism from the mouths of their founders.

Alexander the Great invaded India in 327 B.C., to his sorrow. His armies were beaten and driven off the continent. Between the years 273-232 B.C., one of the greatest of all ancient rulers, Asoka, emerged and unified most of India, establishing Buddhism as the state religion. His empire died with him, however, as so many empires have collapsed with the death of their creators, and India degenerated into a weak and warring conglomeration of small kingdoms, each of which was an easy prey for invaders from western and central Asia.

During the latter third of the first millennium after Christ, the Hindus became ascendant in India, but in the twelfth century the Moslems began to grow in importance. In 1398, the brutal conqueror, Tamerlane, the Mogul, invaded India and captured Delhi. One of his descendants, Baber, founded the Mogul Empire, which became the stronghold of Islam on the sub-continent.

The Moguls produced a series of outstanding emperors and under the ruthless but impressive Aurangzeb (1659-1707) their regime reached unprecedented heights of power and magnificence. The Moguls declined in subsequent years and their lands were invaded by the Hindus, as well as by European armies.

76

The first serious contact between Europe and India came with Vasco de Gama in 1498. England, Holland, Portugal and France were attracted by the vast riches of the sub-continent but, as long as the Mogul Empire remained strong and solid, their ambitions were restricted to matters of commerce. When the Mogul power withered, the Europeans—particularly England (the East India Company) and France—moved in, seizing colonies by force and turning India into a cock-pit in which they fought to create monopolies. The British company finally drove out their rivals and by the 1850's, England controlled most of the land.

Excesses by the East India Company brought about a bloody revolt of its Indian troops (the Sepoy Rebellion, 1857). Reaction in England was so strong that the Company was dissolved, reforms were instituted and the Crown ruled India directly through a Viceroy. In 1877, through the efforts of Prime Minister Benjamin Disraeli, the final step was taken and Queen Victoria was crowned as Empress of India.

The British were not brutal colonizers in the way the Germans, Portuguese and Belgians were inclined to be brutal, but they were peculiarly indifferent to the sensitivities of the Indian character. They blandly assumed that the meanest Englishman was superior to the greatest Indian and operated on that basis. They were efficient and, in many ways, just rulers but they were also obtuse and even in the smallest things managed to annoy, irritate and even infuriate those whom they ruled.

Just as an example, they observed that the Brahmins followed the stupid custom of refusing to eat or drink with anyone who was not of their social caste. The English leaped upon this custom with small, well-bred cries of joy and made it their own. They couldn't have made a worse choice. They alienated Indian leaders and gave them a talking point for the stirring up of the irascibilities of the masses. And, of course, they cut themselves off from important sources of communication with Indian thinking, political and otherwise. As the delightful Indian writer, Aubrey Mennen, has remarked, they couldn't have done worse if

77

they had chosen to follow the native custom of burning English wives alive on the funeral pyres of their husbands!

On another plane, the English assumption of national superiority in everything under the sun, extended to such fields as architecture. (This in the land of the Taj Mahal!) They built railroads but then erected ferociously ugly Victorian Gothic monstrosities as stations, each one of which offended Indians' artistic sensibilities and caused them to doubt the infallibility of their conquerors. After all, it was natural to feel that if the British thought these (and other) excrescences were beautiful, or even practical, they could be wrong in other things, too.

By the same token, in choosing their civil servants the English ignored the dominant races and the dominant religions, and hit upon the Parsees as their favorites. The Parsees were not even considered Indians, by Indian standards, since they had immigrated from Persia only about 1,000 years previously and were felt to be very inferior parvenus. The Parsees became practically deputy masters of certain areas of India, particularly in Bombay.

I cite these examples of British insensitivity just to give an idea of what went on constantly to exacerbate the Indian national pride.

The proud and rather arrogant Lord Curzon of Kedleston almost created a revolution when, in 1905, he coolly partitioned Bengal, dividing the Moslems and the Hindus, without consulting any of the peoples involved! He was forced to back away from this decision to a certain extent, but the Hindus and Moslems remains separate electorates. This has had a most unfortunate effect in that it has emphasized and magnified the historic differences between the two groups.

Indian Nationalism, as a movement, began to be a serious factor in 1885, with the creation of the All-India National Congress, which was dedicated to gaining economic reform and a greater voice in England's Indian policies. Partly because of Lord Curzon's actions as Viceroy, it became a strong, and finally dominant, political party.

During World War I, the Indians supported England and her allies with fervor and courage, mostly because they thought this would hasten the cause of independence. But the English in the postwar period were almost viciously intolerant toward the nationalistic aspirations of their subject peoples. The notorious Black and Tans degraded the reputation of British arms in Ireland to a point almost as low as that which Cromwell had achieved, and in India, British-led troops behaved with almost equal barbarism, particularly in perpetrating the massacre of Indian nationalists at Amritsar in 1919.

Of course, the great figure of the Indian struggle for independence was Mohandas Gandhi, who must be reckoned as one of the truly great men of our age, despite the fact that he was erratic in many ways and inclined to shift his ideological position without notice.

Gandhi, who was born in 1869, was trained as a lawyer in London (Inner Temple) and cut his eye-teeth politically in South Africa, where he fought against the persecution of Indian settlers by the Boers. He worked valorously with a British Red Cross unit during the Boer War and made himself notably useful to the British Crown on several subsequent occasions. He won his battle for Indian rights in South Africa in 1914, and went home to India where even greater challenges awaited him. He was soon at work organizing, in support of the Indian home rule movement, a type of resistance that was to become his trademark: non-violence, use of what he called "soul force", and non-cooperation.

The Amritsar massacre appalled Gandhi and he began to make enormous headway in his campaign of *Satyagraha* ("insistence on truth") which called for non-violent disobedience to unjust laws. He also organized an Indian boycott of foreign (primarily British) goods which was more than usually irritating to the British industrialist community,

The British, once again, behaved without wisdom. They sentenced him to six years in jail in 1922 (he served two) and again in 1930. These sentences made a martyr of Gandhi, angered the Indian people, and adversely affected world opinion against the British colonial policies. The picture of the (at that time) enormous and all-powerful British Empire harassing and bullying this brilliant little, quaint, half-naked symbol of nationalist integrity was not a pretty one. The issues were not as simple as all that, of course, and Gandhi was exasperating to the British authorities, but world opinion turned fairly solidly against the British policies.

By 1935 the British were forced to agree to the establishment of provincial legislatures. The All-India National Congress Party, led by a Marxist Socialist, Jawaharlal Nehru, won thumping majorities in the first elections. The Congress would have used that majority to move for concerted action against the British rule if it had not been for the stubbornness of Mohammed Ali Jinnah, head of the Moslem league, who insisted upon the creation of a separate Moslem State, independent of India. (The poison introduced by Lord Curzon in 1905 was still working.)

When World War II broke out, India behaved far differently than she had done in the first. In that war she had hoped that her valour and her sacrifices would be rewarded with independence. Nothing of the sort happened. This time, India refused to co-operate unless she were given instant independence first. This was refused and a civil disobedience program was instituted. In desperation, Britain outlawed the Congress Party and imprisoned its leaders.

After the War, the British Labour Government (1946), offered India her freedom on condition that the Congress Party and the Moslem League would settle their differences. In August, 1947 India reluctantly agreed to the partition which made Pakistan (population 103,000,000; area: 365,528 square miles) an independent State, albeit awkwardly divided into two separate, far distant entities.

The partition, which was a poor idea in the first place, was dismally carried out. Millions of Hindus and Moslems were forced to move from one part of India to another in order to be with their own religious group. Brutal religious riots broke out in which tens upon tens of thousands were killed.

Gandhi did everything possible to stop the senseless bloodshed. But, in 1948, during a peace demonstration in New Delhi he was assassinated by a fanatic Hindu who blamed him for permitting India's partition to take place.

Like so many educated Indians, Nehru who became Prime Minister, was a very complex man, sometimes uncertain when one expected him to be bold, and inclined to philosophize in situations which demanded firm action. He insisted on Indian neutrality to such an extent that he seemed to many observers to be neutral *against* the West. He remained loyal to his friend, the firebrand pro-Communist V. K. Krishna Mennon far beyond the point where such loyalty was advisable or even sensible.

Nehru did keep India safe from her enemies within, and he did, during his seventeen years of power, bring about great reforms in the economy as well as the social life of his country.

He shocked the world in 1961 when he forcibly seized (at Krishna Mennon's insistence) the Portuguese enclaves of Goa, killing a number of innocent civilians in the process. This was a shameful rejection of Gandhi's philosophy of non-violence and a sordid infringement of the rights of a small group of Indian Christians who were quite content with their Portuguese affiliations.

Nehru blusteringly excused the aggression by saying that Goa represented the last remaining vestiges of colonialism on the Indian sub-continent. It would be interesting to see what the world reaction would be if the United States invaded Canada for the same reason! (The Indians would be the first to cry "Shame!".)

The Indians, who demanded political self-determination in seeking freedom from England, have not been willing to accept the same principles in regard to Goa and Pakistan.

The aggression against Goa opened an international can of worms. Since India had lost her virginity in a spectacularly public way, Red China decided to make the process complete and poured over the border into the North East Frontier Agency Territory claimed by India, with rape in mind.

The incident shook India up in many ways, mainly because it soon became apparent that the Chinese, if they had wanted to, could have marched all the way to Calcutta without serious opposition, and, once arrived, would have been welcomed by the Bengali. Why they didn't do this is still a mystery, as are so many things concerning Communist China. Many Indians believe that it was because the Chinese, surprised by this state of affairs, decided they had enough troubles of their own without going out of their way to acquire the further troubles of feeding and caring for millions of undernourished Indians. They had bargained for an impressive show of military muscle on a small scale, not for a full scale invasion.

The Red Chinese invasion did have the salutary effect of destroying V. L. Krishna Mennon as a political factor in India. His strong support of Red China in the United Nations prior to the invasion finally made Nehru's support politically impossible.

When Nehru died in 1964 he was succeeded by the gentle but ineffectual Lal Bahadur Shastri, whose administration was troubled by drought, famine and difficulties with Pakistan over Kashmir, which both countries claim, and which wants no part of either of them. The trouble almost led to war, but a conference (held, significantly, in Tashkent, in the U.S.S.R.) restored some semblance of peace between these sadly divided nations.

Shastri died in Tashkent and was incinerated with great ceremony early in 1966. He was succeeded by Mrs. Indira Gandhi, Nehru's daughter, whose short period of power has been further marred by droughts and famines, as well as widespread corruption which her Government has not been able to control with any consistency.

Her administration received very serious blows in the February, 1967 general elections, both from the far left and from the far right. The majority of the Congress Party in Parliament has been greatly reduced and it seems possible that Mrs. Gandhi, the first woman Premier of any major nation in the world, will not be able to retain power for more than a few years.

These are some very bare bones of Indian history. We must now dig a little deeper into the Indian character and the Indian background to flesh them out with some meaning.

In the first place it is a vast mistake to think of the Indians as a unified race. There are many distinct ethnic strains among them and because of ancient religious barriers, and the natural barriers of geography, these strains are still distinct and recognizable. There are also many religions, some of them, like Islam and Hinduism, almost irrevocably hostile to each other.

There is also a great language problem. There are more than 220 distinct languages recorded as the vernacular in India. The difference among many of these languages is great, far greater, for instance, than the difference between Portuguese and Spanish, or between German and Dutch.

The official language of India is Hindi. Clause 343 of the Indian Constitution proclaims this fact. It also proclaims that English can be used officially for 15 years after independence and then be progressively eliminated.

So far so good. The fifteen years have passed and not much has been done about putting Clause 343 into operation. It is embarrassing to Indian patriots but even now more than two-thirds of the population are completely ignorant of Hindi and many Indians, particularly in the South, refuse absolutely to learn it.

In the Parliament, English is the language of debate. It is the only language in which all the Members can communicate. The Government makes sporadic attempts to carry out the intent and meaning of Clause 343, but they never get very far. The members of the Parliament know perfectly well that if Hindi were established as the *de facto* official language, all the government jobs would go to the minority who speak, read and write it fluently. The Tamil-speaking Indians are particularly sensitive on this point, since their language is completely different in all respects from Hindi, and does not have even the same base. They also feel it is a far more sophisticated and expressive language than Hindi.

All these elements—race, religion, language—are divisive in their effect upon the people. They make united effort for the common good extremely difficult. They emphasize the differences among the people, and it is the Indian nature to nurture and cherish those differences. Old grudges and complaints, even though five centuries old, are still kept alive and can be ignited into a racial or religious riot of serious proportions on very short notice.

Although the Government, through its various five-year plans, has made creditable improvements, the economy still remains, by western standards, dismal.

The problem, of course, is over-population. It is estimated that there will be more than a billion human beings living in India by the year 2,000, and there seems to be no way to produce and distribute enough food and goods to take care of half that many people.

During the 19th Century, when the industrial revolution made its effects felt in India, there was a heavy migration of peasants from the country into the teeming cities. This reduced the agricultural production because there were not enough people to work the fields, and it also magnified the distribution problem. There were 31 serious famines in India during the century.

Famine is still the constant threat. The United States has shipped more than $1 billion worth of food into India in the past two years (1965-66), but much of it failed of proper distribution because of political reasons.

Unfortunately, it is impossible to have freedom without having also politicians, and many of the Indian politicians (not, I hasten to add, of the first rank) have proved to be extraordinarily corrupt and unfeeling toward the people. This is particularly true at the State and local levels. During the famines of 1966, desperately needed food was delayed in transit while the politicians squabbled over who was to get the credit for its distribution. Millions of dollars worth of food was cold-bloodedly shunted off into the black market. Even in the most ravaged areas of India one never saw a thin politician.

And, in the midst of all this famine, the sacred cows wander serene and untouchable! The cattle population of India is enormous. Hindus are by religion vegetarians and are forbidden to harm the cattle in any way. So, the cows eat the crops, undisturbed, while hundreds of thousands of Indians die of starvation.

Faced with a situation like this, almost every western religion would adjust its dietary regulations to fit human needs. (Indeed, on much less provocation, the Catholic Church has modified its prohibition against eating meat on Fridays, and has almost abandoned its Lenten deprivations.) But the Hindu religion is so monolithic that such an arrangement would be unthinkable. Even if the leaders of the religion were to permit the slaughter and eating of cattle, the people would not accept it. Any attempted modification of the rules would lead to unprecedented riots. The people would literally rather starve than eat beef.

And above all, there is the question of birth control. The Indian Government has done remarkably little to promote the artificial inhibition of the population explosion and, indeed, when it has done so, has run into stiff opposition from some of the religious leaders of the land.

Of course, massive measures should have been taken long ago, but an effort should be made to make up for lost time now. The kind of campaign necessary would take thousands of millions of dollars, since it would have to penetrate into every level of Indian society, and into every state and village. Unless something of this sort is done, India is destined to suffer famines, epidemics and all the other horrors and outbreaks of violence, which are bound to occur among over-crowded, underhoused and starving peoples.

Unfortunately, the blessings of birth control are universally accepted by the more literate and more affluent classes in every land—the tax producing classes—and are ignored or rejected by the least affluent,—or tax-eating—classes.

85

I suppose it is unrealistic to preach continence to a people who have so little other pleasure in life but, it seems to me that if the Indians can endure deadly famine rather than eat flesh, they could also be induced to make some sacrifices in sexual matters.

It is disheartening to learn that the biggest selling items in the bazaars of India are aphrodisiacs, love charms and magic potions. The Communists had success in persuading ignorant rustics in India's hinterland, during the famine, to reject American wheat because, they said, it would make men sterile. Many Indians would rather starve than run that particular risk. (If there were any truth in the rumor, then the consumption of such wheat should be made mandatory. India is one of the nations in the world which could benefit greatly by a temporary epidemic of sterility.)

India has more land under cultivation than any country on earth, except China (approximately 45 percent of the total land area), but techniques are generally antiquated and yields are inferior.

There are some bright spots in the economic picture. Thirty percent of the roads (about 45,000 miles) are now surfaced and the government-owned railroads operate over 36,000 track miles. If this trend improves, the distribution problem could be helped considerably.

Air India, the government-owned airline, is internationally known and respected. In Jamshedpur, Tata Steel turns out 2,000,000 tons of high quality steel a year. This is an Indian venture, pure and simple, and it gives the lie to the old, complacent British *canard* that, left alone, the Indians could not even make a decent screw. It is a significant achievement but, of course, only a drop in the bucket when compared to India's overall needs. Tata Steel would have to be multiplied a hundred times (in other areas of endeavour, of course) to make any real impression on the economic distress of the nation.

One of the troubles with India is that it has relatively few scientists, and none of world rank and not enough young

Indians are interested in science as a career. This is tragic in a country that needs scientists so desperately.

When doting parents have a clever son, their first hope is that he will go into politics. That, they feel, is where the money is and where the prestige lies. The universities, therefore, are crowded with professors of law, history and the humanities (the disciplines out of which politicians are most likely to spring) but are almost totally bereft of modern, or even adequate laboratories.

The over-supply of persons educated in the humanities is dramatized by a popular story about the graduate in Indian literature who was so penniless that he was forced to accept employment substituting for the gorilla in a Calcutta zoo. One day, while performing acrobatics, he fell into the lion's cage. He fearfully expected to be mauled and devoured, until he found that the lion was also a graduate in Indian literature.

India has thousands upon thousands of educated people who cannot find occupations worthy of their intelligence and training. The lucky ones find unimportant and often unnecessary jobs in the Civil Service, which pay miserable wages, but at least enable them to keep starvation at bay.

Not unnaturally, this creates a perfect climate for Communism to prosper. The "hangries"—educated people who are both hungry and angry—form a hard core of potential leadership for Communism in India, particularly in large and teeming cities like Calcutta. The big city masses—underfed, underprivileged, underhoused and over-exploited by local politicians—are ideally conditioned for Communist propagandizing. They care nothing about Karl Marx, or Lenin, or Mao, but they do respond when the Communist propagandists promise them better housing and some degree of sanitation. (The Communists won a majority in Calcutta in the 1967 elections.)

There should be a massive national investment in re-tooling the educational processes so the dangerous science gap can be bridged. Almost no effort has been made in this direction and the average, educated Indian feels that common-or-garden workaday science is somehow beneath him. To find a way to the stars, that is glorious; to find a way of increasing crop yields, that is common.

India has enormous resources which still remained virtually untapped. These include oil, iron, coal, bauxite, manganese, chromite, mica and a wide variety of other minerals. These need exploitation. To achieve this will take money, of course, but even more than that it will require a vast army of competent, home-grown scientists who will know the techniques of exploitation.

There is the Institute of Fundamental Research, in Bombay. It has a magnificent building, perhaps the most beautiful modern structure on the sub-continent. But the emphasis in the Institute is on achieving dramatic results in pure science for prestige purposes, rather than on making the humdrum but practical contributions which the people need to survive. This is exceedingly impractical in a nation that still is 75% illiterate.

There are enough scientists in less troubled portions of the world studying interplanetary flight and the more *recherché* interstellar matters. India needs more men who know one end of a Bunsen burner from another, and who can learn and teach others how to increase the fertility of their land (and to regulate, control or restrict the fertility of their bodies), how to produce synthetic foods, and how to do the millions of things that Indians must learn if they are to survive with any degree of hope and security in the modern world.

It would be glorious no doubt, but irrelevant, if an Indian scientist made a dramatic breakthrough and discovered something nobody has ever known. But what India needs most is a great number of scientists who can learn and teach what every scientist in the western world has known and has been teaching for years.

In the Catholic Church there is an old "sacristy joke" concerning three priests, a Franciscan, a Dominican and a Jesuit, who were conversing together when, suddenly, the lights went out. The Franciscan, coming from an order known for its holiness, began to discourse on the first words of Genesis, and how God had said, first of all, "Let there be light!". The Dominican, being a member of an order that has produced many eminent philosophers, started talking philosophically about the implications of darkness as being merely the absence of light. And the Jesuit, as a member of a very practical order, didn't say a word but got up and changed the fuse.

What India needs today is more people who can get up and change the fuse. They have been enriched over the centuries by thinkers and writers, philosophers and mystics. Now they need doers.

In the 1967 national elections, the first to be held in India since the death of Nehru, the overwhelming majority of the ruling Congress Party was cut down to a whisper, and many of Mrs. Gandhi's cabinet officers lost their seats in the Parliament. The opposition won control of five States (and the power of the individual States is far greater in India than it is in the United States) and will share in the coalition government of three others. The new Parliament will have relatively few experienced legislators and even fewer administrators in its ranks.

Famine, inefficient distribution of food and goods, food rationing, high prices, lack of social progress, and corruption all took their toll. The results showed conclusively that the Indian masses have grown weary of the promises without performance which have been their steady diet during the past twenty years.

The bumbling over the insistence upon Hindi as the national language has caused festering resentment in the South of India, where Hindi is not spoken or understood. The elections reflected this anger. In Kerala and West Bengal, the Chinese Communist supporters were victorious. In Rajasthan and Orissa, the right-wing Party supported by the maharajahs, was triumphant. There is serious danger that, unless the Government is capable of acting effectively with unaccustomed vigour, political unity in India may be fractured and some national fragmentation may occur. There is no longer any single great national hero, like Nehru,

89

who can smother the smouldering hostilities under his blanket of personal popularity.

This is, of course, serious. India is one of the oldest nations in the world. but one of the youngest major democracies. She has much to learn in the art of maintaining a democracy in working order.

The free world needs a stable India, and to maintain her stability, India needs the free world.

But if India is to preserve her stability, she must patch up the differences among her various factions, political, racial and religious. Her leaders and her people must learn to forget the centuries-old antagonisms which over the years kept the nation divided and helped to perpetuate British rule through the lack of unity among the Indians themselves.

She cannot afford the luxury of constant hostility toward Pakistan. She cannot afford the luxury of nurturing her internecine grievances. The task of transforming India into a twentieth century State is a staggering one even for a united people. For a politically, racially and religiously fragmented people, it will be impossible.

VI

AFRICA

A FRIEND OF MINE once told me that his teen-age son had said to him, "Father, I want to stand on my own two feet, but I can't do it unless you increase my allowance."

Somehow this little story seems particularly applicable to the Africa of today.

I want to make it quite clear at the outset that I feel that Africa *should* be free and independent. I am morally and constitutionally opposed to the idea of any people being ruled, by others, against their will.

And yet I feel that the whole programme of African independence has been plunged into with unseemly haste. The colonial powers were too eager to get rid of their expensive African possessions; the Africans were too eager to achieve "Independence Now!" without pausing to contemplate what independence would entail. This is particularly true of the responsibilities which are, or should be, inherent in freedom.

I am quite aware that it is unfashionable at this juncture of the twentieth century to express any doubts about the capabilities for self-government among the African peoples. Yet I would be less than honest if I did not say that such capabilities, to say the least, are still unproven.

The negro in Africa is extremely talented in many ways, but I believe that he is not, as yet, sufficiently endowed with those specific talents which are necessary to make him competitive in twentieth century civilization. This is particularly true in the areas of government and commerce.

There are so many misconceptions about the fundamental facts of Africa that it would be well to review some of them.

The land mass is enormous, about three times the size of the United States, including Alaska. A native of Dakar lives at least 4,000 miles away from a native of Johannesburg, and yet both are, by definition, Africans. Unlike India and most other areas of the earth, Africa is not overpopulated. A rough guess would put the population at 250 million, or about half that of India and one third that of China. (Population estimates are tricky. Some nations like Ethiopia, have never conducted a systematic census. Nigeria, on the other hand, habitually inflates its population figures for political purposes.)

To the frustration of those who preach the doctrine of Pan-Africa, there is very little that most of the people of the continent have in common with one another. Even race is not the unifying factor that most people consider it. Although Africa is the only area in the world where the Negro is indigenous, more than one-third of the population is not negro at all. The Ethiopians, the Somalis, the Sudanese, the Malagasy and the North Africans are not negroes. (Shakespeare, in describing *Othello*, Aaron the Moor in *Titus Andronicus*, and the Prince of Morocco in the *Merchant of Venice*, obviously thought Moors were negroes, but he was wrong.) The Pygmies are not negroes, neither are the Hottentots, the Bushmen or the Coloured of South Africa.

The language problem in Africa is even more difficult than it is in India. It is estimated that the natives speak more than 800 languages, some of them having no relationship with any other known tongue. Swahili is widely spoken as a kind of *lingua franca* in much of East Africa, and Amharic, Hausa and Yoruba are also fairly commonly used. But most Africans speak local vernaculars common only to those who live in their immediate vicinity. This has caused many States to adopt a European language (English, French, Portuguese) as an official "second" language, thus maintaining a link with and a dependence on the colonial past which they want to obliterate.

Contrary to most uninformed opinions, the jungle is relatively unimportant in Africa. Early explorers approached the continent from the sea and encountered impenetrable mangrove swamps. They proceeded up rivers that were lined by thick vegetation and dense woods, but which usually concealed open country only half a mile away. The jungle does exist, of course, abundantly, in West Africa and the Congo basin, but rarely elsewhere. The typical African landscape is prairie, much like the Middle West of the United States. This is the famous African "bush".

Most of Africa is a vast, level plateau, except for the Kenya highlands, the narrow coastal plains, the Atlas Mountains of Morocco, and the mountain ranges of the East.

Even many Africans fail to (or refuse to) recognize that their continent, by and large, is not too well suited for agriculture. (They have been told for so long that Africa is a rich agricultural storehouse that has been exploited and ravaged by the colonists, that they are inclined to accept this as gospel even in the face of incontrovertible evidence to the contrary.) Unfortunately, Africa never experienced a glacial age, a fact that has inhibited soil formation. The soils are, like most tropical soils, poor in essential minerals. The violence of the rainfall, combined with seasonal droughts, has caused erosion on almost an epical scale. The arable soil is thin and is unsuitable for deep furrowing, or even for the use of modern mechanical agricultural equipment.

Several new African States have attempted large scale agricultural experiments without taking these conditions into consideration. The experiments have turned out to be monstrous failures. African customs, in many areas, make efficient farming impractical. In Kenya, for instance, white farmers produce 65% more, off the same land, than do black farmers. But the black African farmer refuses to emulate the practices of his European competitors.

Despite these deficiencies, Africa is not a famine area and is not likely to be. The farming potential could be increased by intelligent planning and management, but nowhere near the level which some African leaders once boasted could be reached overnight.

Africa's potential wealth lies not on the land, but under it. There is some oil, and a little coal, but an abundance of iron, bauxite, manganese, cobalt, copper and diamonds.

And, of course, there is the hydroelectric potential. Africa possesses about 40 percent of the world's total. With imagination and scope in planning, Africa could become one of the industrial giants of the twenty-first century. But this will take a far different kind, and level, of leadership than that which has surfaced thus far in the continent's development.

We should also remember that Africa has very little history, as we think of that term. It is the cradle of the human race (almost certainly) but the significant history before the 18th century is sketchy and illusive.

Approximately thirty million years ago, man's ancestors, the great apes wandered about Africa in profusion. Two million years ago there were ape-like creatures who walked erect and learned to make and use rudimentary tools. After millennia of nomadic development, the African peoples started to sort themselves out and by 6,000 B.C. all the major groups now considered indigenous were established on the continent.

The Africans claim that they invented agriculture about this time. If true, then Africans can take credit for one of the major breakthroughs in the development of civilization. However, there is serious doubt among archeologists as to the validity of the claim. There is a considerable body of opinion that holds that this is an attempt to invent history where none exists, and that agriculture really had its start in the Palestine area.

Certainly, almost all the early, identifiable history of any importance in Africa was made by Egyptian invaders and settlers. There was a substantial kingdom of Meroe which lasted from approximately 700 B.C. to 350 A.D., which had its headquarters on the east bank of the Nile and the important kingdom of Ghana which came into being when Meroe was dissolving. In 1067, Muslim historians estimated that Ghana could put 200,000 warriors in chain mail into the field, 40,000 of them armed with bows and arrows. If this is true, then the armies of Ghana would have been considered formidable anywhere in the European or Asian world at that time.

But, by and large, African life was tribal and concentrated around small villages. There was contact with China, until Chinese isolationism cut off trading in the fifteenth and sixteenth centuries. There is evidence of Sung and Ming porcelain being imported from China, as well as stoneware from Siam. And during the sixteenth and seventeenth centuries the Portuguese and the Dutch created footholds in the continent, dealing mostly in cloves and slaves.

The slave trade, of course, is the horror story of Africa. Europeans, well into the nineteenth century, were not interested in "the dark continent" except as a source of strong black bodies to be sold like cattle on the open market. To conduct this trade, all one had to do was anchor off the coast, or build a trading post, and buy black men.

It is conveniently forgotten by present day commentators that the slave trade could not have existed if certain African tribes did not co-operate wholeheartedly in the dismal project. Strong black races had no compunction about selling members of weaker black races to the white man, and profiting considerably thereby. One of the most shocking stories concerns the developments in Liberia, which was founded in 1820 as a haven for freed American slaves. The transported, freed slaves no sooner set up shop in Monrovia than they began capturing tribesmen in the back country and selling *them* into slavery. Those whom they sold were headed back to the same horrors from which they themselves had so recently escaped.

The slave trade petered out in Europe because of many reasons. (It has not died out in Africa, however, and there are an estimated million slaves still in bondage on the continent. These

95

are African slaves, owned by Africans. As a matter of fact, the new African nations are often most reluctant to support any action of the United Nations against world slavery.) There was some degree of moral disgust among the peoples of Europe and America, it is true, but changing conditions, economic and social, also combined to make the traffic less remunerative than it had been. In 1772 Lord Mansfield cleared the way for the abolition of slavery in England and throughout her empire. England, once having made this decision, sought to use her naval and military power to impose the same conditions on the rest of the world. She adopted a high moral tone in doing so but, of course, she did not want to have to compete in the world markets with nations enjoying the commercial advantage of slave labor. In 1808, the United States forbade the importation of slaves (but not their use). By 1820, Spain, Portugal, Denmark and the Netherlands had all made international trafficking in slaves illegal, though they did not outlaw the institution itself.

The slave trade took a long time to die, and it did irreparable harm not only to Africa and Africans, but also to the countries which indulged themselves in it. (The United States was forced by it into a fearful Civil War and is still suffering from by-products of this infamous and degrading chapter in her history.) Quite understandably, the hostile attitudes of many black Africans toward the white race have been created by the tradition of the slave trade, and, less understandably, the attitudes of Caucasians toward Africans have also been affected. European and American writers and politicians, embarrassed by the moral cancer of slavery, sought to assuage their consciences by speaking of, writing of, and thinking of, Africans as if they were subhuman, almost without souls, and therefore fit subjects for subjugation. In its politest form this was exemplified by writers like Kipling ("lesser breeds without the law"), in its more indecent form by the excrescences of racist preachers of the gospel in many lands during the last century, who tried to justify bestial behavior by quoting the scriptures.

96

It has always amused me, incidentally, that these self-anointed Bible-thumpers continue to excuse black subjugation by citing the curse that Noah placed upon his unsympathetic son, Ham, that day on the Ark. They never bother to mention that Noah was roaring drunk at the time! The whole argument is based on the mouthings of a drunken sailor.

In any case, serious colonization of Africa is a recent development, dating from around the middle of the 19th Century. The Dutch had been in South Africa for a long while, of course, and had been joined (geographically, if not spiritually) by the English in 1808. The French had been in North Africa for some while, and the Portuguese maintained certain bases, but the real land grab started when Leopold of Belgium and the rulers of post-Bismarckian Germany began to have delusions of empire building. The English, with Cecil Rhodes as their spearhead, joined in the scramble with a will. Within two or three decades, most of Africa was partitioned among competing European nations with all the superficial neatness, and essential illogic, that attends the development of the usual large real-estate development.

The colonization of Africa was never really totally successful, nor, in most cases, particularly remunerative. Although there were differences in attitudes, and in human treatment, in the various colonies, the black Africans were never treated as "colonials" in the usual sense, but were always treated as hostile, inferior aliens in their own lands. This, of course, has added to the racial animosities which still dominate much of Africa and which, in many places, impede her progress.

African leaders today are inclined to picture the white European nations as having sucked the continent dry and leaving behind them only the husk. This is only partially true. Some individual investors and *entrepreneurs* grew enormously rich out of Africa, of course, but few nations did. And, of course, if Africa were all that wealthy a land, why are not the newly liberated nations doing better economically? It is a question that arises to haunt some of the more optimistic African politicians today.

Perhaps the worst sin of the colonists was that they geared the African production and the African economy to the needs of Europe, not to those of Africa. Most of the great African enterprises were devoted to the development or growth of goods and merchandise to be sold in Europe, and not to be sold in Africa for the sustaining of an African economy or consumption by African natives. When the markets diminished and when the Europeans left, the need was to develop an entirely new economy geared to the needs of consumers in Africa itself. This, obviously, takes some doing and it has not been done yet, nor does it seem likely to come about for some while.

The cause of African nationalism can be said to date from 1896, when W.E.B. DuBois, the first negro ever to receive a doctorate from Harvard University, emerged as a leader of black people by calling for the first Pan African Congress. (He later joined the Communist Party and died, a Ghanaian citizen, in Accra, in 1963.) In the same year, J. E. Casely-Hayford, a wealthy Gold Coast African, the first of his race ever to achieve admittance to the English bar, started the Aborigines Rights Protective Association in England, and began agitating for nationalism at the local level. These men and their disciples and successors, kept agitation for African independence alive during the first half of the twentieth century and set considerable portions of the population, particularly those living in the cities, to dreaming about independence, although the dreams did not often include the responsibilities that freedom involves.

World War II sealed the doom of colonialism in Africa. The Africans who went off to fight against white enemies in Europe, discovered that white men were not, after all, gods, and, at home, often lived under conditions just as degrading as those to which they themselves were accustomed. On the other hand, the European countries were so exhausted by the war that they had not the strength, nor the will, to remain as colonial powers. Africa, simply, was not worth fighting to retain.

This was aggravated by the fact that world opinion (especially among non-colonial powers such as the United States, Soviet Russia and Latin American countries) was turning against the whole idea of colonialism and making the increasingly unremunerative African enterprise more and more embarrassing.

There is a lot of chest-beating among African leaders about how they drove the European invaders off the continent. This makes attractive listening for their constituents, but it is really nonsense. Since the end of World War II the scramble to get out of Africa has been just as frantic as was the scramble to get into Africa in the 1870's.

If anything, the Europeans left, in some cases, with indecent haste. The African nations would have been far better off if the Europeans had remained a little longer and had introduced responsible leaders into the arts of government and economics before taking leave of the land. By yielding too fast and granting premature independence European powers in many cases abrogated their moral responsibilities and hurt the interest of the Africans involved. The process of decolonization was, in short, almost as immoral as the process of colonization had been.

France has been particularly culpable in this regard. Her precipitous and callous departure from Guinea was nothing less than brutal. (In March of 1967 the people of Somaliland voted to retain their colonial ties with France because the French threatened to walk out on them if they didn't, just as they had done in Guinea.)

One of the greatest problems of modern Africa is that the national boundaries do not make much sense *as national boundaries*. They were drawn up by colonial powers (or by *entrepreneurs* like Cecil Rhodes) for their own convenience in administration, and with little regard for the ethnic, religious or linguistic differences among those contained within the boundaries. This worked out reasonably well under an all-powerful European rule, but when it became time for these artificially contrived political entities to govern themselves, the problems became severe. Independence has not eradicated tribalism and it will take years of education if this disruptive force within the African nations is to be eliminated, or even kept within reasonable bounds. If indeed it ever can be.

In Kenya, for example, there are 52 tribes, almost all hostile to each other. The principal political parties are tribal, rather than ideological, in make-up. The two dominant parties control separate sections of the country and civil war and fragmentation are always a distinct possibility. And yet Kenya has far more potential as an independent nation than most other African countries.

The Congo is similarly disrupted by tribalism, and much of its recent bloody history can be attributed to this cause. In Basutoland, the prerogatives of the Paramount Chiefs of the important tribes disrupt orderly governmental processes, since the Chiefs must be consulted on the formulation of even minor national policies. There is a constant clash between the modern, progressive thrust of independence on one side, and the ancient, conservative tradition of the tribal leaders on the other. Too often these differences lead first to hostility and then to stalemate.

Most of the African nations have Socialist forms of government. This is almost a natural result of colonialism since the paternalistic relationship of colonial governments toward the natives was, essentially, socialistic in its effect.

But African-style socialism differs from the classical variety in that it has no truck with atheism or agnosticism. Africans are everywhere religious. Even her Marxist leaders insist upon a belief in God and on supernatural values. They could get nowhere if they didn't.

Almost all Africans believe in the universality of the spirit and that the spirits affect daily life and can be influenced by religious practices. This has made them susceptible to Christian teaching, on the one hand, and to the practices of witchcraft on the other. (Several prominent African leaders openly consult witch doctors, and few have the courage to deny openly their potency.)

Although traditional African religions are in the decline, except in areas far from the larger centres of population, there are more than 2,000 peculiar sects based rather precariously on Christian beliefs. Usually these sects are based on one text of the Old Testament, with all the rest of the Bible being discarded or rejected. Peter Lessing, the eminent British journalist, who is one of the most knowledgeable of all African observers, has listed some of these picturesque cults: The Holy Spout in Zion, The African Noah's Ark Ethiopian Church, the Heaven Church in Zion, the International Four Square Gospel Church, the Bed Bug Church, the African Castor Oil Dead Church. (The rites of the latter consist mostly of ingesting huge quantities of castor oil in order to induce massive purification.) Most of the members of these Churches consider themselves as devoutly Christian. In some of the Churches elaborate, orgiastic sexual rites are of great significance. (Sex has always played a large role in African religious beliefs. In some areas it is not unsual to find tribal women wearing necklaces of smoked male genitals as they go about their daily chores.)

The off-beat neo-Christian cults have considerable importance in the world of African nationalism. Many churches are led by aspiring politicians. Many of the leaders pervert Biblical texts for their own political ends. There is one cult in Tanganyika, for instance, which cites the Bible as proof that the negro is essentially superior to the white man and that it is the will of God that white should be subservient to black.

These free-swinging cults have made little progress in the coastal regions where Mohammedanism is predominant. (There are an estimated 800,000 Muslims in Africa, mostly based in the far north.) But they have made considerable inroads among the conventional Protestant sects and among the Catholics, whose relatively austere beliefs are more difficult to master and impose on the faithful a less enjoyable form of discipline.

The history of religion in Africa indicates that Africans have usually managed to misunderstand Christian teachings, or to pervert them to their own liking. For instance, when the British

101

captured Benin, in 1897, they were horrified to find that the inhabitants had crucified hundreds of their captives as a gesture of supplication against conquest by the white devils.

Although, as I have said, it was rather natural for the African governments to adopt socialism as their form of government in the beginning, most nations would benefit greatly if an opposition party were permitted to question the validity of this philosophy as a permanent *modus vivendi*. Certainly it would be most useful if such an opposition party could challenge the tendency in some new nations to lean toward Russia rather than toward the West. If for no other reason, it would be beneficial to have an opposition party to keep reminding African peoples of Russian Communism's appalling record of exploitation and subjugation wherever it has gained ascendancy.

Unfortunately, most African nations operate under a one-party political system. This is also, perhaps, natural. National independence in most cases took place under the leadership of a popular revolutionary figure like Nkrumah, Nyerere, Touré, Banda, Kenyatta, and it was not likely that organized opposition would arise easily against such leaders. This has been the pattern in most revolutionary societies. It was not until George Washington was several years dead that political partisanship developed in the United States. In India and Mexico the dominant political party is still the original party of the revolution.

Dr. Julius Nyerere, of Tanzania, has expressed the one-party point of view in this way: "The struggle for freedom from foreign domination is a patriotic one which necessarily leaves no room for difference...

"The same nationalist movement, having united the people and led them to independence, must inevitably form the first government of the new state; it could hardly be expected that a united country should halt in midstream and voluntarily divide itself into opposing political groups just for the sake of what I have called the Anglo-Saxon form of democracy at the moment of independence. Indeed, why should it?"

There is logic in Doctor Nyerere's argument. Unfortunately, the one-party system also makes revolution and political take-over more common. It drives legitimate opposition underground. Where there is no accommodation for political compromise, more drastic methods of political assertion present themselves. One-party states seldom provide for an orderly succession of leadership, so every change of ruler precipitates a major political crisis. In twelve months (1965-1966), seven African governments have been toppled, including Nigeria (once considered the most stable of all), Ghana (another centre of hope), Upper Volta, the Central African Republic, Dahomey and the Congo. What Dr. Nyerere failed to realize is that in even a one-party democratic nation there are always two parties: the government and the army. Most of the governments in Africa were toppled by military insurrections or mutinies.

Also, unfortunately, the comparison with George Washington (or even Gandhi and Nehru) does not stand up. George Washingtons have been in distressingly short supply in Africa. The African Founding Fathers were simply not capable of holding their infant nations together. Most of the recent coups were bloodless and remarkably easy. Indeed many of the deposed leaders were openly relieved when they were thrown out of office. They had found impossible the task of administering democratically nations composed of dissident ethnic groups, and capriciously arranged geographically.

Why did the coups take place? Although the reasons differ somewhat in each case, the principal cause has been massive disillusionment. The African people were told that independence would usher in a brave new world, Utopia, an era of unprecedented prosperity, development, progress. Of course, it did nothing of the sort. Many of the countries were almost totally unprepared for independence. Independence brought unemployment, lower wages, inflation, grinding poverty and incompetent and often corrupt administration. Many of the nations, in short, once the dawn of independence broke, found they were worse off from a materialistic point of view than they had been under their colonial masters, and very little better off from a spiritual point of view.

The end is nowhere in sight. As I write these words, Africa is still in turmoil. I have listed the successful coups above, but unsuccessful mutinies and uprisings have also occurred in Togo, Zanzibar, Tanzania, Uganda, Kenya, Guinea, the Ivory Coast, Niger, Chad, Senegal and Burundi. Although these outbreaks have been put down, the elements that caused them are still present and there is no reason to believe, in most cases, that they will not be repeated.

Of course, the picture is not all bad. There are encouraging bright spots in the African landscape. Tanzania, Kenya, Zambia and Uganda are all benefiting from strong and able leadership and they look now as if they might be able to make it on their own. But the objective observer cannot help but be pessimistic about most of the rest of independent Africa.

Racial bigotry has caused great damage in Africa, and is still causing great damage. The bigotry against Europeans, north of the Zambesi, is just as damaging as the bigotry against black men in the South. In most northern nations the need for educated white men sympathetic with African aims is great. The presence of trained white bureaucrats to organize and administer technical aspects of the Government would be invaluable. But, in most cases, the presence of whites is considered an affront. At best, even the most sympathetic whites have been merely tolerated. At worst they have been persecuted, robbed, abused, murdered, or driven away. There is much the Africans can learn from Europeans in their midst, but they do not choose to learn.

Certainly there is no reason for Africans in most areas to love the white man. They have cause for deep resentment and they have memories of implacable racism directed against them on their own land. But, to retaliate with equal unreason and bigotry is merely cutting off the nose to spite the face. Just because the European overlords failed to instruct the African in the technology of government, commerce and modern agriculture and industry during the colonial days, there is no reason why the

104

African should not use the European today to learn such technology today.

African society today is essentially political. Often it is a case of politics being an end in itself, rather than a means of bringing about national prosperity and fulfillment. While this is perhaps understandable in an emerging nation, it is not conducive to national development.

There is a serious lack of native *entrepreneurs*. Those few Africans with administrative or technical skills are not businessmen but employees of large organizations, owned either by Europeans or by the State.

The ruling political class in most African nations actively discourages the development of a prosperous native business community. This is officially excused on the grounds that classical socialist doctrine holds the emergence of a capitalist class to be undesirable. But the real reason is that a successful business class would develop rivals for political power and could conceivably threaten the position of the present political elite. Foreign business *entrepreneurs* are considered safer. They can be more easily managed and they cannot become political opponents. This is, of course, harmful to the nation, but it is reassuring to the political leaders.

The ruling class is composed of politicians and civil servants, and they are distrustful of educated citizens who do not fall into either of these categories. As a result there is a growth in some African countries (as there has been in India) of unemployment among literate or semi-literate natives. This has caused a serious "brain drain" in Africa. In increasing numbers, clever Africans who have been trained abroad in medicine, the sciences and business, are finding ways to remain abroad, rather than return to the discouraging prospects which await them at home.

As an example of this, in 1963, Nigeria graduated 19 doctors from its sole medical school. By 1967, 16 of them were working in American hospitals. And Nigeria is a country in which there is one doctor for every 33,000 people (as opposed to one for every 670 in the United States.) It is estimated that half the

105

Africans who travel to the United States for their college work do not return to Africa when they are graduated.

Socialism tends to create an aristocracy of its own, often indistinguishable from the aristocracies developed by political systems it presumes to despise. The aristocracy consists of the politicians.

The political leaders of Africa are, for the most part, not only authoritarian, but remarkably self-indulgent. ("We have the papacy, let us enjoy it.") As in India, there are no thin African politicians. They pay themselves very well, far more than their counterparts in Europe are paid, and far more than the economy of their nations can afford.

In many cases, a major portion of the national budget is expended for the care and feeding of the politicians. It has been estimated, for example, that the cost of supporting the politicians in little Gabon represents a higher proportion of the national product than was the cost of supporting the court of Louis XVI at Versailles just prior to the French Revolution.

Unfortunately, the already-rich politicians have almost innumerable opportunities to augment their incomes through graft and bribery, both of which are widespread through almost all the African States.

All this has had serious and deleterious consequences, even beyond the unconscionable drain on the national treasuries. The political jobs are so much better than any other jobs available that the politicians will do almost anything to hold onto them. This causes pressures for the maintenance of autocratic government through corrupt elections, intimidation, and other means. There is also a gradual disappearance of a middle class, thus widening the gap between those who are rich solely because they are in power (rather than vice-versa) and the poor, for whom the revolution, presumably, was accomplished, and who have no hope of ever being even moderately well-off.

The disillusionment (as we have seen) is growing and is leading to serious consequences. It could eventually lead to wide-

106

spread and violent rebellion which would reduce the entire African experiment in freedom to chaos and riot.

Many of the African leaders are young and inexperienced. They have been sent off to college, earned their degrees, and then have come home to be accepted almost automatically as important political persons.

Unfortunately, colleges teach theory, not practice. The young African graduates are fairly bursting with political and economic theories, many of which are quite impossible of practical application under conditions as they exist. The attempts to impose theories in unworkable situations have caused a great deal of political and economic unhappiness throughout the continent.

There is a tendency among the new and young African leaders to insist upon cheap victories and the easy way. For so many of the countries, independence dropped in their laps like an overripe fruit and they appear to expect the other fruits, like economic progress, political stability, world-wide acceptance into the community of nations and cultural equality to drop in the same way. These will not drop; they must be nurtured first, and then plucked. In many cases, *independence* in Africa was achieved almost accidentally. The *fruits* of independence must be earned. They cannot be earned by manufacturing slogans or by blind ideological doctrinaire thinking. They must be earned by hard work, by planning, by intelligence, tolerance of other ideas and by political eclecticism.

Up until this point I have discussed, almost exclusively, "black" Africa, the area which extends north of the Zambesi River. Let us cast a glance now at "white" Africa, which lies South of that dividing river.

"White" Africa consists of the Portuguese colonies, Rhodesia and the Union of South Africa. All three are a source of great disturbance on the continent and, under present circumstances, are a threat to the peace of the world itself.

The Portuguese were the first Europeans to gain a foothold in Africa and they are the last European colonial "power" to remain there. The Portuguese have been there since the last decade of the 15th century, and, despite world opinion and the hatred of Africans generally, they intend to remain there.

Portuguese Africa consists of three territories: Angola (5,000,000 inhabitants, of whom 200,000 are white settlers), Mozambique (7,000,000 inhabitants, 60,000 whites), and Portuguese Guinea (50,000 inhabitants, a scattering of them white). In Angola, 50,000 of the white population consist of Army troops.

The Portuguese situation in Africa is unique. Portugal is itself an underdeveloped country and, unlike the other colonial powers in Africa, she desperately needs her African possessions to keep her local economy reasonably afloat.

The Portuguese have traditionally been rugged, even brutal colonizers, much given to the employment of forced labor (a euphemism for slavery) and to employing severe methods for keeping the natives "in line". The history of Angola has been bloody and depressing and it has been particularly distressing since World War II when thousands of poor, ignorant Portuguese peasants were transported to the colony because the economy at home could no longer sustain them. Most of these peasants were just as illiterate as the natives, and scarcely, if at all, more skilled, and they became competitors for jobs, land and food. Like poor-whites everywhere, they brought to Angola a much more virulent racial prejudice than the original Portuguese settlers had ever exhibited. This has led to savage outbreaks, and even more savage reprisals in which black people were indiscriminately slaughtered to "teach them a lesson".

The Portuguese tradition of suppressing African languages, African culture, African religion and of refusing to permit Africans to participate significantly in any function of administration, has caused these colonies to be far less prepared for independence than even the French colonies. On the other hand, this stupid suppression by the Portuguese has caused the nationalist sentiment in the colonies to flourish and spread.

On the surface, the future of the Portuguese colonies, as colonies, would appear to be dim, particularly since Portugal is ostensibly in no position to resist any "liberating" African forces. But the "liberating" forces in Africa, as yet, do not really exist and a reasonably well-trained Portuguese army can probably handle, at the moment, any opposition that is likely to develop. Furthermore Rhodesia and South Africa have a compelling stake in maintaining the white Portuguese colonial power on the continent. The industrial and military power of South Africa is so dominant that any successful attempt to drive the Portuguese off the continent seem, for the moment, remote.

But, continuing strife seems to be in the cards for these colonies. And, if and when the Fascist administration of Dictator Antonio Salazar in Portugal falls (as all dictatorships must finally fall), it is possible that a more liberal administration will see fit to withdraw from Africa in an orderly fashion and return the land to those who originally owned it.

Rhodesia is still a different matter. It is a settler State, in which a handful of white men dominate a large negro population. (Of 5 million people in Rhodesia, 94 percent are black.)

Cecil Rhodes, who created Rhodesia as a kind of personal duchy, about 100 years ago, was himself a frank and practising racist. (His Rhodes Scholarships were designed to create an Anglo Saxon-Teutonic *corps elite* which would perpetuate his ideas throughout the governments of those countries which he considered most civilized. He undoubtedly, if he is permitted to see such things from his personal Valhalla, is greatly disappointed in how things have turned out. The American Rhodes Scholars who have gravitated to the State Department of the United States, for example, represent perhaps the most vigorous and vocal opposition to racism in the U.S. Government.)

The Rhodesians talk a lot about their pioneer heritage and have developed a kind of spurious *mystique* about their background of carving a little empire out of the black African land. But, closer to the truth, is the description uttered by former Southern Rhodesian Prime Minister Garfield Todd, of how it all was accomplished: "We brought out the scum of Europe, as long as their skins were a bit white, to fire engines and get drunk and keep the black man down." Once again, the poor-white immigrants could be depended upon to be most virulent in their racism.

The tradition of racial subjugation in Rhodesia is even stronger than it has ever been in South Africa, where, of course, it has been brutal and continuing. Africans in Rhodesia have been denied land, the vote, and even the most elementary kind of education. The attitude of the whites toward the blacks has been primitive to the last degree.

But, once again, an overthrow of the white supremacy forces (presently led by Premier Ian Smith) in Rhodesia will be difficult as long as South Africa remains strong and prosperous.

When Great Britain tried to bring the Smith Government to heel by imposing economic sanctions on Rhodesia, she failed because such sanctions are almost meaningless unless the Union of South Africa is also included in the ban. England cannot afford to impose sanctions on South Africa (her economy depends upon this market too much) and, of course, the commerce between South Africa and Rhodesia flows easily and naturally across the borders.

So the key to the permanence or impermanence, as the case might be, of white Africa is the Union of South Africa (area, 472,000 square miles; population, 18 million, of whom 4 million are white). And quite a key it is.

South Africa is unique. It is the only real nation on the continent that is of European origin and it has the largest African population that is thoroughly adjusted to a modern, sophisticated industrial civilization.

The negroes, as everyone knows, have been ruthlessly discriminated against in South Africa, but not to the same extent that they have been in Rhodesia or even in the Portuguese colonies. There are several thousand Africans who have been given college educations and many negroes have been given the opportunity of mastering, and using, important industrial skills. (White salaries, however, are often as high as 17 times greater than the salaries of blacks in comparable jobs, and infant mortality among the blacks is 8 times higher than it is among whites.)

The Afrikaners are not johnny-come-latelies in Africa like the Rhodesians. Most of them are of families that have lived in Africa for more than 300 years and which have the same possessive feeling about the land as do citizens of the United States whose ancestors fought at Lexington or Concord. They have built upon the continent a nation that is respectable and modern in every way except in its attitudes toward race. The country is very rich in natural resources, and its economic growth averages between 5 and 7 percent a year, which is well above average. Its Gross National Product is more than twice as large as that of Nigeria, which is several times its size. To the disgust and embarrassment of those who espouse the cause of a totally black Africa, the nation is flourishing, prosperous and dwarfs the rest of the continent in accomplishments.

I want to make it clear (once again) that I believe the doctrine of *apartheid* is vicious, immoral and anti-Christian and I have a suspicion that those who practise it assiduously have a special section of Hell awaiting them when they depart this life. But, disapproval of South Africa's basic cultural *mores* can be no excuse for closing one's eyes to the materialistic advances the nation has made in a world that is generally antagonistic to its racial philosophy.

On the obverse side of the coin, the leaders of Africa north of the Zambesi think that if South Africa were to become a black African state, then the economic problems of the continent could possibly be settled. South Africa could be the powerhouse to fire the entire economy of the immense continent.

So, the attitude of the rest of Africa toward this prosperous white supremacy State at the southern end of the continent, is a mixture of indignation at the way that black Africans are treated there, and of greed.

And, of course, there are such questions as whether or not South Africa should be a black State like, let us say, Nigeria?

Should it belong to black Africans any more than Minnesota, let us say, should belong to the red Indians? Or Texas to the Mexicans? Or Mexico to the Aztecs?

And, also a very unfashionable question arises: Could black Africans manage the industrial complex of South Africa with anywhere near the efficiency with which it is being managed today? Would, in other words, South Africa be the powerhouse for the rest of the continent if it were under exclusively black Africa management? Sadly, I must say I feel this is doubtful.

One of the greatest troubles with independent Africa today is the scarcity of clear and straight thinking. There is too much glandular reaction, not enough hard mentation. Every issue is approached emotionally, not intellectually. Bigotry, prejudice, intolerance, fanatacism count too much on far too many essential issues.

To put the matter in rather naive terms, there is a lack of understanding of the fundamental truth that two wrongs do not make a right. If a person or a nation behaves inhumanely against you, it does no good to react with the same inhumanity. You only descend to the same level of behaviour; you demean yourself without improving your enemy.

There is also, in Africa, an almost complete unwillingness, or inability, to face the facts of life as they are, and a startling unconcern about the necessity of learning those facts.

African leaders have time and time again exhibited a lamentable ignorance about the facts of life in countries in Africa other than their own, and sometimes about even their own countries.

This was, notably, displayed in the discussions during the summit conference of African leaders in Addis Ababa in 1963.

The conference blithely voted to finance (with a million and a half pounds sterling) a Pan African "March on Johannesburg" which would drive the white population in South Africa into the sea, and take with them the whites in Mozambique and Angola as well.

This resolution was passed with a whoop and a holler, but

without taking into consideration certain factors which, at the moment, make the plan impracticable.

Item: Where will the million and a half pounds come from? Most African nations are hard enough put to maintain order and develop a reasonable economy within their own borders, without financing an expensive war thousands of miles away. Also, the interest of an African in northern Africa in a native of South Africa is pretty theoretical. It is about as intense as the interest of an Alaskan Eskimo in an Indian living in the Panama Canal Zone. They both are under American domination; they both are, vaguely, Indian. And, so what? Neither feels any compelling necessity to die for the other. (The African Liberation Committee, after much struggle, was able to raise about one-tenth of the sum proposed.)

Item: They conveniently forget that South Africa has the most formidable army on the continent. Portugal has stationed 50,000 troops in Angola, and 20,000 in Mozambique. They may not be *Wehrmacht* in quality, but they are far better trained and far better equipped than anything Africa is likely to produce as a striking force. Most importantly, Portugal and South Africa have small but modern Air Forces which could paralyze any African invasion plans before they got started.

Item: There has been no success, to date, in creating effective military intelligence, or even ordinary intelligence on a government-to-government or a people-to-people basis among the various African States. The newspapers are primitive and most of them are little more than puff-sheets for the administration in power in each particular nation. Most newspapers are heavily censored and controlled. There is little free flow of information among the African States, and without this any combined military effort would be futile.

Item: Northern African leaders fail to differentiate between the attitudes of purely colonial powers, and the attitude of Portugal and South Africa. South Africa is not a colony, it is a nation. Its white settlers have roots in the land just as deep as have the white "settlers" in Minnesota or New Mexico. They

113

have been on their land longer than have the Minnesotans and New Mexicans. They will not just pack up their belongings and leave, because they have nowhere else to go. They cannot go home, because they are already home. The same goes for the Portuguese whites in Angola and Mozambique. They do not live in colonies, they live in Portugal. These sections of Africa are integral parts of Portugal just as much as are Braganza and Castello Branco. Portugal feels that a history of 400 years of possession in this particular part of the world is sufficient to give her legal title. She will not give in as she did when India raped Goa, because the stakes are a very great deal higher in Africa. (If Portugal were to lose her African provinces, her economy would collapse. Goa was unimportant to her internal economy.) And though Portugal may not be one of the formidable military powers of the western world, she is far more formidable than any power that the African nations can, at this time, mount against her. And, of course, she can depend upon complete military and ideological support and co-operation from South Africa.

Item: It is the worst kind of foolishness for African nations, at this stage of their development, to talk about spending millions of dollars on extravagant and doubtful military adventures. Any money that could be spent on conducting a war against the Union of South Africa, Rhodesia and Portugal could be better spent on development at home. There is a need for far less hotheadedness and for a great deal more patience. If African nations concentrate on building up their own interior strength, it may never be necessary to fight a war against the white South. And even if, eventually, the black nations north of the Zambesi do find it necessary, they would be in a far better position to win than they are right now. Any military effort under present conditions would be an economic, social and moral catastrophe.

I hasten to add that I am not speaking of things as they ought to be. I am speaking of things as they are.

And, above all, I am not speaking of things as they always must be.

The intransigence and brutality of the South African white community toward the negro is stupid and short-sighted. South Africa is building up an enormous store of hatred and resentment against herself among all the other nations of Africa, and, certainly, she has no divine assurance that her present position of impregnability is permanent. World conditions could change swiftly and make it no longer necessary to refuse to impose economic sanctions on South Africa. She could very well find herself cut off from the rest of the white world which, for the most part, looks upon her programme of oppression with distaste. Another global conflict, for example, could do this overnight. Nations which tolerate South Africa today would find themselves far too busy to indulge in such luxuries and the South African nation would soon find itself bereft of defense against a black invasion.

If a really serious black uprising were to take place in either South Africa or the Portuguese possessions now, it could, no doubt, be put down. But the putting down would entail such a blood-bath that the stomachs of the western white world could be irretrievably turned and nations might seek other alternatives than toleration of present policies.

Portugal has been making concessions to its black population. Not enough, and not in any significant depth, but, nonetheless concessions. The South Africans have not only made none, but the Government tends to get tougher.

And Rhodesia, which could not last ten minutes if South Africa did not stand behind her, amuses herself by thumbing her nose at the rest of Africa and the rest of the world. In fact, the Ian Smith administration is being threatened politically by an opposition which claims the Government is too "soft" on the blacks.

It is all madness.

The time for these nations and provinces to make concessions is now, when concessions are not compulsory. Concessions made under compulsion are meaningless and would do nothing to appease the wrath of the black Africans if such wrath ever became assertable.

Intransigence in human affairs is always stupid. The leaders of "white" Africa have been just as intransigent as have the leaders of "black" Africa, and with less excuse.

The African revolution is by no means complete. In many areas it was started prematurely. In many areas (such as the Congo) it has thus far proved to be a failure. But the revolution exists and it will continue.

But, if the revolution is to be a success, African leaders must learn that revolutions do not succeed, and man does not progress by negation alone.

Africa must first discover herself and preserve those elements that are good and which are common to most African peoples, and use them as a means of creating on the continent a viable form of Pan Africanism. She must find a way to establish her identity in the world. Mere blackness, or negritude is not enough. The identity must be deeper than the skin. It must permeate the bone and inspire the soul.

And Africa must *learn to learn* from Europe and Europeans. The Europeans have been in the civilization business for centuries. They have the technology, the training, the expertise which Africa needs if she is to become a truly significant part of the world, if she is to realize her potential, if she is going to be anything more than a conglomeration of cultural backwaters sustained by the sporadic guilt-feelings of the white world.

This is not easy for Africa to do. Her resentments are deep and legitimate. But her hope for the future lies in collaboration with the white world, not in insistence upon a kind of *apartheid* of her own.

The hope of Africa lies in her ability to find and then establish her own identity. She cannot prosper if she continues to exploit the hatred of everything white and if she rejects white ideas, white medical techniques, white economic and agricultural expertise. Unfortunately, the modern world as we know it has been shaped by European and Asiatic forces and, to survive

116

successfully, Africa must adjust, in her own way, to those conditions. She may be able to affect and influence the world as it exists, but she cannot remake it.

Africa can eventually contribute something unique to world civilization, but she first must develop the means of making such a contribution within herself.

There are so many new African nations, almost forty at last count, that they can eventually dominate the United Nations Organization. They have the votes, if not the leadership and prestige. She can conceivably, if she will, be the unique force which can soften the attitudes between the East and the West and be the leader in the ultimate effort to build a new world of broherhood and equality among all men.

No political entity in the history of the world has ever had such a unique opportunity for accomplishment and service. Unhappily for Africa and for the rest of this greatly troubled world, there has been little to encourage one to believe that she has, as yet, the will or the ability to assume such a burden of responsibility.

VII

JAPAN

I AM CHINESE.

I try, but I cannot be wholly objective about the Japanese. The Chinese have suffered much from Japanese savagery and indifference over the ages. One does not forget these things entirely. They are bred in the bone and borne along the bloodstream. But, one must try. The whole peace of the world depends upon individuals, first, trying to overcome their prejudices and to forget their wrongs (or the wrongs of their forefathers) and then to impose their individual and united sense of tolerance upon their governments. This rarely works from top to bottom (no matter what the diplomats say); it must work from bottom to top, if it is to be effective and permanent.

It is amazing to me that the United States of America has shown such a magnanimity toward Japan, and has taken in recent years with equanimity certain occasional slurs and insults when she could redress them with a mere flick of the hand.

Although I shall have more to say of this later, it seems to me a mark of greatness and maturity in a nation that it can forbear from over-reacting when it is tormented with pin-pricks.

I cannot help but think of the bitter resentment of the French against the Prussian aggressor, which lasted in full force for a half century, at the very least, and exists in part even today, because of the War of 1870, to the complete detriment of relations between France and Germany, and then contrast it with the American attitude toward Japan since World War II. The

United States had many reasons, valid reasons, to be totally vindictive against Japan after World War II, and, instead, behaved with unique charity and solicitude. And yet one sees anti-American demonstrations in Japan! It is hoped that the Japanese do not mistake idealism and magnanimity for weakness.

The western world thinks the Chinese are inscrutable. Perhaps we are. But I must admit that *I* find the Japanese inscrutable, or, at least, more than occasionally, beyond comprehension.

They have imitated the Chinese for centuries, but, somehow, they have always got things a little wrong—culturally, artistically, politically, socially and morally. (For a much briefer time the Indians have imitated the British and have also got things essentially wrong, copying the form but not the substance.)

How can one reconcile the almost servile Japanese politeness and insistence on meticulous and refined artistic effects with their cruelty and grossness toward their American and British enemies in World War II? How can one reconcile their almost absurd observance of the forms of religion with their almost complete disregard for the substance of religion of any sort? How can one reconcile the almost unbelievable and fragile beauty of Nara, for example, with the equally incredible bestiality of Bataan?

It is a puzzlement.

But, nonetheless, even the most prejudiced person must admit that the Japanese are an incredible and, in many ways, an admirable people.

For twelve centuries they slavishly imitated China, and then for two centuries pulled down the blinds and shut the gates and went into seclusion. When they emerged from isolation they found to their dismay that the world was no longer dominated by Chinese culture, but by European gun boats and cannon. They were centuries behind the western world in all the areas that mattered if they were to be competitive.

The Japanese promptly turned their nation into an industrial State and built an army and a navy along western lines. They began to use their military forces aggressively and, in doing so, gravely affected the history of the world. In all probability, neither Russia nor China would have turned Communist if they had not been first severely damaged by Japanese blows.

Japan seems almost totally resilient. In 1946, her condition seemed hopeless. She was a beaten nation, despised by free men everywhere. Her empire was gone, her factories in ruins. Two of her major cities had been demolished by the Bomb. She was overcrowded to a point where she could not possibly feed her own people. Four fifths of her military and mercantile fleet was at the bottom of the ocean. She had only 17 ships to her name.

After twenty years, Japan has emerged once again as the great power of the East. She is the world's greatest ship builder. She makes more steel than does France. Her standard of living is the highest in the Orient. And, miracle of miracles, she has apparently entered upon a massive program of voluntary birth control. Prior to 1948, her birth rate was among the highest in the world. Since that time the rate has fallen even below that of England, and is one of the lowest in the world.

Fecundity has traditionally been Japan's greatest problem. It led her into a disastrous war because she felt it was necessary to find *lebensraum* for her teeming millions. Her chances for continued prosperity and peace now depend upon the ability of her people to keep the propagative instinct reasonably controlled.

Of course, Japan is still overcrowded. Her land area, consisting of an archipelago of more than 1,000 islands, covers only 142,726 square miles, or considerably less than the land area of California. However, 99 million people live in Japan, and only 18 million in California. One out of every 9 Japanese live in Tokyo which, with more than eleven million inhabitants, is probably the largest city in the world.

The latest statistics on Tokyo show that it has twice as many cinemas as has New York, and more neon lights by far than any city in the world (alas!). It has 78 universities with over 400,000 students. There are 2,500 bath houses and 11,000 cemeteries; 35,000 bars; 5,500 beauty parlors; 1,455 Shinto shrines, and 2,753 Buddhist temples. There are 1,600 publishing companies, and more than 100 magazines publishing, exclusively, poetry.

Only about 500,000 households have flush toilets, or one out of every five.

Tokyo, and most other Japanese cities, are essentially garish and ugly. As civic developments they are monstrosities. I cannot escape the conclusion that the Japanese ruling classes planned them that way. It gives them that much more aesthetic satisfaction when they escape the gaudy, bawdy outside world and enter the exquisite, quiet beauty of their own homes. It makes possible the Pharasaic pleasure of breathing a word of thanks to whatever gods they think there be for not being like other men. It is a kind of extension of Japanese flower arrangement, or sand and stone garden planning. Crazy, but entirely possible.

The present day Japanese are a mixture of many Oriental races. The only distinctive ethnic group is the Ainu, considered to be aboriginal. The Ainu have Caucasian faces, and were relentlessly persecuted and despised for many years.

The language is also hybrid, though it leans heavily on the Chinese and is almost equally complicated. There are twenty equivalents of the English pronoun "I", for example and they are not interchangeable but are to be used in special circumstances. There is one system of pronouns for men and one for women. And to be able to read and write Japanese with any facility one must have first memorized more than 1,500 characters, at a minimum.

The principal religion of Japan is Shinto, but Buddhism is tolerated and, today, there are many Christians. This seems like an amiable arrangement, but the fact is that the Japanese are not really a religious people at all. Religion, with them, is a device to preserve law and order. It is a convenience to the Government. Before World War II few intelligent Japanese actually believed that their Emperor was a god descended from the Sun Goddess but the appearance of belief was maintained in order to justify the operation of an autocratic form of Government.

122

There are more than 200 Buddhist sects in Japan and many Japanese consider themselves both Buddhists and Shintoists. Since the war, new cults have grown up in some profusion. Some worship the Pole Star. One even considered making Rutherford Adcock, Great Britain's first Ambassador to Japan, an object of serious worship. (The British put a stop to this. They like to be admired, but not adored.)

The Japanese Christians were disturbed at first by Japan's program to conquer the world and rule it "under one roof". However, some bright theologian decided that the Trinity was really a Quaternity and that the Emperor was the fourth Member. This made everything all right.

Few Japanese believe in sin or in an after world. When they pray, they do not ask for admission into Paradise, they pray for temporal comfort and success.

There is, I think, a hunger among the Japanese for a belief in something beyond themselves and in something beyond temporal advantages. The war killed most of what was left of the old beliefs, in the gods, in the Emperor, in their traditional religions. With some justification, they felt that their gods had let them down. The Buddhist temples and Shinto shrines have suffered from declining attendance and support since Hiroshima and Nagasaki.

It is hard to say whether the Christian revival in Japan is superficial or sincere. Christianity is "new" and "western". It seems to have served the western people well, perhaps it can do some good to us, seems to be the prevalent mood. But it has accomplished a purpose. It has helped to counteract many of the vicious introverted traits that have made the Japanese so dangerous in the past.

And, who knows?, maybe it will really catch on. If the Japanese become as enthusiastic about Christianity as they have become in the past over other, less admirable, creeds, this circumstance would have a profound effect on her national development.

Like China, Japan might have been a Christian country if human stupidity hadn't intervened. That remarkable Jesuit, St. Francis Xavier, landed in Kagoshima in 1569 and within 12 years the missionaries were operating more than 200 Churches in Japan. Communications were set up with Rome and the progress of the new religion seemed irresistible.

But the Christian lords became fanatics. They were convinced that Buddhism was the invention of the devil and they began to burn temples, destroy Buddhist art treasures and murder Buddhist monks in wholesale lots. This led to drastic reprisals. Catholic missionaries were tortured and crucified and Japanese Christians were hunted down and slain.

Japan then closed her doors to the rest of the world. The Government forbade the building of ocean-going ships and made it a capital offense for any Japanese to leave the country. This decision was disastrous, for it prevented Japan from building an empire, along Elizabethan lines, which would have provided living room, in later years, for her population.

Lafcadio Hearn summed up the influence of Christianity in Japan, in this fashion: "This religion, for which thousands vainly died, brought to Japan nothing but disorders, persecutions, political troubles, and war."

And yet, when the period of isolation (1639-1853) came to an end, Europeans found devout remnants of a Catholic community still in existence, worshipping as best they could, underground, without ordained priests or hierarchial direction.

Japan's earliest history is veiled in mythology. It is said, but not really believed, that Jimmu, the direct descendant of the Sun Goddess and the alleged ancestor of the present Emperor, founded the empire about 660 B.C. There seems to have been an organized civilization based on the clan system in the earliest days, and some connection (probably hostile) was established with Korea. (Artifacts from Korea, dating from the first century before Christ, have been found in Japan.)

The Chinese conquered the islands and their cultural effect was great upon the people. Buddhism was introduced in the sixth century of the Christian era and became the religion of the upper classes. The Japanese also adopted the Chinese language and certain elements of Chinese art, philosophy and science. This did not make for a highly creative culture, but the early craftsmen of Japan, following Chinese models, turned out art objects which were essentially of the same quality of achievement that the artists of China were producing.

The earliest years of the developing Japanese monarchy were marked by violence, civil war, assassinations and the inordinate influence of the Buddhist clergy.

In 782 A.D. the first really able Emperor appeared, in Kwammu. He strove to diminish the power of ambitious clergymen and in 794 moved the capital from Nara to Kyoto, to get away from excessive clerical interference. (The capital remained in Kyoto for almost 1100 years.) Kwammu tried to create a primitive form of Civil Service by abolishing hereditary succession among territorial governors. He was only temporarily successful in this. He also attempted land reform by returning land owned by these hereditary governors (and by the Buddhist monasteries) to the people. He failed in this, but he at least tried to effect a measure of justice and in doing so, he was considerably before his time. In addition, he won a campaign against the Ainu, who rather naturally, resented the ascendancy of stranger tribes upon their land.

It was after Kwammu's death that a persistent feature of Japanese history began to assert itself: the separation of real authority from titular authority. The emperor became more or less the figurehead while the Shogun ("Barbarian-subduing Generalissimo") became the administrative head of State and the real power in the land. The Fujiwara, one of the greatest families in the land, were the first Shoguns and the era takes its title from them. They ruled for 200 years.

The Royal Household was treated with enormous outward respect but, as it happened, whenever an Emperor tried to exert any authority on his own he usually found himself driven to enforced retirement in a monastery, or if he were not so fortunate, he died conveniently.

Civil war was constant in Japan, as it was in China. The great families fought for power among themselves and resisted any attempts to develop an efficient centralized government. In 1184 and 1185 two of the greatest families, the Minamotos and the Tairas conducted a large-scale war against each other. The Minamotos won, and their leader, Toritomo declared himself to be the Shogun of all Japan. For 700 years following Japan was a feudal State run by a Shogun who was also a military man.

As we have seen, Japan turned her back on the rest of the world and isolated herself in 1639. There was a Dutch trading post at Nagasaki, and that represented the only window she had on the world. The following 200 years were remarkably peaceful, but they also brought about a stagnation in Japanese development. Japanese society during this period was organized into a tight feudalism which broke down into four strata. The samurai, or warrior cult, was at the top, followed by the peasants, artisans and merchants.

In 1853, Commodore Matthew C. Perry of the United States Navy rather arbitrarily opened up Japan to trade with the West and for the admission of foreigners. The fear of foreign influence was so great that Perry's action caused a long period of civil strife, ending in the recognition of the Emperor as the true head of State (1868), and the elimination of the Shogun rule.

This development (the Meiji Restoration) enabled Japan to move a great deal closer to the 19th Century. Feudalism was abolished in 1871, modern laws were enacted, education was made compulsory and a new constitution, based on that of Prussia, was acknowledged by the Emperor. The Japanese studied and imitated successfully the western ideas of manufacturing and production.

The Japanese also imitated, and outdid, the western nations in imperialism and land-grabbing. In 1894-95 she attacked China and annexed Formosa, the Pescadores and the Liao-tung

126

peninsula in Manchuria. In 1904-1905 she fought and beat the seemingly invincible Russians. In 1910 she seized Korea.

During World War I Japan was on the side of the Allies. She did not contribute very much to the victory but she was (foolishly) rewarded by being given the mandate over numerous Pacific islands that had previously been the property of the Germans. (These Japanese-held islands became a source of great woe to her former allies during World War II.) She also moved into parts of Siberia.

During the 1920's nationalism in Japan went amok. The old lie about the divine origin of the Emperor was dusted off and revived. The warrior class once more became dominant, as it had been in the Shogun days.

In 1931, Japan overran Manchuria. (When the League of Nations criticized the action, Japan quit the League.) She continued to create incidents to justify her growing involvement in China and her pursuance of the "undeclared war" with that country. In 1938 and 1939, Japan almost became involved in war with Russia because of some border incidents in Manchuria.

This record of constant aggression was capped, on December 7, 1941, by the sudden and devastating attack upon Pearl Harbor. Japan swiftly built up an enormous but ephemeral empire stretching from the borders of Alaska to those of India. But, the tides of battle turned inexorably and Japan lost everything she had conquered, and a great deal more besides.

After two atomic bombs ruined two of her great cities, she surrendered in August, 1945. A completely demilitarized Government was formed and an American occupation was organized under the direction of General Douglas A. MacArthur. A new constitution was approved and, finally, a peace treaty with the U.S. was signed in 1951. In the following year the treaty became effective and Japan, once more, assumed a position among the nations of the world. The years since 1952 have been prosperous and productive.

The system of government is *demokurasu,* or democracy, Japanese style. It has interesting variations from the American version of democracy, and has changed the entire social organization of Japan.

One of the most important developments has been the comparative liberation of the women. Traditionally, females had been treated like chattels. Up until the middle of the nineteenth century the population was kept down by the practice of murdering unwanted female infants at birth. Midwives would keep a wet paper at hand so, if the baby were an unwanted girl, she could instantly smother it. In the second half of the nineteenth century, lower class families learned to profit by letting their female children live a little. As soon as the girls matured they were either put to work in the cotton mills or sold to the brothel keepers.

Today women have the vote and freedom almost equal to that of men. Half of Japan's industrial workers are women (although they are not as well paid as the men). They have the right to divorce their husbands, a privilege formerly reserved for the men. They attend the universities and generally play a useful and productive role in Japanese life.

In many ways the Japanese have been overimpressed by what they consider to be "democratic". They are still dangerously ready to swallow anything that is fed them in the name of *demokurasu*. They associate democracy with the West, and think the two terms are totally interchangeable.

Curiously enough, both Communism and Christianity are the beneficiaries of this misconception. Both are western ideas so, many Japanese feel, both must have something to do with *demokurasu* and must therefore have some good in them. This has caused a revival of interest in Christianity and a rather disturbing increase in the ranks of the Marxists.

For the first time in history, there are opposing political parties in Japan and there is political choice and complete political freedom. There is, unfortunately, a strong and vocal Communist Party but it seems, to this writer, inconceivable that Communism should flourish excessively in Japan. The Japanese have been the beneficiaries of the benevolence of the democratic na-

128

tions, particularly the United States. What totalitarian nation would have treated a defeated enemy with such beneficence as the United States has treated Japan? As a contrast, one need only recall the way Russia has treated her former enemies. And, of course, the free enterprise system has proved to be the key to Japan's unprecedented post war success. It has worked so well that it would be madness to turn away from it.

Everywhere in the world that we look—if we are honest enough to look objectively—we see free enterprise succeeding, and the controlled, socialistic or Marxist economy failing. The greatest example, of course, lies in West and East Germany. In the Middle East we need only look at burgeoning Israel and floundering Egypt. And in the Far East Formosa and, especially Japan are thriving, full of hope and ambition, while India, Cambodia, Indonesia and Red China, depending heavily on a Marxist, planned economy, are in dreadful condition.

The development of Japan since the Meiji Restoration of 1868 has been remarkable and in many·ways a triumph for her people. In 1868, after two centuries of almost complete isolation from the western world, Japan was an anachronism, almost a medieval state. Her economic and social structures were practically stagnant. She was at least two centuries behind the west in scientific knowledge and in productive techniques.

In fact, Japan's condition in 1868 can be compared to that of India in 1948. In both cases, a major political change made it possible for sensible and dedicated men to make sweeping changes in the economic structure and to abolish the rigid and out-moded class distinctions among their people. Both countries had, at the time of their emergence, a very distinguished tradition of artistic achievement. Both countries were far behind their contemporaries in technology but both had the chance of inheriting industrial techniques which the western world had developed at great cost, and which could make the newly-emergent nations economically powerful and self-sufficient.

If anything, the differences favored India. India had and has enormous physical resources, Japan has relatively few. India, though held in subjugation by the British, still had considerable contact with the western world; Japan had had none for 200 years. The British left behind them in India a good railroad system and a highly-efficient, trained Civil Service. The Japanese had to begin from nothing. And, India, in 1948, and ever since, has been the beneficiary of billions of dollars of resources and aid from other nations (roughly equivalent of a quarter of her entire capital formation). Japan had no such advantage. She provided the whole of her own capital from domestic sources.

Japan emerged and took her place among her sister nations with confidence and success. The feudal structure was dismantled, social and economic opportunities were vastly expanded, economic growth was achieved and the lot of the common man was remarkably enhanced. Unfortunately, in the political sphere, there was not, at that time, any thought of democracy.

In India, despite all the advantages she has had, things have not turned out so well. The caste barriers have not really been dismantled. (This is a real blot on the Indian record to date.) The rich have grown richer, the poor have grown poorer. Famine is a seasonal terror. The lot of the common man, after almost 20 years has not improved, but deteriorated.

Why have things developed in this manner? I suggest strongly that it is because of the different economic systems the two countries followed. Japan, in 1868, followed a capitalistic, free market policy based on the British system of time. When the State took a hand it was to make the free enterprise system more effective. It did not try to control production or direct investment artificially, but it did subsidize the training of Japanese with a potential for leadership and it did import experts from abroad to teach modern techniques.

The Indians, in 1948, attacked the problem differently. Her leaders were either Marxists or Fabians. They regarded capitalism and imperialism as synonymous, and have depended heavily on central planning. They have adopted the Russian system of five-year plans under which the opportunities for private investment are carefully controlled. The government controls wages and prices and prohibits private industry from building factories or even making extensive investments without a government permit.

Reliance on the market and a free economy has developed tremendous initiative in Japan and has uncovered unsuspected resources among its people. Reliance on governmental controls in India has frustrated initiative; it has substituted bureaucratic fussiness for free enterprise; it has protected its own vested interests against the inroads of progress and has produced a kind of dynamic inertia among its people.

Japan's experiment in 1868 was a success from the start. In 25 years she was a formidable power. In 35 years she was a *dangerous* power, capable of defeating one of the strongest nations in the world in a major war. I am not saying that the ability to wage war against a great power, and to do it successfully, is a totally reliable yardstick for measuring a nation's development, but it does tell a great deal about the industrial and economic condition of a nation. After almost 20 years of independence, and with enormous technical and material assistance from other nations, India finds it difficult to preserve order within her own borders, and the incidents with Red China give rise to doubts as to whether she could successfully defend herself against a major attack.

It is unfortunate that those responsible for the Meiji Restoration in Japan in 1868 cared so little about individual freedom or political expression by the masses. They were interested only in making their country powerful in an industrial and military sense. They believed in an all-powerful aristocracy and the government by an elite class. These doctrines caused the tragedy of World War II. But, despite the lack of interest in the common man, the common man did prosper under the free enterprise, capitalistic system. He prospered despite the indifference of his rulers.

The Indian leaders in 1948 were primarily interested in political freedom and the economic improvement of the masses. But they chose the wrong system of achieving these goals, while the

131

Japanese, embracing the right system, achieved the goals almost as a by-product. The Indian masses have suffered because of the ideology of their masters.

With such an illuminating contrast available to them, it is amazing that anyone in Japan should actively espouse the economic system that has produced in India, misery, and to abandon the system which has given to Japan so much.

Democracy is still a foreign concept in Japan and it sits uneasily upon a great number of the people. It is inevitable that a people so steeped in tradition should resent the almost total freedom which now prevails among Japan's *après-guerre* generations. The traditionalists complain that reverence for the family has broken down. The men complain about the lack of subservience among the women. Conservatives have attempted to have the old order of abject obedience taught once again in the schools. The teachers' union has fought, successfully, against this bit of retrogressive brain washing. The Japanese people are constantly suspicious that the Government wants to turn the country back to a police state, or a neo-fascist state, and are alert to an abnormal degree, to such a possibility. This has led to an over-reaction in favor of Socialism in some quarters, although the people do not realize that Socialism is more likely to create the conditions they seek to avoid than is *demokurasu*.

The Liberal-Democratic Party is still dominant in Japan's politics, but it is the only conservative party. The Socialists, the Democratic Socialists and the Communists are constantly threatening its power and, if they ever succeed in overthrowing the present regime, the remarkable recovery of Japan since World War II could well come to a temporary, or even permanent, end.

And the recovery has been astounding. In 1964 the increase in the Gross National Product was 18.3 percent. In 1965, it tapered off to (a still high) 9 percent, but in 1966, it rebounded once again. Starting from scratch in 1946, or, more accurately, a considerable distance behind the scratch line, Japan, through the free enterprise system and *demokurasu* has grown to the point where she is the world's largest ship building country, the second largest producer of electric and electronic equipment; the third largest in steel production, and the fourth largest in the manufacture of cars and trucks. The unemployment rate is less than 1 percent of the total work force, and there is an acute labor shortage. Exports, which are vital to Japan's well-being, topped the $9 billion mark in 1966.

Before World War II manufacturers of other nations complained bitterly about "cheap" Japanese products, copies of their own products which were being sold for less in foreign markets. Ironically, as the Japanese standard of living has increased, and wages have gone up, Japanese manufacturers are suffering from the same problem in their own bailiwick. "Cheap" Formosan and Red Chinese products are being offered in Japanese markets at lower cost than the local products. There is some agitation to increase tariffs on imported goods so as to minimize the competition. This would be a reversal of Japanese tradition, which has always been opposed to high tariffs in Japan and in those countries with which she does business.

The average industrial worker in Japan gets the equivalent of $100 a month, plus $25 in fringe benefits. This is a high wage for Asia, but there is evidence that Japanese workers are getting sick and tired of being treated as Asians. They want to get the same share of the economic pie that workers in the United States or the United Kingdom get. The labour unions are strong and insistent and it seems apparent that the day of "cheap" Japanese products will soon be over. Certainly Japan is exporting more "quality" merchandise than it has ever exported before, and the standard of materials and workmanship in many products equals those of any other nation in the world.

The labour unions of Japan are, for the most part, considerably more left wing than are the labour unions in the United States, and even more to the left than the unions of Great Britain. The Japanese industrialists will have to find a way of sharing Japan's prosperity to a greater extent with the workers, or they will find a greater degree of Fabian socialism forced upon them, to the detriment of the entire nation.

Japan is the most westernized of all the Asiatic nations and it should be the dominant force in the East. It may one day even become the peace-maker of the world, mediating between the East and the West.

But Japan has taken up western thought, western methods, western political ideas on her own terms, not as colonials. She has rebuilt her cities after the war in her own way (according to adaptations of western designs) and with her own money. This makes her unique among the nations of Asia.

She has always been eclectic about the West and still is. The average Japanese thinks the average westerner is very comical and very rude. He respects the strength of the west, and admires and imitates its products, but he does not really understand or like the citizens of the other hemisphere.

She likes our manufactures but cannot abide our manners. This is not as trivial as it seems in a people with whom manners play such an important part in their everyday life and their thinking. It is very unlikely that there will ever develop between the Japanese and the west the essential feeling of brotherhood which binds together so many nations of Europe. We must not sentimentally confuse peaceful co-existence and co-operation with amity.

The Japanese have been deadly dangerous in the past, and may be deadly dangerous in the future.

There is no sign, at present, of any tendency for the Japanese to return to the virulent militarism which at one time exalted them, and then ruined them, but they have shown time and time again that it is perilous to crowd them.

If Japan is to prosper and grow she must be allowed total freedom of competition with the western world in industry and commerce. She must be permitted to build up her avenues of trade with her Asiatic neighbours, not excluding the enormous potential market of Red China.

There is an inevitable tendency on the part of politically powerful nations to inhibit the economic competition of a politically weaker nation. The temptation is particularly strong today when

Japan is capable of competing on equal terms in almost any market place. The temptation must be resisted. If Japan is to be a useful ally, and not a foe, she must be given economic elbow room. The United States, Great Britain and the rest of the non-Communist world must work with Japan as partners in the peaceful development of Asia.

The future welfare of the world could well depend upon how Japan prospers and how she develops in the community of free nations. She could become the primary force for good in the East and she could become the force for evil. Her dynamism can go either way, and if thwarted and frustrated, as we have all learned to our sorrow and horror, it can cause permanent damage to the fabric of the world's peace.

The western world will have at least as much to do with the future course of Japan as the Japanese will themselves.

VIII

EUROPE AND THE COMMON MARKET

I T WOULD BE FUTILE for me to try to recount in capsule form the history of the principal European countries. This history is too well known; it is taught in schools, it is part of the heritage of most of those who will read this account and it is readily available in hundreds of good and accessible books.

Therefore, in discussing Europe today, I shall confine myself to some commentary on the three dominant nations of that continent, and perhaps draw some conclusions that will help attain an understanding of what has been going on.

Western Europe today consists of a group of second and third class powers which are intensely irritated, psychologically and politically, by their exclusion from the first class.

There are only two first class powers in the world: Russia and the United States. If a third one emerges it will probably be China. No Europeans need apply.

On the whole, Europe resents the ascendancy of Russia less than it does that of the United States. Russia, after all, is *almost* European and she has been a major power since the time of Peter the Great. The United States is the *parvenu*. She could have been a great power any time after the end of its Civil War, in 1865, but she did not choose to be so until here entry into World War I, in 1917.

Europeans resent the United States for her newness almost as much as they resent her for her benefactions. Rule One of international policy is never to forgive a benefactor and, talk as they might about the Common Market and other helpful devices, Europeans cannot get away from the fact (as much as they would like to) that their present prosperity would have been impossible if it had not been for American generosity and American altruism.

It could well be that if Red China were to become the third first class power in the world, she would not be resented as much as the Americans are resented. China has been in the major power business for a long while. She was uniquely powerful for two millennia, from 221 B.C. to 1839 A.D., and is therefore a Charter Member of the Power Club, and if she ever finds herself able to pay the dues necessary for a renewed membership in that select group, she would probably be met with cold, but open, arms.

But America is composed, mostly, of the descendents of people who rejected Europe and who shook her dust from their shoes in order to build a new life in another world. It is intolerable to Europeans that such people should assume world leadership and should have the effrontery to spend their treasure almost indiscriminately in order to rescue their paternal homelands from ruin and desolation. The donations are, of course, welcome; the donors are not.

Almost all the major European countries have had a run at the Great Power Business. France stayed at it the longest, from 1494 to approximately 1940 although she was only a bogus power, really, between the two World Wars. England shared the summit from about 1701 (beginning of the War of the Spanish Succession) until 1945, (the end of World War II). Prussia lasted as one of the kings of the mountain for about 200 years, Holland and Sweden for about a hundred apiece. The Danubian Habsburgs under various guises stayed near the top for 400 years, mostly by fancy footwork and carefully-planned bedwork. Spain held on for less than a hundred years, losing out when "God blew a great wind" and helped the English demolish the Armada.

So, there is nothing permanent about Great Powership, really, But, in today's world, the prize belongs to those nations that have the control of atomic power, and those which dare to explore and conquer space.

The dominant figure in Europe today, of course, is the brilliant but difficult Charles de Gaulle, and he has made France dominant in her milieu of second class states. She is powerful enough to cause embarrassment to the first rank, and seems to take delight in exacting satisfying little humiliations from her peers.

France is the largest European nation, with approximately 50 million people, located in an area of 211,208 square miles. It has always been rich in industrial and agricultural resources, and, since World War II (thanks to American aid, to a great extent) it has greatly expanded its industrial complex. It is thriving today, perhaps more so than at any previous time in her history.

DeGaulle is an extraordinary man. If he were not quite so extraordinary he might be one of the great figures of our troubled century. (Though, of course, it would never occur to him that he is not one already.)

His military career was brilliant but inconclusive. Between World Wars, on the question of the production and use of armored tanks, he was correct, of course, and the French high command was wrong, but his intransigent manner of presenting his case made it all but impossible for his less gifted superiors to accept his ideas, even if they were so inclined.

In its last years, the Third Republic of France was betrayed by its leaders and collapsed shamefully before the German onslaught. The English, the Americans and, later, the Russians, were engaged in the business of fighting a war to the death and they could not find the time to take the Free French as seriously as General de Gaulle felt they should be taken. The Free French were treated as a symbol, and their fighting men were used to a

139

limited but inconsequential degree, but de Gaulle, despite his gallantry and prickly brilliance, was never admitted to the inner councils of the great strategy.

De Gaulle, it was felt, demanded more recognition than the performance of his countrymen had warranted. And, certainly, since the end of World War II, France has claimed more credit for victory than she deserved. A tour of the beaches, monuments and battle fields of Normandy would lead the uninformed visitor to believe that the Free French had liberated their own country with only an assist from their allies. The fact of the matter is that only a handful of French participated in the storming of the beach heads, and none before the crucial first six days of fighting were over.

In the official recapitulation of the Normandy invasion, issued by the United States Congress, twenty years after the fact, the contribution of all the allies is meticulously listed and evaluated, but the Free French are not even mentioned.

This is brought up with no intention of denigrating the courage and the purpose of the French fighters and their leader. It is said merely to counteract the attempts by modern Frenchmen to rewrite history.

Winston Churchill once said that the heaviest cross he had to bear was the Cross of Lorraine. He and Franklin Roosevelt and, later, Stalin, had no time or inclination to soothe the wounded pride or appease the injured *amour propre* of the leader, no matter how valiant, of a rather small faction of a nation that had been ingloriously vanquished at a most inconvenient juncture of the war. De Gaulle, on the other hand, never forgot or forgave the slights, real and imagined, which the Americans and English visited upon him, and many of his attitudes today are the result of those frustrating experiences.

But, with all his personal shortcomings, De Gaulle has been of inestimable value to post-war France. He emerged as the only really national hero of her war, the only man of stature upon whom she could hang her tattered pride.

140

The post-war Fourth Republic in France was a disaster, despite the good intentions of many of its leaders. It lacked stability, which is an absolute essential for political success. As government after government toppled, serious thinkers throughout the free world began to doubt that France had retained the ability to govern herself effectively under the democratic processes.

When de Gaulle took over as head of the Fifth Republic in 1958, he laid these doubts to rest. As a national hero of almost monumental stature, he has been able to stabilize government in France, almost through the sheer power of his own personality. He has been autocratic and maddening, and at times (as in May, 1967) he has appeared to reach out for dictatorial powers, but he has made France once again the most powerful power in Europe.

And he has done it in such a way as to make the French feel they have done it all by themselves! He has minimized the enormous aid which the United States poured into France (and without which France would have found it impossible to recover) and goes out of his way to insult America and Americans. He knows full well that the United States will have to protect France from aggression, if aggression ever comes, and can do so through her sophisticated nuclear umbrella. So, he imperiously orders NATO off French soil and tells all American military personnel to be gone. He realizes, of course, that this will make the defense of France more expensive and difficult for the Americans to achieve, but he also knows that such a defense *will* be achieved because a free France is necessary to the peace of the western world. He can afford to show-boat and tweak Uncle Sam's nose because this makes Frenchmen believe in their own honour, and makes votes at home, while causing very little risk to French sovereignty.

The de Gaulle attitude toward Viet Nam is almost incredibly audacious. He recently delivered a speech, wildly applauded by the faithful, in which he claimed that France had graciously and willingly left that area because she felt the Viet Namese had the right to self-determination.

The fact is that France fought as long as she could to hold onto what she called Indo-China and was trounced ignominiously by an embattled people who were tired of her brand of colonialism. She left because she was kicked out. But, of course, it would be disturbing to French "honour" if the Americans succeeded in an area where France had failed. So de Gaulle and the French hope America will fail.

The French attitude toward Great Britain is more complex. There is more than spite behind her opposition to England's admission to the Common Market, but the spite is there in ample supply, also.

England, before joining the Common Market, must insist upon some concessions favouring the products from her Commonwealth. If she fails to do this, then she runs the risk of losing what is left of her Empire. The European nations are generally willing to make such concessions but de Gaulle is adamant against them.

DeGaulle, undoubtedly, remembers always the wartime days when he was snubbed by the English and the Americans. Now, when England needs some understanding and compassion from him, he is not prepared to give them to her.

Above all, de Gaulle wants to call the shots in Europe, and with a prospering England as part of the Common Market, his ability to do so would be severely limited.

One of the unique phenomena of post World War II life is that the vanquished have prospered just as much as have the victors, and in some instances, to a greater degree. Germany, Japan and Italy are all in excellent economic condition, far better than that in which England finds herself. France cannot be considered a "victor" in World War II. She was an early loser, and was liberated finally by forces other than her own. France was eliminated in the quarter-finals.

When the war was ended, the politicians were determined that the mistakes of the Treaty of Versailles would not be repeated. They bent over backwards. Someone has compared the American officials who roamed about Europe after the hostilities to

142

rich, childless aunts making peace after a nursery brawl. Nobody was spanked. There was a kiss and candy for all.

German industrialists had their pockets stuffed with dollars and were told to carry on as if nothing had happened. Italian entrepreneurs found themselves, for the first time in their lives, supplied with undreamed-of capital.

Marshall Plan money, which was intended to build schools and put roofs over homeless people, was, in many cases, diverted into vast industrial complexes.

Americans got little thanks for this. In fact, they were greatly blamed by the common people of Europe because they were doing so little to restore what their guns and bombs had destroyed!

The European magnates, and the European press did little or nothing to correct this apprehension. When prosperity returned to the Continent, it was attributed to the cleverness of the politicians and the hard work and the vision of the industrialists, the inherent superiority of the European people and their capacity for thinking constructively. None of these sterling qualities had been especially noticeable in Europe prior to World War II! It is surprising that they should have emerged so suddenly, full blown, from the brains of their fathers. Of course, they did nothing of the sort. The recovery could never have occurred without American beneficence. But, in Europe it has become a sacred patriotic duty for the politicians to tell polished lies about America to their constituents.

Still, the re-emergency of Germany as a thriving second-class power has been a remarkable post-war phenomenon. Her recovery from almost total destitution has been, for the rest of the free world, an inspiration and a source of serious concern.

It is important to Europe and the rest of the free world that Germany be prosperous. But nobody wants Germany to become so successful that she will be tempted to try again for world dominance. She has tried twice within the memory of living man, and came close to succeeding each time.

The attitude of the free world toward Germany must be ambivalent. She will never again be wholly trusted. She will always be viewed somewhat like a potential bomb, which could still be ticking long after Viet Nam is defused.

Thoughtful Germans are inclined to be equally ambivalent about their own national character. Like the Japanese, they are fearful of any resurgence of the Fascist spirit and are inclined to search it out and discourage it whenever it appears.

Politically they are somewhat like epileptics. They know they are subject to fits; they know they have had serious fits before. They hardly remember the attacks, but they know they were terrible. And they fear further attacks.

When the present Chancellor, Kurt Kiesinger, was elected to office, a goodly part of the western world (and a goodly part of the German population) winced with apprehension because he was once a member of the Nazi Party. "Aha!", people seemed so say, "here it comes at last, the neo-Nazi revival." But the forebodings were probably unnecessary. Kiesinger seems a convinced convert to democracy, and, to be perfectly frank, it would be very hard to find any prominent German over 50 years of age who wasn't, in some form or another, a Nazi during the Hitler years. Party membership was the key to survival.

But the Nazi generation is dying out, and to the new generation, World War II is remote, just as it is to the new generation of Americans and Englishmen. It is history. It is past. It is academic.

It is unreasonable for us to expect this new generation to continually bear the burden of guilt of their fathers. It is even unreasonable to expect present day Germans to come to terms with their own history. How can you come to terms with the fact that your father was a monster, or the pliable tool of monsters?

On these conditions, it seems probable now that Germany has developed a capacity for political health. But yet, those nations who fought her twice already in this century, and were almost overcome by her, must still experience apprehension. The new

Germany may be remote from the temptations of Fascism, but the genes are still there.

It has often been said "Scratch a German and you find a sheep." There is some tragic truth in this oversimplification. There seems to be in the Germans a compulsion to say "Yes" to anyone in authority. *Anyone.* At its worst it was manifested in the huge and noisy demonstrations during the Hitler era, the obedient acceptance of the most atrocious policies.

At Nuremberg and elsewhere convicted Nazis looked wide-eyed at the Court when accused of the most dreadful inhumanities and bestialities, and with wondering candour exclaimed: "But I was only doing what I was told to do. I was only following orders!"

There is evidence of this obsession in Germany today in the field of labor-management. In German industry today in the field of labor management. In German industry in an average year, only 60,000 working days are lost through strikes, as contrasted with about 5,000,000 days in France. At first glance, one is likely to say: "How sensible!, How orderly!" And then one must have a troubling second thought: "How *docile!*" If workers will follow the leadership of their bosses so obediently, are they not likely once again to follow the leadership of a politician who acts like a boss?

The Germans have an enormous respect for law and order. That is a good thing. But it may be too much of a good thing. The respect extends to law, even when order is not present.

Certainly, the Federal Republic's record over the past two decades has been extraordinary. West Germany, with 95,928 square miles, and a population of 60 million, is prosperous and booming under the free enterprise system, particularly in the chemical, metallurgical, automotive, electrical and consumer goods industries. There is almost no unemployment in West Germany, and slums are almost non-existent.

By contrast, the so-called Democratic Republic of Germany is much smaller and less successful. In the eastern Communist sector there are 41,659 square miles and only 17 million people.

The state-controlled industry is in somewhat better shape today than it was several years ago, but it is almost totally dependent upon Soviet Russia as a customer and as a provider of raw materials. The farms are collectivized but in 1965 they produced no more than they produced in 1953. East Germany must import food to supply its people; West Germany is self-sufficient. (Except, of course, for the isolated West German half of Berlin.)

There is very little possibility that both halves of Germany will be joined into one State in the foreseeable future, and most Germans today seem, at least tacitly, resigned to this.

Germans, for the most part, seem to accept the fact that under present conditions their country cannot have much significant impact on world affairs, and on the whole, are rather relieved by the knowledge. When Germany has been strong enough to affect the rest of the world, the effect has been disastrous not only to the world, but to Germany itself.

This includes atomic weapons. Germany once was inclined to demand a voice in the dispensation of atomic weapons. Now, the Germans would like to see all atomic warheads, and all atomic bases banished from their land.

There is one disturbing factor in Germany's sociological climate, which may have an effect on future events. There has been no intellectual renaissance since World War II, as there was, to such an enormous degree, in the years after World War I.

This is probably due to the fact that the Jewish community was annihilated during the Nazi terror. The Jews led the intellectual revival in Germany during the twenties.

However, there has been an intellectual revival in France and Italy since the end of the war, and it has not, necessarily, been spearheaded by Jews, although they have played a prominent part in it.

It is possible that the 12 years of violent Nazi anti-intellectualism has had a stultifying effect on German minds of today.

Education in Germany is compulsory for eight years, but there is very little pressure on youngsters to continue beyond that limit. As in France (and, to a lesser extent, in England) college is reserved for the intellectually and/or the economically elite. This rather haphazard approach to higher education served European nations adequately in the past, but it will not serve them adequately in the highly technological society of tomorrow and the day after tomorrow.

The six Common Market Countries (France, Germany, Italy, Belgium, the Netherlands and Luxembourg) have a total population about equal to that of the United States, but they are turning out only about one-fifth as many college graduates. In America, one out of every three youngsters of college age is actually attending some kind of college. In the Common Market Countries the average is one out of every 20.

Furthermore, in the Common Market Countries less than 2 percent of all college students specialize in science or technology, as compared to 4 percent in the United States and Russia.

The universities of Europe are ancient and distinguished, but mostly for their achievements in the humanities, in philosophy and the classics. In all Europe there is no institution anywhere nearly equivalent to the Massachusetts Institute of Technology, to California Tech or even to Rice University. There is nothing even remotely comparable to the Harvard or Stanford Business School, and most European educators would look down their noses at the mere suggestion that there should be such an institution. Nonetheless, the lack of such distinguished, specialized institutions of higher learning has caused a serious and continuing "Brain drain" from Europe to nations where special talents are better recognized and rewarded.

The French have even further inhibited the potential of their universities by decreeing that nobody except French citizens can teach in them. This leads not only to intellectual inbreeding, but makes unavailable to French students the enormous pool of academic talent throughout the world. It is very doubtful, for example, that either Russia or the United States could have reached their present status of world leadership without the assistance of German scientists. It is equally doubtful that France can reach the pinnacle without borrowing from the best that other nations offer.

The technological gap that exists between Europe on one hand, and the United States and Russia on the other, will not be narrowed unless these deficiencies are cured. The European countries are not likely to become first class powers again unless they develop a more technologically sophisticated society.

In the United States and in Russia it is taken for granted that a youngster should be given the opportunity to be exposed to as much education as he can absorb. This philosophy is quite foreign to Europe and it is Europe's loss that it remains so.

There is a further disquieting consideration. When the vast majority of young people are only half-educated, by modern standards, a nation is developing a mass of academically frustrated drop-outs, and they form the material out of which dictatorships are carved. This has happened in the past, and there is no assurance that it will not happen in the future.

Italy is, of course, the third largest European country. It covers 116,303 square miles and has a population of 53 million people. It is therefore about one-thirtieth the size of the United States in land area (roughly equivalent to the State of Arizona), but has about one-fourth the population. Her national income is a little more than one-twelfth of that of the U.S.

However, to estimate the prosperity of Italy is a tricky business. It is like estimating the depth of a river, which is at some places three feet deep, and in others a hundred. The northern provinces of Italy are very highly advanced, industrially and economically, while the provinces in the far South are about on the level of the underdeveloped countries.

In the northwestern part of Italy, in the triangle cornered by Milan, Genoa and Turin, economic conditions are just about as prosperous as they are in Switzerland. South of Rome, and particularly south of Naples, conditions are no better than they are in impoverished North Africa. In the south, an annual wage equivalent to $500 a year is considered far better than average.

148

In the industrial north, a wage equivalent to $3,000 a year is considered adequate, and no more.

Despite strong Socialist influences in Italy, there is a very inefficient distribution of the wealth. Taxation is a haphazard matter, and little of the money seeps down to the masses. The institutions of the Catholic Church (to which 99% of the people, at least nominally, belong) are sometimes enormously wealthy, but they do not concern themselves unduly with the problems of the poor. According to the Government, more than 10 million Italians, or 20 percent of the population, lack adequate food and shelter. This is a potentially dangerous situation and explains, in part, why Italy has the largest, and most active and efficient Communist Party in the western world.

After her disastrous and ineffectual participation in World War II, Italy has made a remarkable comeback and is more prosperous, comparatively, than she has been at any time in her history since the greatest days of the Caesars.

Once again, American money and American compassion made this possible. At the end of World War II, when Italy was ravaged by both the international conflict and by bitter internecine stife, American aid, both from the government and from private sources, saved the nation from starvation. The Marshall Plan, that great American programme for the restoration of prosperity in Europe, was extended to include former enemies as well as former allies, and Italy was a notably beneficiary. Foreign Aid was poured into Italy. In 1964 the United States made a loan of a billion dollars to Italy to bolster her faltering currency. (This came at a time when the U.S. currency itself was not in the best of shape.)

But still, one finds anti-Americanism there! It is not as virulent as it is in France, but it still exists and thrives and grows. And almost nowhere in Italy does anyone give credit to the United States for having made the rehabilitation of Italy possible. The politicians, the industrialists and the ordinary people give the credit to Italian know-how, Italian ingenuity, Italian perseverance. Gratitude is clearly not a virtue of nations.

In 1964 the Gross National Product of Italy had reached $40 billion. This was twice as high as it had been in 1953. And, despite the wreckage of the war, it was 50 percent higher in 1953 than it had been prior to World War II. Unemployment is well below 3 percent, and most of that is in the south.

But this, too, is misleading. Italy is almost unique in that only 40 percent of the population is counted as part of the labor force. This figure reflects the large number of independent *entrepreneurs*—small shop-keepers, small farmers and so on—within the economy. While this condition sounds healthy, it should be added that less than 20 percent of the available capital is divided among the small independent producers and businessmen. The rest is concentrated in large corporations controlled and owned by a handful of industrialists. Hundreds of thousands of small farmers and small shop-keepers must live a precarious hand-to-mouth existence.

The Government owns and controls a great portion of the national industry, more than in any other non-collectivist nation in the world. The public sector includes more than half of the steel industry, a sizeable portion of the mechanical industries, most of the banks, most of the chemical industry, most of the insurance businesses, plus all the railroads, shipping, airlines and communication media. The Government controls about 15 percent of the total industrial output, and, indeed, in Italy, socialism and capitalism seem to exist more harmoniously in harness than in any other European nation.

The Communist Party in Italy in the local elections of 1964 polled 26 percent of the total vote, or about the same as it polled in 1948. On one hand, you might say that the Party appeal hasn't grown any, but, on the other hand, it should be pointed out that it hasn't *decreased* any, either.

The power of the Communist Party lies in the fact that no political Party in Italy controls a majority of the votes. The Catholic-Socialist-Social Democrat-Republican coalition of parties controls about 56 percent of the vote. But, the coalition is artificial and, at times, uneasy, and serious defections within it could make the Communists a part of the ruling Party and enormously enhance their power and prestige.

Many observers optimistically claim that the Communist Party in Italy is different from the Party in Russia, or elsewhere. They point to the fact that its leaders have divorced themselves from International Communism's goal of world domination. They claim that most Italians who vote the Communist ticket are merely making rude gestures toward Holy Mother Church and giving expression to the traditional Italian antagonism against authority. They say that most Italians who vote Communist would not do so if they felt the Party had the slightest chance of capturing control of the Government; that they do so only to let the *intelligentsia* (who have always controlled Italy's democratic governments) know they are there.

Maybe so. But, maybe not. I remember so well when the same things were being said about the Chinese Communists; that they were merely agrarian reformers, and not Communists at all! I also remember when sentimentalists were saying that the Italians weren't really Fascists at all; that Fascism was just a thin veneer over the Italian people which really didn't amount to anything significant. This turned out to be nonsense. The Italian brand of Fascism may have been relatively inefficient, when compared to the German brand, but it was Fascism all right. At least two million people, inside Italy and out, died before their time before it was extirpated—if it has been extirpated.

There may be a basic, ethnic reason why Fascism worked more successfully with the German people than it did with the Italians. *Deutsch,* it should be remembered, means *tribe,* and, this is basically the German orientation. Look at their monuments, for example: huge tribal manifestations of doubtful taste, impressive mostly for their size. Their churches and cathedrals are generally out-size. Even their beerhalls are cavernous.

Fascism is a *tribal* belief. The emphasis is on the State. This fitted in with the German *ethos.*

But, in Italy, the emphasis is almost totally on the *family,* not the State. The family means everything. Most Italians are fundamentally anarchists in that, while they will go along with the State in affairs that, they feel, do not matter, they will rebel when the State tries to interefere with the integrity of the family. This is a national characteristic basically opposed to the totalitarian ideal.

During the Hitler days, for instance, the Nazis were able to persuade youngsters to turn in their parents, their brothers and sisters, for "crimes" against the State. Youngsters by the thousands did this in blind obedience, often watching with smug complacency as their kin were dragged off to concentration camps and certain, horrible death. They salved their consciences with the sure knowledge that they were being "good citizens".

It is inconceivable that such a tactic would work in Italy. The average Italian youngster would cut off his hand rather than betray his parents, or his siblings, or even his cousins or his aunts. And, if he were so despicable as to perform such a monstrous act, the vengeance of the community would soon catch up with him. Whether the State approved of him or not, he would not be long for this world.

Democracy was more or less forced upon the Italian people at the end of World War II as a necessity for survival. It was accepted without enthusiasm, because Italians were unfamiliar with it. It had been tried over the years, in relatively small doses, and never with notable success. Up until the post World War II period the Italian people never showed any great talent for governing themselves democratically. They have shown some talent since that time, but not enough, really, to allay suspicions that the talent may not be permanently durable.

There are some hopeful signs. The efficiency of government institutions has increased significantly in recent years, and the Civil Service, though not free of corruption, is functioning better than it has ever done previously in Italy's history. Local self-government, eliminated by the Fascists, has come back strong and plays a highly important part in national life. Public education has been vastly extended and, particularly in the north, illiteracy has been all but eliminated. (Though, far too few Italians, as

152

we have seen, can manage a college education. The ratio of college students to young people of college age is about one to 30.)

Although the degree of Government control of industry and business is great, the growth of the Government's participation has taken place pretty well without inhibiting the growth in the private sector. The growth is greater in the private sector than in the public.

In 1950 the Government acted intelligently in creating the *Casa del Mezzogiorno,* a fund which has poured about $4.5 billion into the development of the impoverished South. This has not produced a standard of living above the mere subsistence level. But it has accomplished a great deal, and it is difficult to think of what would have happened in that area if this effort at enlightened planning had not been initiated. Italy needs more of the same.

By all odds, the most significant fact in Italian life is the Roman Catholic Church, which enters actively or passively into every area of human activity. Ironically enough the Church has been the principal reason for Italy's resistance to Communism and the principal reason for its receptiveness to Communism.

The Church is, of course, intransigently opposed to Communism and, in Italy, where there is no prohibition against the mixing of Church and State, it has fought the Communists at every level—from the pulpit, on the hustings, at the ballot box. (In one notable case, in a hotly-contested election, Pope Pius XII personally persuaded a Texas Catholic oil millionaire to build a school in an area that was likely to go Communist because the Government and the Church had neglected to do so previously. He did as he was asked, spent a million dollars, and the Communist threat was blunted.)

On the other hand, the Catholic Church in Italy, as in most Latin countries, is far more conservative and far more authoritarian than it is in countries where it has to fight for survival. (The Church is nowhere so attractive as in countries where it is a minority.) The Church is tremendously rich in most areas, but contents itself with providing inadequate charity to the poor, rather than providing dynamic programs which could help the poor help themselves.

It has followed a policy that the spiritual needs of the faithful are far more important than the physical needs. After all, why should man worry about the woes of this world if they prepare him for the inconceivable blessings of all eternity? This has for centuries been a comfortable doctrine for the well-to-do, relieving their consciences of the necessity of hard-core philanthropy, but it no longer works in the second half of the twentieth century. The poor would prefer to be as well off as the Monsignori, and take their chances with eternity.

The Church in Italy is also anti-intellectual and tries to exercise a strong right of censorship over the production of the nation's artists, literary and graphic, as well as over the newspapers and journals of opinion. This, naturally, creates rebellion, and rebellion in Italy often leads to some kind of accommodation with the Communist Party.

The reforms which have swept through the Catholic Church in recent years have not been of Italian manufacture, even if they did originate with that great Italian Pope, John XXIII. They were, indeed, resisted by the Italian Cardinals and Bishops, and were placed in effect over their opposition. Not surprisingly, the Church in Italy has not been affected by modern trends to the same extent that it has been affected in the United States, England, Germany, Holland and a score of other countries where it is an embattled minority.

And yet, if the Italian Church does not soon resolutely join the twentieth century, it could find itself a minority in its own homeland. It is not possible that Italians will turn Protestant, of course. That would be unthinkable. But, the proportion of faithful Catholics to merely *soi-disant* Catholics is steadily dropping and the impatience of the faithful as well as open anti-clericism is growing at a pace that should give serious concern to the Vatican. The fault does not lie with the people of Italy, it lies within the Italian Church itself.

154

The political future (as well as the religious future) is still in doubt. While the nation seems stable and reasonably prosperous, there is a constant and very real danger in any society where wealth and land are so unevenly distributed. (After all, one-fifth of all the people are living on the margins of starvation!)

Massimo Salvadori, one of the great authorities on modern Italy, and a Professor at Smith College, in the United States, has summed up the situation as follows: "The survival of democracy depended on the success with which Italy could solve her social and moral problems within the frame of free institutions. On this, too, depended in great measure the position Italy would occupy on the international chessboard, success leading naturally to closer co-operation with the United States and Western Europe, failure leading to growing neutralism and a rapprochement with adversaries of the United States."

Failure would be a very serious matter. A Communist Italy could conceivably be a dire threat to the security of the entire free world.

However, if Italy does escape the ruin of Communism, it will not be so much because of the astuteness of her politicians, or the power of the Church, as it will be because of the strong and pervasive sense of *family* which is incompatible with the totalitarian State.

As these words are being written (June, 1967), a great international celebration has just been concluded in Rome honoring the tenth anniversary of the birth of the European Economic Community, or European Common Market. The star of the show, and the guest so greatly honoured that all others faded into insignificance, was France's leader, Charles de Gaulle. He acted, as always, as if he were the progenitor of the Common Market and its leading inspiration. There even was one titillating moment at the Vatican when there was speculation as to whether the Pope would confer his blessing on *le Grand Charles,* or vice-versa.

This was a typical example of European statesmen trying to rewrite history. Nobody at the celebration deserved honor less

155

than did de Gaulle. He opposed the idea of the Common Market in the beginning, and since its inception has done more than any man to stunt its growth and harm its development.

The idea of the Common Market originated in the Benelux nations. (Belgium: 11,778 square miles, population 10 million; the Netherlands: 12,978 square miles, population 12.5 million; Luxembourg: 999 square miles, population 333,000.) William Beyen, the Dutch Foreign Minister, started campaigning for an inter-European economic organization as early as February, 1953. In 1955, he and Paul-Henri Spaak, Foreign Minister of Belgium, and Joseph Bech, Foreign Minister of Luxembourg, presented to the foreign ministers of France, Germany and Italy (May 20) a program for "comprehensive supranational integration" of such sectors of the economy as electricity, transport, and nuclear energy, as well as for the formation of a Common Market.

The French held back from the proposal because of political considerations at home. The German and Italian representatives made the initial decisions, based on the Benelux Memorandum, which eventually brought the Common Market into being.

The French finally went along with the idea, mostly through the constant prodding of the great Jean Monnet, one of Europe's outstanding world citizens. (At de Gaulle's insistence, both Spaak and Monnet were ignored at the tenth anniversary celebration in Rome. Monnet was not invited, and Spaak was invited so late that he could not accept.)

On April 21, 1956, at the Brussels conference, Spaak sounded the keynote which was persuasive to the other future partners in the treaty. "Europe cannot . . . sustain itself with the present rhythm of expansion with its present economic organization," he said. "None of our countries is large enough to support the extensive research and basic investments that will give impetus to the technical revolution which the atomic era promises."

In his report, Spaak urged the gradual elimination of customs barriers among the member states, the elimination of import quotas, and the establishment of a common investment fund for specially ambitious projects. He also urged that there be a common policy on competition, including equal pay for men and women, equal policies on overtime and vacation pay, and so forth. This latter was especially important since the labor-management policies in France were far more liberal than those in Germany, thus making production costs higher. There was also a recommendation for a free interchange of knowledge and expertise on production methods and management procedures.

All the interested nations agreed with the recommendations, in substance, except France who (according to *Le Monde*) was "Postponing for as long as possible the disagreeable moment for throwing herself into the cold water she knew to be good for her health."

France delayed her approval until she gained some special concessions for herself, which were rather grudgingly granted. Then, in Rome, on March 25, 1957 the Treaty among "The Six" was finally signed.

Unfortunately, Great Britain and the Scandinavian countries abstained from the discussions and the agreement. This has weakened the overall strength of the Community, and has caused disturbance ever since.

From the very beginning the Common Market was a success, a fact that has been admitted freely even by its critics. As a result of its operation, the German industrial production increased 39 percent (between 1959 and 1963), and the French index, 30 percent. In the important chemical industry, production rose even more sharply: 73 percent in Germany, 59 percent in France.

On July 23, 1961 Prime Minister Harold Macmillan, of Great Britain, announced that Great Britain would seek entrance into the European Economic Community. Five of the partners were enthusiastic about this possibility, even though Great Britain asked for certain concessions protecting its preferential trade with Commonwealth nations. But, on January 14, 1963 General de Gaulle coldly and personally vetoed the proposal.

The psychological reasons for this opposition have been touched upon earlier in this Chapter. There was also a selfish economic reason: trade with the English Commonwealth nations was not nearly as important to France as it was to Germany.

In eleven years, between 1950 and 1961, German exports to Canada had risen from $10 million a year to $133 million a year, and her imports from Canada had risen from $10 million to $236 million. In the same period, the exports to Australia had risen from $27 million to $111 million, and the imports from $64 million to $91 million. France's business with these countries was less than a third of that, and de Gaulle felt that permitting Great Britain to join the club would help Germany, which already had the inside track, more than it would help France.

In the summer of 1967, Great Britain is once again making a determined effort to join the Common Market. Five of the six nations are in favor, but, once again, de Gaulle is opposed. However, there is a growing dissatisfaction among all the partners except Germany, with de Gaulle's paternalistic approach to the market. (Italian President Giuseppe Saragat, for instance, almost spoiled the tenth anniversary party by calling for British admission. He compounded his "sin" by publicly thanking the United States for its unselfish role in re-building war-shattered Europe.)

In recent years France, under de Gaulle's leadership, has been accustomed to treating the Common Market as if it were a purely private arrangement between herself and Germany. The other nations have been somewhat slighted and shunted aside, and this could cause serious difficulties in the future. In any case, it seems likely that Great Britain will eventually be permitted to enter the Market, after she does public penance before de Gaulle, somewhat like Kaiser Heinrich IV before Hildebrand, (Pope Gregory VII,) at Canossa, 900 years ago.

Meanwhile, de Gaulle's narrow and proprietary approach toward the Common Market has vitiated its power and slowed its impetus so it is not now so great a success as it was in its earlier years.

The question naturally arises, whether the European Economic Community will eventually be expanded into some form of political integration along the lines of the United States of Europe, with a common parliament, common monetary exchange, and so forth.

It is not valid, I think, to talk about the racial or ethnic integrity of the various European countries. It doesn't exist. The ethnic variations *within* each European country (except, perhaps, for France) are as great, if not greater, than the variations among the various countries.

A Genovesan, for instance, is an entirely different breed from a Sicilian; a Tuscan is entirely different from a Roman or a Neapolitan.

The Genovesans are, as a matter of fact, different from *anybody*. They are the bankers of Italy *par excellence*. The Bank of America, the largest privately operated Bank in the world, was originally the Bank of Italy in San Francisco, and it was founded and is still largely operated by Genovesans. The Jews, the Armenians and, I must admit, the Chinese, all have a reputation for being hard bargainers. But, in this field, they all must yield, in some ways, to the people of Genoa.

Scientists have been trying for centuries to achieve Centigrade Zero, the absolute absence of heat, the epitome of refrigeration. They have been looking in the wrong places. They could find it in a Genovesan's eyes during a business transaction.

Similarly, the Prussians have little in common with Bavarians, and the Hamburgers and Berliners are completely different tribes, as different at least as are the Czechoslovakians from the Jugoslavians.

In fact, as recently as 1800, when the United States and France were established nations, what we call Germany today consisted of 77 major principalities, 51 Imperial cities and 1,475 territories ruled by Imperial Knights. It was not until 1871 that Bismarck, with his *Realpolitick,* created any semblance of a United Germany.

159

If these racial distinctions can be accommodated within the artificial (and often disputed) borders of the present European nations, they could be equally accommodated in a United States of Europe.

Surely the advantages of this latter accommodation would be far greater than its disadvantages.

Such a development would automatically raise Europe to first class status in the community of nations, and would be a strong factor for maintaining world peace. But, this is not likely to happen as long as Charles de Gaulle is with us. He scoffs at the idea, and has pressured out of positions of power within the Common Market organization all those who stress the supra-national aspects of the community. He views the Common Market only as a means of improving the economic potential of France. If other members prosper, that is all right with him, as long as they don't prosper too much. He is unalterably opposed to any extension of the scope of the Treaty, and, as of now, his will prevails.

But Charles de Gaulle cannot last forever. When he has left the scene, there may be hope for some degree of political integration on the European continent. It depends pretty much on how permanent the infection of his narrow nationalist philosophy has become within the European peoples. His influence (along with the seeming fading away of the threat of attack by the USSR) has caused a steady growth of isolationist thinking among European peoples. It seems impossible to say definitely whether or not the influence will survive the man.

Personally, I feel that common sense will prevail and that the path will one day be cleared for political integration in Europe. De Gaulle's ideal of a *Europe des patries,* a concatenation of separate, self-sufficient, States is old fashioned and sentimental, and not at all suited for the challenge of the 21st Century, if there is going to be such a century.

I feel that European peoples, except for the citizens of Russia and her satellites, are growing together through travel, which has been accelerated in recent years to an unprecedented extent. The

160

cheap automobile and universal paid vacations, plus unparalleled personal prosperity, have combined to send Europeans hurtling across national borders in search of other peoples and other customs. This has done much to dissipate many of the old prejudices and fears. They have even, to the horror of traditional Europeans, begun to develop their own *lingua franca,* a kind of pidgin English which allows them to communicate with some adequacy with other nationals. Since most European children are taught some English in school, this is the natural choice for a common language.

I also feel that the pressure from European industrialists will be greatly in favor of integration. They cannot compete on equal footing with such American industrial giants as General Electric and General Motors unless they can expand freely across the melting international boundaries. In many areas, such as airplane and automobile production, the manufacture of computers, the petrochemical industries, American interests dominate the European field. European industrialists are not likely to remain content with this situation, and the only way they can achieve equal footing is by expanding production and markets and thus making it possible to turn out comparable products at competitive prices.

Finally, I have faith in the innate good sense of the people. They have too much pride to settle for a second class status in the community of nations. They must realize that the only way to regain their stature in the world is by the development of a joint effort. The only way they can defend themselves adequately is through this course. It will be a difficult course, and perhaps a painful one, but it makes far too much sense to be ignored.

Unfortunately, it is impossible to talk about Europe without discussing some of the aspects of anti-Americanism, its causes and its possible cure. Anti-Americanism pervades ever stratum of life in most nations of Europe and it is a very real and injurious factor at both the official and the personal levels.

Much of it is based on frustration. Much of it on jealousy.

161

And a whole lot of it is based on an atavistic urge to crawl back into the ever-loving womb of Mother Europe.

Part of the trouble lies in America's actions and attitudes. As I have mentioned before, the United States is perhaps the only large country in the world capable of performing, or willing to perform acts of altruism and generosity.

Europeans do not understand this. They have almost no altruism or generosity themselves, and they are darkly suspicious of the motives of anyone who has. They feel that anyone who displays generosity is either a fool or a knave with some vicious, hidden motive.

They cannot believe that America has poured billions of dollars into a Europe ruined by war unless she intends to undermine European sovereignty, or take over European markets, or gain some other similarly sinister end. This is the basis of so much talk about "American Imperialism".

And, of course, if America does not have such an ulterior motive behind her giving, then she is, in their eyes, a nation of clowns, and deserving only of contempt.

Philanthropy, as the Americans know it and practise it, is almost unknown in Europe. As an example, when the floods attacked Florence in 1966 and caused almost irreparable damage to the greatest treasures of Italian art, only one Italian millionaire came forward with a substantial donation to finance the restoration. The other solvent Italians sat back complacently, knowing that the Americans would rush forward with checkbooks in their hands. And, this is precisely what happened.

Americans would do far better in Europe if they foreswore generosity for a while. They would do well to emulate the attitudes of Charles de Gaulle, who is the most respected figure in Europe today. De Gaulle does not exude love or generosity. He drives hard bargains. He gives away nothing unless he is certain of getting far more in return. Europeans understand this. They do not understand a nation acting like a romantic spinster demanding to be loved, and lavishing gifts in order to achieve

162

international affection. In Europe, there is no such thing as international affection.

Americans also should realize that the post-war period is over in Europe. Immediately after the war, Europe needed American leadership and the Marshall Plan was her salvation.

That's all done with now. Europe is on her feet and she no longer needs or wants American leadership. She resents it and opposes it.

The United States would also do well to assume an attitude of greater detachment, to be a great deal more pragmatic in her dealings with Europe. She should hesitate to give advice, and she should learn not to over-react to signs of European unfriendliness.

In short, she should make Europeans worry about how America feels about them, rather than be continually concerned about how Europeans feel about her.

Any one experienced in the art and practices of love knows that it is fatal for the lover to appear so devoted that he can be taken for granted. There is a lesson here for Americans to learn.

Europeans feel that American concern for their welfare, and American preachments on their political behavior, indicate a lack of respect for their new status in the 1960's. They feel that America does not realize that they are no longer occupied countries, or war ravaged countries, but modern States fully capable of handling their own affairs.

And America has been slow to realize this. It is about time she does. If she learns to be more detached and more pragmatic, she may find that she will get along a great deal better with her European friends.

IX

ENGLAND

T HE AVERAGE THOUGHTFUL ENGLISHMAN today feels he is trapped on a downward escalator, and that there is something very nasty waiting for him in the basement.

The terrible thing is that he may be right. The economic condition of post-war England is dreadful. Her morale is low. Her leadership has become almost psychopathically pessimistic. Unless she can achieve some major breakthrough, like membership in the Common Market, and with it effect some kind of moral and spiritual renaissance, her future in the world of today is very doubtful indeed.

I write these words in sorrow. As a Jamaican, I feel a very deep affection and loyalty to the Mother Country. I consider London as my second home and, indeed, I am writing these words in that city.

The wonder, of course, is that England ever became a major nation in the first place.

The entire United Kingdom consists only of 94,220 square miles. This is approximately the size of the State of Oregon, which ranks only tenth among the United States of America. (England itself has only 50,331 square miles; Scotland, 30,411; Wales, 8,016; Northern Ireland, 5,462.) The total population of the United Kingdom is around 56 million, of whom 49 million live in England and Wales; 1½ million in Northern Ireland and 5½ million in Scotland. These are not the kind of statistics which would lead one to expect world greatness.

In a way, England became great because she had to. There was no other way to survive. She could not feed her population by herself, so she was forced to build and maintain the greatest navies of the world. She could not consume sufficient of her own manufactured goods to maintain a prospering economy, so she found it necessary to build an Empire greater than Caesar ever knew, the greatest in the history of humankind.

All this would have been impossible, of course, had it not been for the innate power of the English character. The English have always been tough. Julius Caesar found them too hard a nut to crack. Once King Alfred of Wessex was able to weld them into a cohesive nation, they drove the fearsome Danes out of their land. The bastard conqueror from Normandy, leader of the only successful invasion of England, succeeded more through good fortune than through good management, and the Normans made their success permanent only by allowing themselves to become absorbed. The Spanish, the French and the redoubtable Hollanders all came to grief against the oaken walls of English ships and the oaken hearts of English men.

And, of course, there were the German onslaughts of 1914 and 1938. These were almost fatal victories for the English. They gave England her finest hours, but they drained her of so much manpower, so much treasure, and so much energy that she is today only a pale shadow of her former self. Her empire is all but dissolved. The once-sacrosanct Pound Sterling is in shaky condition. As the most industrialized nation in the world, her productivity has not kept pace with the increases in wages. England's exports lag far behind her imports. Twenty-two years after the end of the war England is experiencing wage-price freezes, extortionate taxes and a rugged austerity program. Ironically, these have been imposed by a Socialist Government, which had formerly derided such measures as Tory devices. A Tory Government, of course, would never have been able to persuade the labour unions to accept such an oppressive program.

One of the most significant changes in English life since the

166

end of World War II has been the emergence of the working class.

Over the years the British upper classes were almost incredibly indifferent to the welfare of their social inferiors. Reform was slow in coming and opposition, particularly in the House of Lords, was implacable. It took decades of heart-breaking labour on the part of dedicated men to stop in the mid-nineteenth century the bestial practice of working children as young as seven years of age, 15 hours a day in the mills of Lancashire and Yorkshire. In the 1830's it was estimated that 300,000 children of 13 or younger were working from 6 a.m. to 10 p.m. in the bowels of the earth, digging coal for wages of 2/6 a week. Many of them did not see the sun from one year to the next, and they were treated like animals. It took half a century to pass the Reform Bill, which took absolute control of the House of Commons out of the hands of the aristocracy and eventually led to the enfranchisement of the working man.

As late as 1836, children of 9 years of age were hanged for stealing as little as a bushel of potatoes.

Even during the period between the world wars, years defaced by widespread depression, there was a singular lack of concern on the part of the still affluent upper classes for the unemployed, or even for the employed lower classes. Wages were, in comparison with those paid in other civilized countries, a scandal. It was quite common, for example, to have a cook, living in and working six and a halfdays a week, for as little £60 (about $300) a year. Other domestics, of course, were paid far less.

The rigidity of the social structure wreaked further and more subtle injustices. If a man or woman had an "accent", if he or she dropped an "h", or added an occasional one at the wrong place, or indulged in somewhat tainted vowels, he could not hope to be accepted socially within the upper classes and upper middle classes. They could never hope to be referred to as a gentleman or a lady or even be addressed on an envelope as "Esquire".

Even so eminent an industrialist as Lord Nuffield, who built his huge automobile empire from a bicycle shop in Oxford, was derided and snubbed by the Establishment because of his "non-U" speech. In the United States, of course, such self-made men were national heroes.

Up until World War II, it was very difficult for a working class boy to get into Oxford University, and almost impossible to get into Cambridge. Scholarships were few and rather skimpy, and most colleges within the Universities were decidedly stand-offish when considering the applications of lower-class applicants. The Provost of Worcester College, Oxford, in 1933 summed up the general feeling of his colleagues, when he was heard to remark: "I prefer to hear the voices of *gentlemen* in the quad."

This rigidity in the social structure was costly. It deprived England of an enormous pool of talent by denying hundreds of thousands of clever youngsters with the opportunity of going to a university. It also created class hatreds which are yielding harmful dividends to this day.

To digress a little, the whole basis of the claims of superiority on the part of so-called "educated" or "accepted" English are more than a little spurious. The English broad "*a*" was borrowed from the Cockney! It was not until the period 1825-1850 that this hallmark of cultivated English speech became accepted in British society. As late as 1791 an English pronouncing dictionary classified the broad "*a*" as vulgar and the flat "*a*" as "characteristic of the elegant and learned world". Queen Elizabeth spoke more like a modern American than like a modern Englishman. Shakespeare also used the flat "*a*", but with a strong Warwickshire accent. He would not have been accepted as a gentleman in England in the 1930's, although up until around 1850 moderately regional accents were more common among educated people, and were far more widely accepted.

Of course, this is all changed now, particularly under a Labour Government. The cockney accent is almost "chic", and when Prime Minister Wilson goes on radio or television to address the people he puts a touch of the cockney into his speech to produce a bit of artificial homeliness as a veneer over his rather chilling academic, doctrinaire background.

Tradition has always played an important part in every level of English life; perhaps, too important a part. Ever since the Industrial Revolution, England has produced more goods than could be consumed locally. She has also produced too much history for local consumption.

In too many cases, British management executives love the traditional too fondly, and distrust the modern and the new. Europeans and Americans may lean somewhat too violently to the other point of view, but their attitude is more conducive to progress than is that of the English industrialist.

> *"Be not the first by which the new is tried,*
> *Nor yet the last to cast the old aside."*

In England there is an almost frenetic resistance to casting the old aside. New machines are bought sparingly and disapprovingly and in many shops the old surviving Edwardian monstrosities are babied and pampered out of all proportion. "That's British workmanship, that is," a proud foreman will say. "Works almost as good as it did back in 1907 when it was bought." He does not care to mention that it costs about five times as much to keep operating, and consumes about five times the number of man hours than does the despised modern machine, and produces about one-fifth as much.

By the same token, British industrial design has always lagged approximately a decade behind the competition. Until very recently British automobiles generally looked like the American automobiles of a previous generation. They were excellent from a mechanical point of view, but they had a certain old-fashioned stolidity which made them unattractive to the foreign market. British products generally were known for their excellent workmanship, their superior materials, their durability, and their almost total lack of sex appeal.

169

It may be that the British executive, when reaching the higher echelons of his industry, has sought unconciously to ape the *mores* and the prejudices of the aristocratic classes by whom he hopes eventually to be accepted.

It is certainly true that the evolution from rags to riches, always difficult in even the most progressive lands, is particularly arduous in England. An industrialist who has made it, and has his son in a topflight public school or at one of the two major universities, is particularly loath to risk his new riches on expensive technical innovation. The cost of failure is so great and would lead inexorably to a slide down the social ladder the industrialist had worked so hard to climb. As Norman Macrae, a brilliant editor of *"The Economist"*, in London, has said: "The pains of going down the social ladder are greater than in America, and the joys of going up, from being a millionaire to being a multi-millionaire, are much less here." The risks, in short, are greater, and the incentives less.

The fact that the British Establishment, which sets the tone of leadership in England, comes almost exclusively from Oxford and Cambridge, may have something to do with England's lack of industrial progressiveness. These are two of the greatest universities in the world, none greater, but they are fundamentally traditionalist in their approach and they are inclined to produce traditionalists. These are not the seed-beds from which industrial innovation can be expected to spring. It is to be hoped that the development of the new red-brick provincial universities will eventually break the deadlock of the traditionalist Establishment on British progress.

As a dangerous hangover from older times, the British are still inclined to feel that "What was good enough for my dad is good enough for me", and to be suspicious of innovation. The truth of the matter is that what was good enough for dad is *not* good enough for today and, ironically, "dad" wouldn't have thought so either! The industrial revolution in England, cruel as it was to its servants, was characterized by enormous imagination and courage on the part of its managers. But it was through the

170

Industrial Revolution that industrial management achieved a certain amount of social respectability, and the present managers are determined to hang onto that finger-hold with raw and bleeding hands, even at the expense of progress. The industrialist in the nineteenth century had little or nothing to lose; in the twentieth century he has (he believes) everything to lose. The British Establishment has traditionally despised the "pusher" and so pushing is eschewed, even though it is desperately needed in the England of today.

There are further and more tangible reasons for England's precarious and peculiarly dormant position today. For instance, the pound sterling is over-valued. This is a result of winning the war instead of losing it.

As a victor in World War II, Great Britain, with America, became one of the peace-keepers, and she was poorly equipped to assume the role. She had suffered too much herself and was too economically exhausted to perform the function history forced upon her.

In 1949 the present exchange rates were set. This was a time when most of the important countries of the world were in ruins, their economies buried under their own rubble. It is silly to maintain that the pound should have the same relative value to the *yen,* let us say, in 1967 that it had in 1949. Japan in the subsequent years has become, in her way, a forward-looking industrial giant, far more impressive than England. A sensible devaluation of the pound would cheapen British exports and make them far more attractive to foreign markets. But this would, in the minds of many traditionalists, be an admission of defeat for the pound sterling "upon which", as Prime Minister Wilson so often says, "so much of the strength of Britain depends."

A part of England's unwillingness, or even inability to adapt to changing conditions or to admit past mistakes springs from the *doctrinaire* quality which dominates her politics. The English people are traditionally unattracted to blends. They like their tea "India" or "China", and would not dream of mixing the two. They like their tobacco "Turkish" or "Virginia", and so on. By the same token, they like their politics Labour (i.e. Socialist) or Conservative. Since the withering away of the Liberal Party after World War I, the reasonably liberal Englishman has had no ideological or political Party to call his home.

When England went Socialist after World War II, and then reverted to Conservative, the pendulum swung too sharply back and forth for the economic well-being of the country. The railroads and some basic industries were "nationalized" and then were "de-nationalized", to the confusion of almost everybody.

When Mr. Wilson's Socialist Government took over again, it acted with more caution. In many respects its policies are indistinguishable from the policies of the Tories, and some of them are a little to the right of the policies of the liberal wing of the Conservative Party! This homogeonization of English political life today apparently pleases no one. The powerful Trade Unions charge that their leaders have betrayed the Socialist revolution. The Colonel Blimp conservatives believe the nation has gone to the "demnation puppies", and the average middle-of-the-road Englishman just wishes that somebody would exhibit some inspired leadership and employ some imaginative planning that will get the economy rolling again.

Actually, the Labour Party is caught in a kind of cleft stick. Although its leaders must continue to pay lip service to Socialism, they know that Socialism is not the answer to England's problems, if, indeed, it is the answer to the problems of any nation. They also know that the average Englishman, while somewhat to the left of the official policy of the Conservatives, is not at heart a Socialist and never will be. So the leadership tries on one hand to appease the hard-core Union leaders who make up the viscera of the Labour Party without offending the average voter. This is not the climate in which social or economic progress is made.

Unfortunately, there is considerable doubt as to whether England *can* make much economic progress under existing conditions. Her domestic market is far too small for a country desir-

172

ous of being an industrial power in the final third of the twentieth century.

As new industries have become more and more sophisticated, it has become increasingly necessary to develop a wider economic base to support them. Thus, it is possible to maintain a reasonably thriving traditional industry in a smallish economy, such as the cotton or the steel industry, but when one gets into automobiles or airplanes the base must be much larger than England can supply.

Competitive prices depend upon the ability to produce in volume. Potential investors shy away from putting their capital into industries that do not have free access to a market considerably larger than England's 56 million people can offer. Englishmen traditionally buy automobiles to last a decade or so. They are not accustomed, nor are they likely to become accustomed, to trading old cars and buying new ones every few years. This has made the expansion of the industry more difficult.

All this has led to a complication of woes. English industry does not have the capital to invest in research and the development of new and more efficient techniques, and money is not being invested in new ventures. Thus there are few new industries in England, and the older industries are becoming old-fashioned and comparatively inefficient.

It must be added that the attitudes of the British trade unions have not been helpful during this period of approaching crisis. The restrictive labour practices dictated by the unions have grown more rigid, instead of less, as times have worsened, and they seem to have grown most oppressive in the industries that have been suffering or declining the most. Labour's co-operation with management is minimal in industries that are threatened by new competition in their fields (such as ship-building, coal mining, the railroads); in industries which are seasonal and dependent upon the vagaries of English weather (construction), and industries that are cyclical in nature and highly sensitive to existing economic conditions (automobile manufacturing).

173

This curious and hurtful condition is influenced considerably by the traditional Socialist doctrinaire philosophy of most labour leadership in England. The union heads dislike or distrust the profit system and challenge the rights of management in this area. But, since British industry must and does operate on the capitalistic system (no matter what the philosophy of the Government might be), profits are necessary for the provision of full employment, decent wages and humming production lines. There is abundant evidence that the Trade Unions are not as popular with the rank-and-file workers as they used to be but the leadership is so entrenched that successful challenge is all but impossible. Leadership in British Labour Unions goes almost entirely by seniority and a modification of current philosophies can come only by slow degrees, through death or retirement throughout the present hierarchies.

The fault, obviously, does not lie solely at the door of labour. Management has to bear its share of guilt. The managerial class in England has always been indolent, and still is. Despite the changes wrought by two great wars, the English executive establishment still considers hard work as a pretty coarse and degrading exercise, fit only for Americans, Germans and other lesser peoples.

English executives, even in a period of economic distress, rarely get to their offices before 10 a.m. The heavy two-and-a-half hour lunch with claret is by no means extinct. Nothing, not even the Bomb, could interfere with the afternoon tea ritual.

The fact that business and industrial executives are more likely to have come from the ranks than they were before World War II, has not had much effect on the customary languor at the top. These men observed their superiors indulging in the practices of indolence while they were working their way upward, and they envied these prerogatives as the enjoyable fruits of success. Now that they have won the prerogatives, they have no intention of giving them up.

These lackadaisical work habits served reasonably well in former days, since the competition was mostly domestic and equally self-indulgent. There was enough money to go around and everyone could get his share, in a decent gentlemanly way, without breaking his neck over it. But, since World War II the "competition" no longer consists of a tightly-knit society of English *entrepreneurs,* it consists of the entire world, where even the Chairmen of the Boards rise early and work steadily and long at their jobs. The English approach to management is more enjoyable but, unfortunately, it is inadequate for world-class competition, and it sets a tone of slackness throughout the entire spectrum of industrial activity. In the international rat race, unfortunately for British complacence, the foreign "rats" get up earlier, and work harder and longer.

We hear a great deal these days about "the English sickness", the inability and even the unwillingness of the people of England to start moving again. There is a great deal of truth to the talk. The sickness is based upon an endemic disillusionment among the people. Since World War II they have taken a long, hard look at their gods and have found them wanting.

Even after World War I, the English had an almost childish faith in the quality of their "Establishment". The ruling class of gentlemen had their faults, to be sure, but somehow the Holy Ghost had breathed into them the divine quality of leadership which permitted them to muddle through every crisis.

It was natural, therefore, that in time of war, nice young boys right out of Oxford or even just out of Eton or Harrow or Winchester should be given officers' commissions, and be placed in command of battle-tried veterans from the working classes. This was, presumably, the way God ordained things.

It was natural, also, that the real leaders of the political parties should come from the ranks of the privileged. This was just as true of the Labour Party as of the Conservative. The Labourites may tuck a few Cockney former boilermakers or railroaders into their Cabinet, but the significant leadership came (and comes) from the power elite. The difference is that in a Labour Government the top leaders are likely to be dons from Oxford or

Cambridge rather than the younger sons of peers, who seem to dominate Conservative governments.

After World War II the English had good cause to be skeptical about the mystical leadership qualities of the upper classes. If they were so good at managing, then why did things get into such a mess? The diplomatic debacle prior to the War, leading up to and beyond Munich, was an upper class mess. The comparative unreadiness of the Army and Navy when war came, despite years of warning, was another. The fact that a despicable little man like Hitler, who was certainly *not* a gentleman, could come so close to bringing England to her knees, did not enhance the prestige of the upper classes. Despite the fact that Winston Churchill was every inch a patrician, the Battle of Britain was essentially a victory for the Common Man and had little to do with any particular quality within the Establishment.

Since World War II national events left the reputation of the Establishment in shreds. The Empire was peeled off, bit by bit, like an artichoke, so that only the heart and a few bristles remained. The Suez Crisis disheartened the people even more, disclosing as it did, an alarming weakness and ineptitude in Britain's governmental leaders. The failure of the United Kingdom to gain admittance to the European Common Market has also been blamed on upper class leadership.

The Profumo scandal did not help matters. However, it was not as basically serious as some observers seemed to believe. It showed evidence of considerable moral deterioration at the heart of the Establishment, but the English have never demanded that their leaders be especially monogamous, or even spectacularly chaste. The list of successful legislative lechers in England is long and the populace has been remarkably tolerant of dalliance, as long as it was kept within certain bounds and was conducted with taste and with a person of the opposite sex. (The Parnell-Kitty O'Shea case was an exception, but it was an Irish case, and most of the moral indignation was imported from the homeland of the principals.) The damaging point of the Profumo case was that it was so tawdry and low class, somewhat as if the Old Vic Company were to make a stag movie and then show it in Buckingham Palace. Ordinary Englishmen felt they had a right to expect more *style* from their leaders. Mrs. Fitz-Herbert was one thing. So was Wallis Simpson. But — *Christine Keeler*?

Far more significant was the fact that financial improbity started showing up in hallowed places. The bastions of British finance, the Bank of England and the Bank of Scotland and the Government itself were duped by dishonest practitioners. The most trusted institutions showed themselves to be just as credulous and gullible as, let us say, a small and inexperienced merchant in Twin Forks, Idaho!

Next to the Bank of England, perhaps the most reliable household gods in the nation were Scotland Yard and the British constabulary in general. These were symbols of incorruptibility and efficiency, the best and most reliable police force in the world. Even these were found to have feet of clay. A new breed of English criminal inaugurated a new type of English crime and, in doing so, made Scotland Yard and the local police look little better than Mr. Mack Sennett's Keystone Cops. There were well-substantiated charges of corruption and police brutality. And when criminals were apprehended and imprisoned, the supposedly impregnable British gaols turned out to have about as much security as a tin of sardines. Scotland Yard detectives are no longer the national heroes; the criminals are. The remarkable men who engineered the Great Train Robbery are looked up to and even admired; the detectives of Scotland Yard are derided.

Englishmen used to be able to feel a complacent well-being about their railroad system. They were certain that their principal trains were the fastest, most reliable and most comfortable in the world. When they began to travel on the continent after the War, they looked about them and found that this was no longer true, if, indeed, it had ever been true. British trains, compared to those in France, Germany and even Italy were slow, often late, dirty, drafty and antiquated. Half-hearted attempts at nationalization, combined with inadequate funds for the development of new techniques and new equipment, have reduced the once-proud British railroads to a point where they are very little better than the abominable passenger trains in America.

Another household god was the Church of England, which has lost most of its relevance to the life of modern England. It is the official Church, of course, and the Queen is its nominal head, but its rôle has been fairly well reduced to that of a comforting conductor of ceremonies which are important more for their historic values than for their influence on the world of today. Although the Anglicans are, by far, the dominant religion, numerically, in England, the number of Englishmen who attend the Church regularly is distressingly small and grows smaller every year. Some estimates put the percentage of practising Anglicans at about 10 percent of the whole. The people just don't believe in the Church any more, and from a number of statements I have read, and of conversations I have heard, I have come to the sorrowful conclusion that not very many Anglican clergymen believe in the Church either.

It could well be that the Methodists and the Roman Catholics have more *practising* members in England than does the Established Church.

It was almost inevitable that, as the working classes rose in importance and power, the Church of England should decline in influence. Over the centuries, the Church had performed a peculiar social function, to indulge the rich and keep down the poor (*"parcere superbis et debellare subiectos"*). This has been the role of "Established" Churches everywhere. If it were not, the Churches wouldn't have been "established" in the first place.

The Bishops of the Anglican Church are peers of the realm and sit in the House of Lords. They almost always come from Establishment families. There is little chance of their ever being a Cockney Archbishop of Canterbury, or even one with as humble an origin as that of the Roman Catholic Pope John XXIII.

For centuries Anglican parsons in country churches, who more often than not owed their ecclesiastical "livings" to the local aristocracy, preached earnestly to the poor that they should be content with their station in life and obey without murmur

178

those whom God, in His infinite wisdom and justice, has placed over them to rule. The English workmen listened to this inspired balderdash with amazing patience over the years because attendance at Church was almost compulsory, and dissent from the established way of thinking, not healthy. (Victorian and Edwardian families would hold communal prayers on Sunday nights which the servants were compelled to attend.) But when the working classes began to achieve a certain degree of economic and social independence, it is not surprising that their enthusiasm for the Establishment and "established" Church waned.

Methodism was something else again. The Methodists preached a kind of down-to-earth (or, perhaps, down to Hell) fire and brimstone religion which recognized no distinction among the classes. If the Methodist preachers failed to find much good in their congregations, they were egalitarian in that they found just as much evil among the rich as they did among the poor.

In the 18th Century, this approach shocked the aristocracy, and alarmed them because such thinking could easily lead to speculations about the rights of man. If a rich man could be just as evil as a poor man, then a poor man could be just as good as a rich man.

This point of view is explicity and delightfully expounded in a letter which the Duchess of Buckingham wrote, in the latter part of the 18th Century, to the Methodist Countess of Huntingdon:

"I thank your Ladyship for the information concerning the Methodist preachers; their doctrines are most repulsive and strongly tinctured with impertinence and disrespect towards their superiors, in perpetually endeavouring to level all ranks and to do away with all distinctions. It is monstrous to be told you have a heart as sinful as the common wretches that crawl the earth."

The more worldly Churchmen of the Establishment saw Methodism as a threat, not so much to the chances of eternal salvation among the poor (which was unimportant), but to the political *status quo* (which was very important indeed). The

Bishop of Lincoln, in 1799, saw in Methodism a double threat. "The same means," he said, "might with equal efficacy, be employed to sap and overturn the State, as well as the church."

Under such circumstances, it is not surprising that the average British workman should feel less than enthusiastic about the established religion. If he is religious at all, he is more likely to be a member of a "chapel", one of the dissenting sects.

The role of the Roman Catholic Church in England has been · interesting and, to members of that faith, frustrating, ever since Henry VIII led his country away from Rome. We have seen, in other chapters of this book, how the Roman Church muffed glorious opportunities in other lands, to become the dominant religion. In England she missed the boat twice, and on each occasion a touch of common sense or common decency on the part of the English Catholic ruler could have insured permanent victory.

Henry's daughter Mary, while no more bloody-minded than his other daughter, Elizabeth, was a fool, while Elizabeth was not. She married the Spanish King, Philip, and turned England for a few years into an enclave of Spain, thus making Protestantism a patriotic duty on the part of all proper Englishmen.

In the succeeding century, James II, the younger and stupid brother of the clever Charles II, tried to force a French version of Rome upon the English people and was, in turn, chased out of the kingdom. If he had had half the brains, and half the tolerance and charm, of his brother (who was a crypto-Catholic but chose not to make an issue of the fact), he could have quietly made Catholicism not only respectable, but dominant, in England.

The English are not, by nature, a religious people, but they are a patriotic people. Mary made Catholicism in their minds synonymous with Spanish oppression; James II made Catholicism synonymous with French oppression. The English were not likely to become excited about matters of dogma, unless the dogma threatened their liberty or sovereignty. If the Vatican had thought to indulge in just a touch of tolerance in either reign, it could have re-won England. But, as with all Churches of international power, the political aspects far outweighed the simple consideration of saving souls and of bettering the condition of humankind.

The Roman Church has won many converts in England, particularly since the dramatic Oxford Movement of the latter part of the 19th Century. But its appeal has been mostly among the *intelligentsia,* backed up by a hard core of Irish immigrants and descendants of families who were able to withstand the pressures of the centuries to abandon their traditional faith. (In a very snobbish land, there is nothing or no one more snobbish than a member of an old Catholic family that kept the faith! And, oddly enough, they are far more snobbish against the converted Catholics than they are against the English Protestants. Newman found this out to his sorrow; Chesterton found it out to his amusement.)

I am aware that I have digressed somewhat in discussing the role of religion in England, but it is a question that fills me with a kind of horrified fascination. So many tens of thousand of people died—the brave, the noble, the stupid, the ambitious, the bigoted, the innocent, the zealous—because of dogmatic disagreements which did not matter a ha'-pennyworth, except that they had political undertones. It is a terrible thing when religion falls into the hands of people who are fundamentally irreligious!

In any case, the Church of England, which has always been a political force more than a religious force, is now in a condition of almost terminal decline. It is a household god that has lost its meaning, and even its reason for being.

These disillusionments have plagued and numbed the English. They have always been traditionalists. Perhaps too much so. Now they have been going through a period of realizing that the old traditions have less value than they had believed, and perhaps never did have as much as they had supposed. Subconsciously, many Englishmen, of all classes, feel they have been victimized by a massive confidence game perpetrated by the Upper Classes. They have been seduced by the elegant manners (and the sometimes equally elegant rudeness), the classical education, the superior attitudes, and have been blinded by the very real deficiencies that lay behind the impressive facade.

The English have been so beaten down by dull failures in endeavours where they once were triumphant that they over-react hysterically whenever a success is achieved. When England, for the first time, won the soccer championship of the world, the nation went into delirium. When Sir Francis Chichester completed his wonderful solo sail around the world, the reaction was equally frenzied. The English behaved in a way they used to find amusing in the Americans! But, at this point, the average person is looking desperately for *some* reassurance that the spirit that made England great is not totally defunct.

Is the English sickness fatal? It is hard to say; but, probably not. The English people have endured so much and overcome so much that it would be foolhardy and almost impertinent to contemplate the arrangement of obsequies.

It could be the illness has been treated wrongly. The Governmental doctors have been prescribing tranquilizers when they should have been prescribing benzedrine. It is useless for the politicians to keep pouring out soothing syrup and telling the patient he will pull out of his vapours in time. He won't, unless he gets up out of bed, pulls up his socks, and starts moving resolutely toward the necessary goals.

The recovery depends also upon England's acceptance into the Common Market. Despite the opposition of De Gaulle, this development cannot, surely, be indefinitely delayed.

England's future lies in Europe and her industries and economy cannot possibly flourish until they have free access to larger markets. For years, the ties with the United States have been sentimental rather than helpful. The "special arrangement" between the two countries has had its advantages, but, recently, the disadvantages have prevailed, particularly in regard to the linkage of the pound with the dollar. (America would also do well to loosen some of its ties with the Mother Country, especially in the field of diplomacy. The preponderance of Rhodes

Scholars in the U.S. State Department has made American foreign policies almost a tail to the kite of Great Britain's policies, and often to the disadvantage of both countries.) This does not mean that the friendship between the two countries should be diminished, but it does mean that the value of continuing an excessive inter-dependence should be thoughtfully examined. England would do better if her orientation were more toward Europe than toward the United States.

And, although General De Gaulle has not seemed to grasp this fact yet, Europe needs England just as much as England needs Europe. The Common Market is still not large enough to compete with complete success against the massive enterprises of America. The addition of British industry to the complex of the European Common Market would put Europe in an exemplary competitive situation which she cannot achieve in any other way.

In 1967 two teams from the important British chemical industry travelled to America to investigate, in depth, the differences between the industrial operations in the two countries. The findings were more than interesting; they were potentially instructive for all British industry.

The most obvious finding was that the average American worker produced 2½ times more than did the average British worker.

This is partially explained by the fact that the plants are larger and the mass production techniques, which the Americans have developed to perfection, are more possible. But this is only a partial explanation.

The Americans also enjoy the advantage of bulk transportation of their products, bulk handling and bulk buying. And, of course, the American companies have a far larger domestic market and are not as dependent upon exports as are the English companies.

These are built-in American advantages, but they do not tell the whole story of the British lag. The investigating teams point an accusing finger with almost equal emphasis at comparatively hide-bound and inefficient English management and the crippling, maddening restrictive practices which the unions impose upon the industries.

The English managers operate in what the report terms "a well-intentioned haze". They do not make sufficient use of computers or modern executive techniques in setting and achieving goals and evaluating performance. They do not supply to line management the specialist assistance that American industry provides. They are not sufficiently profit-minded, and their techniques are as hopelessly old-fashioned as their machinery.

On the other hand, labour is also a generation behind the times. The English workman has been accused, by the spokesmen of the Establishment, as being "bone lazy". This is simply not true. The British workman is by and large eager to work more, and do a better job, than his union will permit him to do.

British labour is senselessly compartmentalized into overlapping unions which make the efficient operation of a plant almost impossible. The overlapping results in payroll padding, a plethora of superfluous workers created by needless demarcations among the duties they can perform.

The report points out that in the United States all chemical workers belong to the same union. In England the workers in a chemical plant will belong to a proliferation of competing unions. For instance there are separate unions for unskilled workers, for machinery maintenance men, process workers, and other skilled workers performing numerous functions. An unconscionable amount of time is wasted while workers hang around waiting for members of other unions to perform jobs they could just as well do themselves. The English unions resist the development of new processes, and this too often discourages management from insisting upon the institution of labor-saving, cost-cutting techniques.

Also, it was found, that the chickens of the old class-distinction have come to roost with a vengeance. Blue collar workers in British industry are treated like a second-class citizens, and they feel far less interest in the success or progress of their company

184

than do American workers. American workers are far more profit-conscious than their Socialist-indoctrinated brothers in England. Many large American companies have incentive and stock-sharing programs which make the interests of the worker identical with the interests of management. This is not common in England and, if proposed, would probably be opposed by the hide-bound union leaders who would view it as a "speed up" device. The United States, having originated as a classless society, is reaping enormous dividends from that conception. There is a sense of industrial team work in America which is almost totally lacking in England. The average English worker feels he is as different a human being from a member of top management as an alley cat must feel he is different from his cousin, the jaguar. The worker resents the manager, envies him his freedom and economic security, and feels very little kinship with him. Very few British workers carry the baton of a Field Marshal in their knapsacks. Hundreds of thousand of American workers do. In England, a job is usually just a job, but in America a worker is far more likely to consider his job a career. This has created a completely different atmosphere in the industries of the two nations, and the advantage is all on the side of the Americans.

Sociologically, England is healthier today than it was before the second War. The "grand scheme of subordination" which was more or less accepted by all classes for many centuries, has been broken up beyond repair. Full employment, fairer (if oppressive) taxes, improved social and medical services, and the subsidization of basic foods have combined to narrow the division between the ruling and the working classes.

However, there is still a great disparity in the distribution of property. The nation's wealth is held by a very limited group. Rent, interest and profits make up one-third of the Gross National Product, and only two-thirds are accounted for by wages. One-third of the incomes are less than £300 a year. When he dies, rarely does a British workman have anything to leave to his survivors.

185

Socialism has achieved very little for the common man, except, perhaps to make him believe that the Government is actively on his side, and not arrayed against him. The results have been more psychological than actual. There is a growing feeling that the English working class is becoming sick and tired of living in another world from that of the Establishment and is going to insist more and more upon the demolition of the barriers which separate him from the better life.

England cannot progress economically until the buying power of the worker is significantly enhanced. Too little attention has been paid to developing the working class as a lucrative market for the goods they produce.

It is inconceivable that Great Britain should go under and become a minor nation, small in stature and influence, warmed only by the memory of a glorious past. England has meant, and does mean, far too much to the world for this to happen. She has gallantly withstood the shocks and machines of war, the steeled cunning of most troubled times. It is beyond belief that she could be permanently diminished by the pressure of modern economics.

As the nineteenth century Italian statesman, Camillio Cavour, said: "I venerate her because I regard her as one of the principal forces in the world; as the rock on which liberty has found, and may perhaps still find, inviolable sanctuary."

But England will not, and cannot, recover from her present perilous position merely on the strength of her reputation. If she is to make the leap into future, she must adjust her thinking to the 21st century. She must re-discover the boldness, the imagination the grandeur of spirit which made her for so many centuries one of the "principal forces" in the world.

The battles of peacetime may be even more difficult to win, and more trying to the soul, than were the glorious battles of war. But they must be fought, and for the benefit of all mankind, they must be won.

X

THREE COMMONWEALTH NATIONS

THE COMMONWEALTH OF NATIONS, formerly known as the British Commonwealth, is all that is left of the globe-encircling British Empire. The nations are joined together by varying degrees of allegiance to the Crown and by certain mutually satisfactory trade agreements.

The British Empire really began to break up after World War I, and in 1931 the Mother Country, through the Statute of Westminster, rewarded Australia, Canada, New Zealand and South Africa for their enormous contributions to the allied victory by formally recognizing their status as nations. (South Africa has withdrawn from the Commonwealth in recent years, and now is totally independent.)

After World War II, as we have seen, colony after colony achieved independence, but most preferred to remain within the loose Commonwealth. At latest count, the Commonwealth included (in addition to the States mentioned above): Barbados, Botswana, Ceylon, Cyprus, The Gambia, Ghana, Guyana, India, Jamaica, Kenya, Lesotho, Malawi, Malaysia, Malta, Nigeria, Pakistan, Sierra Leone, Singapore, Tanzania, Trinidad and Tobago, Uganda and Zambia. The list may be a little longer by the time these words are read. The British are very industrious in granting independence to out-of-the-way possessions, many of which have little idea what to do with it. Would the British were equally industrious about more constructive matters.

CANADA

Canada is the most powerful and perhaps the most interesting of all the Commonwealth nations. Among all the nations of the world it is second only to Russia in size (3,851,809 square miles) and is ranked tenth among all countries in overall power and effectiveness. Her standard of living is second only to the U.S.

Canada may well be the most powerful nation in the world in the 21st century. She has almost incalculable natural resources, most of which are virtually untapped. All she lacks are people and climate.

The population of Canada is only 20 million. By far the vast majority of the people are strung along the southern border in close proximity to the United States. Above them, to the north, lie millions of square miles of virgin forests and inhospitable arctic desert, under whose ice and snow lies a bonanza of minerals and natural resources. All that is needed to exploit this untapped wealth are enough rugged and adventuresome people willing to live under primitive and freezing conditions. In recent years Canada has been attempting to entice immigrants from the Scandinavian lands, but with only fair success. About 44 percent of the population are of English origin, and 31 percent of French. The other 25 percent come mostly from other European nations, except for a handful of native Indians (205,000) and Eskimos (13,600)

Like the U.S., Canada is a land of dramatic contrasts. It contains some of the most stunning scenery in the world, and some of the most wearisome expanses of featureless flat lands. British Columbia is in many respects like an English colony of the 19th century, while frontier communities like Winnipeg and Calgary

188

are roaring, vulgar, vital cities with more than a touch of the Wild West about them. Ottawa, the Capital, is among the dullest cities in the world, while Montreal is perhaps the most fascinating and cosmopolitan community in North America, rivaled only by San Francisco and Mexico City. In the city of Quebec and, particularly, on the beautiful Ile d'Orleans, one is in the heart of France, a million light years in culture and outlook away from Toronto. Canada is almost disturbingly kaleidoscopic, and is almost entirely fascinating in its diversity.

It is possible that the Vikings were the first Europeans to visit Canada, but the first recorded landing was by the Italian-born English explorer, John Cabot, who claimed the "new found land" for Henry VII in 1497. In 1534, Jacques Cartier arrived and planted the lily flag of France on the Gaspé Peninsula and claimed the area for *his* King, Francois I. Seventy years later, Samuel de Champlain founded the first French settlement on North American soil, on the coast of New Brunswick. In 1607, Champlain moved inland and founded Quebec on an almost impregnable bluff above the St. Lawrence River, and made it the capital city of New France.

Meanwhile, the British claimed the entire territory on the basis of Cabot's voyage more than a hundred years earlier. The warring between the two nations ended when the red coats finally defeated the French arms on the Plains of Abraham, at Quebec, in 1759. The subsequent Treaty of Paris (1763) renounced French claims in Canada, but it did not settle the controversy. While the vast majority of French *Canadiens* are loyal to Canada as it is now constituted, they are totally French in language, culture and point of view. And since Protestantism is the religion of Great Britain, the average French *Canadien* is considerably more Catholic than the Pope. The incredible behaviour of Charles de Gaulle in Quebec in the summer of 1967 demonstrated dramatically that there is still a great deal of difference between Canadian and *Canadien*.

Canada is celebrating its centennial this year, for it was in 1867 when England, under the North America Act, granted her

Confederation and a certain amount of autonomy. However, Canada's real history as a national entity begins with the Treaty of Westminster of 1931. The earlier date had to be recognized as the birth of Canada in order to provide a peg on which to hang the motivation for the magnificent "Expo '67" fair in Montreal, and so the centennial was declared.

The important thing about Canada is that it is not a part of the United States and has no intention of becoming one. On at least two occasions (during the Revolution and during the War of 1812), the U.S. made ill-advised attempts to invade and conquer Canada or, at least, to "rescue" her from British tyranny. Both attempts were fiascos. The beleaguered maiden, who was presumed to be imprisoned in her tower, showed no gratitude whatsoever toward her would-be "rescuer". Instead, she grabbed her flintlock and drove him off with a charge of buckshot in his britches.

Despite superficial similarities, Canadians are not very much like their U.S. neighbors. They are inclined to be far less outgoing than Americans, far less exuberant. Canadians, by and large, are more comfortable in the company of Englishmen than they are in the company of people from the States.

Canadians are solid Church goers, to a far greater extent than are citizens of the U.S. It is estimated that 80 percent of all Protestant Canadians go to Church regularly, a far higher percentage than one would find south of the border. In all Canada, in 1966, there were only sixty divorces! Family life is very strong, but the dominant figure is the father, not the mother, as in the U.S. Yet, Canadians do not share with Americans the urge for personal, private philanthropy. No Canadian has gone in for philanthropy on anywhere near the scale that the Fords, Rockefellers, Carnegies, Whitneys, Mellons and other great U.S. families of wealth have gone in for it. A Canadian multi-millionaire would consider the founding of a Foundation as somewhat foolish and more than a little vulgar.

Considering the proximity of the populations, and the constant cultural and personal exchanges, it is remarkable that the citizens of Canada and the U.S. are not more similar than they are. But it is just as well that there are these differences and that, on the whole, Canadians and Americans respect each other for them.

The relationship between the all-powerful U.S. and Canada is friendly, co-operative and usually pleasant. It is also occasionally prickly and always a little uneasy.

It is almost inevitable that the U.S. should dominate Canada in many areas: culture, higher education, research, finance, fashion. This causes resentment among the Canadians, but there is really no way it can be helped.

U.S. interests today control 60 percent of Canada's productive capacity, and they continue to buy Canadian industries at a quickening pace. Recently this matter was brought to a head when the First National City Bank of New York bought the Mercantile Bank of Canada. Parliament then passed the Canada Bank Act of 1967, and is now asking the First National to sell its Canadian acquisition, because *post hoc facto* it is in violation of the new law.

Like the Europeans, Canadians resent the fact that American money is "calling the shots" for their major industries. But Canada needs money if she is ever going to develop her potential, and the States is where the money is. It would be irresponsible for private interests in the States to invest their money in Canadian enterprises without demanding a proportionate share of control.

Canada is in a far better bargaining position than is Europe, since she has almost unlimited natural resources, and European nations have few. But she is also in danger of permitting chauvinism to impede her own progress.

Maurice Suave, the Canadian Minister of Forestry and Rural Development, made a speech in the spring of 1967, in which he explained the dilemma in sensible terms:

"Our persepective of foreign investment should not be one of fear, concern and nationalism for nationalism's sake. Our approach should be positive, and should be based on our assessment of the overall needs of the Canadian economy. In our acute sensitivity to the imagined effects of foreign ownership on the performance of our economy, I believe we have allowed ourselves to be distracted from more important problems facing us. Our objective should be to develop the full economic and social potential of our nation. What should concern us is whether foreign investment and Canadian investment are being effectively used to reach this objective."

Nonetheless, the Canadian *angst* against U.S. financial domination continues, and could eventually impede Canada's progress in the field of world leadership.

The cultural domination by the U.S. is even more seriously resented, and it is even more inevitable. Except for Montreal, Canada is a cultural desert. She has no writers of world rank (except for one or two French Canadians), no painters, few musicians. If a Canadian book is to gain recognition in Canada, it must be published in the States. Canadian publishers consider a sale of 1,000 books better than average for a successful Canadian writer.

As late as 1954 there were no more than 50 English-speaking bookstores in all of Canada. Although conditions have changed somewhat, for the better, a bookstore is still somewhat of a curiosity. The best way to kill interest in a forthcoming Canadian book is to announce that it is being published in Toronto, instead of New York.

Canadian culture has been described as "Here a professor, and there a poet, and between, thousands of miles of wheat and indifference."

There is no national library in all of Canada. There is no art gallery equal to those even in smaller U.S. cities like Minneapolis and San Francisco.

Although McGill University in Montreal is greatly respected abroad, its excellence is in certain specialized fields. If a Canadian scholar is to gain recognition, either at home or abroad, he must do his post-graduate work in the United States or in Europe.

Outside of Quebec Province, which is a special case, there is not a really first class restaurant in all of Canada, and very little demand for one.

There is no great newspaper in Canada, certainly none of national status like the New York *Times*, the Wall Street *Journal*, the Christian Science *Monitor*, or other U.S. papers of al most equal distinction. There are no magazines or learned periodicals of superior quality.

It is only natural that this cultural vacuum should be filled by the cultural powerhouse on the U.S. side of the border. Canadians read American books, listen to American music, watch American plays and movies, subscribe to American newspapers and magazines, learn from American-trained scholars, buy American paintings, and hate themselves for doing these things. But, there is no other way they can fill their needs.

The cultural relationship between the two nations has not been helped by the constant "brain drain" which Canada is experiencing. In 1966, Canada lost 50,000 of its most talented young men to the U.S. through emigration. The opportunities are so much greater south of the border and the pay and recognition so much more rewarding, that one cannot really blame young Canadians for emigrating. But the situation exacerbates relationships, since Canada can so ill afford losing valuable citizens. As A.M. Lower, the Canadian historian, has written: "It has tended to be the more able and especially the spontaneous who have gone . . . Canada has retained the withdrawn, the sedate and those with the least energy and ability."

Aside from the usual nationalistic drives, there is a subtle but more important reason why Canadians fear domination by their U.S. neighbors, and it involves the relationship with minorities within the borders of each country. The United States is the great melting pot. The national thrust is to absorb minority groups and meld them into a reasonably homogeneous whole. This is not the Canadian way. Canada is not a melting pot. The people make no attempt to absorb the minorities, and these groups are inclined to live among themselves and retain their national characteristics.

The French *Canadiens* are possibly more anti-American than the English Canadians and much of their distrust stems from this cause. The *Canadien* is fiercely proud of his *Frenchness*, and he would fight to the death against any attempt to homogenize his people into a kind of bland Canadian entity. Curiously enough, the *Frenchness* of the *Canadien* is of the pre-revolutionary vintage. Even his language has become strangely mummified. Although he writes modern French, his speech is somewhat closer to the language of Corneille than it is to the language of Charles de Gaulle. The effect of a *Canadien's* speech on a modern Frenchman is somewhat like the effect would be on an Englishman if he could converse with a cockney who had once seen Ben Jonson plain.

Of course, there is no real desire on either side of the border to amalgamate the two nations. The Canadians have no wish to inherit the negro problem in the U.S., and the United States has no wish to inherit Canada's Quebec problem.

Canada's international policies do not run automatically in harness with those of the United States, and sometimes they run counter, as in the matter of Viet Nam. Before World War II, the policies of the two nations were inseparable, but since that time there has been considerable divergence.

This is not to say that Canada assumes hostile attitudes, or that it has a tendency to be "neutral" in the way that India is neutral. Canada is solidly pro-western. She could not be anything else if she wanted to be. She is still almost totally dependent on American arms and American protection.

But Canada's diplomatic forces represent the most distinguished department of her government, and they are probably unsurpassed in skill by any corps in any other nation. Certainly Canadian diplomats are respected throughout the world more than are the diplomats of the United States.

Ever since Canada created a Department of External Affairs in 1909, she has built her diplomatic corps toward this ideal.

She reserves her top positions for career diplomats and makes the positions attractive to talented persons by paying the highest salaries of any major country in the world. Her diplomats have consistently served in the most delicate situations in the United Nations and have held in that body positions requiring the utmost in responsibility and trust. The Canadian people have every reason to be proud of the performance of her diplomatic corps, and, naturally, it is to be expected that such a distinguished group of policy makers will not always be content with serving as a tail to the U.S. State Department's kite.

Canada, in short, is in a transitional stage. She is a large and important nation, but she is still something of a satellite in the U.S. orbit. Canadians feel that their U.S. neighbors are condescending toward them, and, certainly, Americans can learn some useful lessons in tactful behavior in this area.

Canada is growing, and frustrated because she is not growing faster than she is. This serves to abrade her relationships with the United States because she would dearly love to be as strong and as independent as her neighbor.

But Canada's destiny, with luck and God's blessing, seems to lie in ultimate greatness. She needs American protection and she needs American money, if she is to survive and prosper. It is absolutely essential to her that America remain strong, for geographically Canada is also a neighbour of the Soviet Republics. Her problem is to maintain this dependent relationship with the United States and still maintain her national identity and her ideological independence.

Canada's progress to world greatness must be made upon an interesting and tricky tightrope, but it seems inevitable that the progress will be made.

AUSTRALIA

To most people living in the northern hemisphere, Australia is the upside-down country. Its winter falls in June, July and August and its summer in those months we usually consider winter.

Since it is an island, and has been an isolated island for so many geological periods that it hardly matters any more, the land abounds in forms of animal and bird life which don't exist anywhere else on earth. In Australia the giant birds cannot fly, some mammals lay eggs, and many of the animals, caught in the middle of an arrested process of evolution, cannot walk on all fours. The trees shed their bark instead of leaves.

Because the pull of gravity is different south of the equator, the water in sinks and water-closets goes down clockwise, instead of counter-clockwise, as it does in the northern hemisphere. This is very unsettling to the uninitiated.

Australia is so confusing that geographers disagree as to whether it should be considered a continent or an island. It is either the largest island or the smallest continent on earth. Take your choice.

Certainly Australia's dimensions are impressive. It measures 2,971,081 square miles, which is just slightly smaller than the area of the 48 continental States of the U.S. However, its population is only 13 million, of which 2½ million are concentrated in Sydney.

The curious thing about Australia is that it was originally populated by losers, many of whom have eventually learned to become modest winners. But the heritage of the losers still infects the social life of the nation.

It is a curious phenomenon that whole cities, and even territories, of the world can suffer from what the psychologists call an inferiority complex, which makes a surprisingly large percentage of their citizens carry a chip upon their shoulders. In Great Britain, the citizens of the northern industrial cities suffer from this malady (particularly Wigan!), but so, also, do most of the people of Wales. In the United States, half the State of New Jersey is so infected, and almost all the State of Texas, as well as inhabitants of certain cities which are overshadowed by nearby communities. St. Paul, Minnesota; Forth Worth, Texas; Oakland, California, and Brooklyn and other satellite cities surrounding New York City come to mind immediately.

Australia has this disease in depth. Most Australians carry a large and brittle chip upon their shoulders at all times. Many of them are quite good at dishing out insults to others in a matey sort of way, but it is madness to try to retaliate in kind. In this area, Australians are much better at giving than receiving, but it is doubtful that they are twice blest because of it.

Part of the attitude comes from the fact of Australia's humble, and rather embarrassing beginnings. Nobody tried to colonize Australia until Captain James Cook stumbled on it in 1770 and, almost absent-mindedly claimed it for the crown. (He was later eaten by the Hawaiians.) In 1788, the administration of George III of England, searching desperately for a dumping ground for criminals not worth the hanging, hit upon Australia as the perfect solution. (The State of Georgia in the United States was begun in the same way.)

The typical Australian attitude can be estimated by the fact that the males have assiduously cultivated the cockney accent while English-born persons elsewhere have done their best to get rid of it. (Oddly enough, this is a masculine phenomenon. Australian women of the upper social class do not speak cockney.) For many years before World War II, relationships between Australian leaders and English leaders were impeded by the determined cockney accents of the men from "down under". Class-conscious English gentlemen found it very hard to take seriously any man with a cockney accent, and as Australian frustrations grew, their aggressiveness grew apace.

Unlike Canadians, Australians are not religious by nature. The average citizen scorns to go to church, and attendance is scanty.

The penal colony phase of Australia's existence started to decline rapidly when gold was discovered in Victoria Colony (the Southeast portion) in 1851. Settlers started streaming in in great numbers, and the practice of importing criminals became more and more inconvenient. Besides, a gradual relaxation of England's savage penal laws eased the pressure on local prisons. In 1868 the practice of transporting criminals was abandoned.

197

The six colonies of Australia were separate entities until late in the reign of Queen Victoria, but, in 1891 a constitution was finally drafted and Australia entered the Commonwealth in that year.

Australia is not designed for heavy settlement. There is a 2,000 mile strip down the east and southeast coasts that is remarkably fertile. There is a small workable area in the southwest. Most of the rest of the vast land is desert, stern and unpredictable. It is comparatively easy for an imprudent traveller to die of thirst in Australia's interior.

Still, Australia, a predominatly agricultural nation, produces enough food for her population, and even exports food. She is rich in natural resources, and may eventually become a major oil producer. Australia is the largest producer of wool in the world. There is coal in abundance. The major obstacle to ultimate greatness is the uncertainty of her water supply. Despite this deficiency, the economy of Australia is more than ordinarily healthy, and could be much healthier if the Australians worked seriously at the task of making it so.

In Australia, not only does the water seems to run in reverse, but the ambitions of many of the people seem to run backwards also.

Australia is perhaps the most egalitarian of all countries. *Égalité* is a national mania to such an extent that anyone who tries to be "different", socially, intellectually or economically is in danger of being shunned by his fellows.

The average Australian is complacent and likes things exactly the way they are. He has almost none of the competitive, industrial drive that Americans have. In an egalitarian society, where there are few class distinctions, there is little incentive to better one's self or the status of one's family. A recent poll shows that only half the skilled Australian workers surveyed wanted their children to have a university education, and no unskilled workers—absolutely none—desired such a boon for their offspring. To harbour such an ambition would be considered 'side" and would mark a man for derision among his associates.

Americans are inclined to see, or imagine, certain aspects of kinship with the Australians, but an attitude like this is almost completely incomprehensible to the U.S. mind, where the almost compulsive national drive is to better one's self and build a better future for one's children. The Australian sees nothing wrong with the world he now inhabits and doesn't see why that world shouldn't be perfectly all right for his children as well.

This is the distressing inheritance from the losers who first inhabited the land. Men order things differently, and better, in the States.

In the States, the compulsion is to get on in the world. In Australia, there is great distrust and dislike of the man who tries to live more elegantly than his neighbor, or who reads books his neighbor does not read, or who listens to music his neighbor doesn't understand. The insistence on retaining the Cockney accent is a manifestation of this peculiar national attitude. If an ordinary Australian male started cleaning up his vowels and speaking with an accent that would be considered "standard educated English" in most other parts of the world, he would be derided and shunned. The way to success in Australia is to make believe you are the same as everyone else, even if you are not.

Australia is predominantly a Socialist nation, and, because of this odd insistence upon *sameness*, socialism seems to work on the continent-island about as well as it does anywhere else on earth.

But, in a society that is so aggressively 'liberal" in its politics, Australia is about as conservative as South Africa in its treatment of its coloured minorities.

The aborigines of Australia, like so much of her other fauna, are originals. They are not black or brown or yellow, but a unique shade of grey.

When the white man found them, the aborigines were living in the Stone Age, and the 100,000 of them still existing there are, for the most part, still living in the Stone Age.

The white Australians forced the "abos" into the desert and have pretty much kept them there. Aborigines have many noble characteristics, but they are the poorest and most backward of all native minorities in any civilized nation in the world.

In truth it must be admitted that some of the aborigines are almost unbelievably backward. A survey taken (by white Australians) some years ago claimed that some tribal groups were so incapable of logical thought, and so sexually promiscuous, that they had never worked out the relationship between cause and effect in procreation. When a woman became pregnant, the male who was most responsible for her upkeep would take up a club and go out and whack away at a rock or a tree as a way of punishing the evil spirit he believed to be imprisoned there, and who was presumed to be responsible. The evil spirit idea is an interesting variation of the stork theme and the male aborigines, in shifting the blame for pregnancy into the realm of the supernatural, may be considerably more intelligent than the white sociologists thought they were.

Only a few Australian States permit even some of the aborigines to vote, and ordinary civil rights, taken for granted even in capitalistic nations, are denied the "abos". Aborigines are paid far less than white men, even when working side by side on the same job.

The official policy of socialist Australia is "assimilation" of all races, but the actual practice is far short of the theory. The same discrimination which oppresses the aborigines extends to Orientals, despite the fact that Australia is technically an Asiatic country. Australia desperately needs more people and hunts for them all over the world, but still makes it almost impossible for an Oriental to immigrate. And, once an Oriental does manage to slip into the country, he is treated far worse than the negro is treated in the United States. Far worse.

In many parts of Australia the labour unions have become dictators to an extent not experienced elsewhere in the world. In areas of New South Wales, the state which includes Sydney, the Barrier Council (equivalent to the Central Labour Council) controls almost every aspect of life. It exercises censorship over all newspapers and magazines, and if it does not approve of the

200

editorial contents of a publication, it declares a strenuously enforced boycott. The Council itself publishes a daily newspaper and all union members in a household must subscribe—a device which can result in four or five copies of the same edition of the same paper arriving at the doorstep every day. If a merchant does not see fit to advertise in the union newspaper, he is put on the blacklist, and woe betide the citizen who continues to patronize him! Such a citizen, whether he be a union member or not, will suddenly find that no deliveries of any kind can be made to his home, and members of labour unions are forbidden even to speak to him.

This is a kind of tyranny that would be intolerable in any other nation of which I have experience.

Oddly enough, businessmen and industrialists from other parts of the world, find the rugged Australians peculiarly inefficient in managing business matters of even minor complexity. The older Australian is so impatient of detail that he tends to move ahead without knowing where in the world he is going. Movement is an end in itself. He wears the chip on his shoulder so aggressively that he will not admit, particularly to foreigners, that he does not understand what they are talking about. Rather than admit his ignorance, the Australian businessman will nod his head vigorously and say, "she'll be right", and trust to luck and slapdashery to muddle the project through. American and German *entrepreneurs* have sometimes escaped insanity by the barest of margins trying to do business with Australians.

There are some indications that the modern generation in Australia is breaking away from its suffocating past and is eager to burst into the twentieth century, intellectually, culturally and socially.

Australia has produced some extraordinary musicians in her time, particularly in the field of opera. The ineffable Nellie Melba, probably the most spectacular coloratura soprano of all time, was a local product. So was the heroic and great Marjorie Lawrence, whose supremacy as Wagnerian singer was cut short in mid-career by polio. Joan Sutherland, the greatest coloratura soprano of the 1960's is an Australian. So is John Brownlee, the great Metropolitan barytone of former years. The Australians have taken pride in their singers to the same extent, and in the same way, that they have taken pride in their superlative tennis players and cricketers.

There are signs of a cultural boom of sorts in Australia, and in Sydney a magnificent Opera House has been abuilding for many a year. When completed it will undoubtedly be one of the wonders of the world, but, because of the typical Australian slapdash approach to important matters, nobody knows when it will be completed. It is already four years late, and the end is nowhere in sight, and the cost of about $70 million will be about nine times the original estimate, and will have to be financed by a national lottery. There are some Australian writers coming to the fore, and perhaps a painter or two but, as in Canada, most of the talented ones cannot wait to get out and away from down under.

Australia has a developed society, but is still an underdeveloped country. Her position in the world is as unique as is most of her flora and fauna. She is a western nation located in Asia, and she has done very little to make herself agreeable to the Oriental nations who could conceivably imperil her security and her freedom.

Because she is a nation of strong and rugged individuals, her people believe that the nation itself is strong and individualistic. This is a mistake. Australia's potential in the free world has hardly been scratched. She has not nearly the industrial capacity, as yet, to protect herself in case of serious trouble in the Orient, and yet she will not face up to her own incapacity. She has been particularly lukewarm about the American effort in Viet Nam, for example, because she refuses to admit the obvious fact that if U.S. arms permitted Communist aggression to run wild in the Orient, Australia would be the principal target for aggression and the principal prize in that area of the world.

Australia has been fortunate up until now, because other nations have permitted her to be fortunate. She must learn to make

202

her own fortune in the future, and time may be running out on her. She cannot afford to continue to be satisfied with an easy--going agricultural-pastoral economy in the face of the steeled industrialism of an Asia that could well become a unified and hostile Communist empire.

It is not enough to be a nation of strong men. The strong men must build upon their great island a strong nation. That is the task that lies ahead.

JAMAICA

I am a Jamaican, and I love my country very dearly. I have reason to be proud of her, and reason to be grateful.

Jamaica was discovered by Christopher Columbus on May 3, 1494. The "Admiral of the Ocean Sea" was subsequently stranded on Jamaica's north coast for a full year, during 1503-1504. He was our first "tourist" and, I might say that if one has to be stranded somewhere in the world, Jamaica is the place to go.

The Spaniards called the island Sant' Jago, but its native Arawak name was Xaymaca, or "Isle of Springs" and this was the appellation which, with variations, has prevailed.

The Spanish colonized Jamaica in the early 16th Century, but were fairly constantly harassed by British raiders who for more than a hundred years carried on a series of looting and burning forays. The entire island during these years was owned by eight Spanish families and immigration was so discouraged that the entire population, free and slave, never was greater than 3,000.

In 1655, Cromwell attacked the West Indian Empire of Spain, and in three years' time drove the Spanish off Jamaica.

The Puritans in Jamaica behaved with characteristic nastiness. Cromwell's men distributed cheap bibles to the natives and then plunged with a right good will into the slave trade. Not only were black slaves imported in great numbers from Africa, but white slaves were rounded up and shipped over from Ireland and Scotland. Cromwell declared his intention of ridding those countries of "vagabonds and light women" by sending anyone accused as such to Jamaica as slaves. Unfortunately, he interpreted "vagabonds and light women" as anyone professing the hated Catholic religion, and several thousand young boys and girls, as well as priests and nuns, were hunted down and shipped across the sea. The white slaves proved to be uneconomical and soon died out under miserable conditions. However, the Puritans enjoyed the girls while they lasted.

The early history of Jamaica was blighted by violence and elemental catastrophe. In 1692 an earthquake pushed the capital city of Port Royal into the sea. In 1712, 1714 and 1722 vicious hurricanes all but destroyed the island and caused the capital to be moved to Kingston, which is located so that it is less disaster prone. Another earthquake, in 1907 practically levelled Kingston, and other towns of the island.

The Jamaican negroes did not accept slavery with docility. Thousands of them escaped the sugar plantations and fled to the mountains. They were known by the Spanish name *Cimarrones,* or Peak-dwellers. The name was perverted into "Maroons". In 1734, after years of sporadic guerilla warfare, the Maroons began an uprising in earnest, marauding, burning military installations, killing white men. The Maroons proved to be fearless and able soldiers. The British were helpless against them, and even after reinforcements landed, were fortunate to escape annihilation. They finally sued for peace, and the Maroons were granted their freedom and 2,500 acres of land, as long as they swore allegiance to the Crown.

The British learned little from their humiliating experience. In 1795, the authorities had two Maroon leaders publicly flogged by a slave of the Crown. This was intolerable to a proud and free people. The second Maroon War broke out, and with the same results. The Maroons knew the terrain and were excellent marksmen. They maintained a fabulous intelligence system, and anticipated and thwarted every British maneuver.

The British once again had to sue for peace and granted honourable terms. But this time the authorities behaved despicably and deported 500 of the Maroon leaders to Nova Scotia much to the indignation of public opinion in England. The English indigenous love for the plucky underdog made minor heroes of the Maroons and the Government was finally forced to remove the brave blacks from the unsuitably cold climate of Nova Scotia and transplant them to Sierra Leone, where they were established as free men. There are still Maroons living in Jamaica on the free land granted them by the original treaty of 1738.

Slavery was abolished in 1833, an action of undeniable moral rectitude, but which caused serious economic collapse. The sugar plantation economy withered away in importance, and the succeeding years were marked by dissension between the government, operated almost exclusively by white planters, and the negro freedmen.

In 1866 Jamaica became a Crown Colony, but that didn't seem to do much good. A great social and economic wall divided the white colonialists from the black islanders. Overpopulation added to Jamaica's troubles and during the Depression of the 1930's a serious banana blight brought matters to the desperation level.

In 1944, as the result of an investigation by a Royal Commission, Jamaica was given a wide measure of self-government. In 1953, this was broadened even further so that Jamaicans were given full political autonomy.

Three years later Jamaica joined with other Caribbean islands in a West Indies Federation. However, it soon became apparent that she would have to carry the other members economically and, after three years, withdrew from the Federation. In August of 1962 Jamaica was given her full independence, within the Commonwealth, with the successful and colourful labour leader, Sir Alexander Bustamante as Prime Minister.

It has come as rather a shock to many Jamaicans that independence has not solved overnight all the problems that had beset their island, and has even created some of its own. Jamaica can make a success in the world of free nations, but it will take time, and it will need a great deal of assistance from the United States and from Great Britain.

The island contains 4,232 square miles. This makes it slightly smaller than Connecticut, the 48th ranking State in the U.S.A. Jamaica has 2,000,000 people, which is too many *under present conditions,* if the nation is ever to become self-sufficient. More than 90 percent of the Jamaicans are of African origin, and more than 80 percent of the population are literate.

The land is beautiful and varied. It abounds in rivers, impressive mountains rising as high as 7,400 feet, and magnificent beaches. Jamaica is the world's largest producer of bauxite (essential to the production of aluminium) and recent American investment of $175 million in building a plant for the processing of aluminium will undoubtedly help the economy greatly. The second most important industry is agriculture, occupying 49 percent of the labour force. The principal crops are sugar cane, bananas, cocoa and coffee. The third largest industry is tourism.

It is perhaps natural in a new country that national exuberance should sometimes supersede good sense, but Jamaica, to date, has had a tendency to put emphasis on the wrong things. There has been a great deal of attention paid to building luxurious Government buildings and too-super super highways, and not enough attention paid to re-organizing the nation's agriculture and putting it on a more practical and more dependable basis. The Agricultural Department, for example, is a huge bureaucratic colossus (on a smaller, Jamaican scale, of course) in which well-trained specialists are confined to desk jobs, pushing papers around, when they should be out in the field solving important problems where the problems exist.

I have said that a population of two million is too much *under present conditions.* Jamaica could sustain five million people if her agriculture were modernized and re-organized. It is patently ridiculous and wasteful to employ the best farm land for the production of sugar cane, which ties down so much of the land and the people to a chancey one-crop economy. The growing of sugar cane is traditional in Jamaica. It made a pleasant life, some of the time, for some of the planters, but it has never been consistently remunerative except under slavery conditions.

Because of her obsession with sugar cane, Jamaica has yet to produce a single plant—hardwood, fruit tree or what have you —which is of significant economic value to the nation. The small farmers should be encouraged, through Agricultural Loan Banks and through education, to grow a wide variety of fruits and vegetables suitable to the Jamaican soil and climate. The Government has created a Marketing Department to help the farmer dispose of his goods, but it has limited its activities to a few selected crops. This beneficial activity should be extended to all crops, and American experts should be imported to help the farmers learn the most effective modern techniques, and the arts of diversification.

Jamaican leaders must plan ahead. The land is alive with beautiful rivers and streams, but there are times when there is not enough water to sustain the economy. The country needs numerous storage dams to retain the water at strategic places, instead of permitting it to run wastefully to the sea. I don't mean big, pompous multi-million pound dams; I mean a network of useful, inexpensive little reservoir dams which will make the plenitude of water available at the points where it is most needed, and at the times when it is most needed.

The Government should increase the incentives for the farmer. At the present time, the farmer is being taken advantage of by every other element in the economy. Last year, the average farmer received 36 shillings a ton for sugar cane, but after expenses, he could realise only 3 shillings a ton. The rest went into cultivation costs, the employment of union labour, transportation costs, the percentage to the middle man, and so on. A farmer averages about a penny ha'penny for a pound of bananas, which will not sell for less than 2 shillings a pound in England. Certainly, other elements in the economy are taking more than their just share of the profits. The coconut industry in Jamaica is a monopoly. The company does not issue balance sheets, but it prospers mightily. The farmer who grows and harvests the crop does not share sufficiently in its prosperity.

The Government *must* make agriculture more attractive and more rewarding to the farmer. It *must* offer more incentive, more protection and more security. The migration in Jamaica, as elsewhere in the world, is from the country to the city. Even a huge and powerful nation like the United States is having serious troubles because of this relentless movement. Jamaica is not strong enough to adjust to the imbalance. It needs more productive farmers in the field, not more unproductive consumers in the cities.

The Government must also stop *entrepreneurs* from building housing developments on the most productive farm lands. Such developments should be restricted to otherwise useless land. Every inch of productive land on the island must be utilized.

Jamaica is plagued by a proliferation of exotic "religious" sects whose adherents wear colourful clothing but refuse to contribute anything to the economy or to the national welfare. They are "above" hard work and live off the alms of the superstitious or the over-tolerant. The Government should crack down on these unproductive groups. In a struggling, emerging society there is no room for "free riders". Everyone must do his share, everyone must pull his weight in the national boat.

Tourism is very big in Jamaica, but not big enough. Tourism is a highly competitive business, and if Jamaicans do not make themselves and their island totally attractive to visitors, other Caribbean paradises will be only too glad to take over for them.

There is a great deal to be done in the field of tourism. Arrangements must be made with airlines to make Jamaica more available to Americans and others and at attractive rates. Jamaican hotel staffs are often inadequately trained; it would be no difficult matter to school them and train them to world class performance. Jamaican cooking too often lacks verve and imagination. The tourist situation could be improved greatly if efforts were made to develop *cordon bleu* quality chefs, enough to entice and satisfy the fastidious. A few two or three star restaurants would work wonders.

Tourism is not an accidental thing, it is a highly competitive business. Jamaica depends on it, and the Government should act as if it realized this fact. The Caribbean is overloaded with glamourous beaches and breathtaking vistas. Luxury hotels are a shilling a dozen. The weather is so pleasant and the tempi so relaxing that the Caribbean will probably be the "in" vacationing area of the next decade. This could be of enormous value to the Jamaican economy, if steps are taken now to make ready for the future bonanza. Jamaica, in short, must develop reasons why a vacationer or a tourist should *want* to come here, rather than go to a dozen other competitive isles scattered so attractively upon our azure sea.

Tourism is our third largest industry. It could be just as important as the big two, if the Government and the people would only work at making it so.

Fortunately, Jamaica has been blessed with many talented politicians, possessed of superior leadership, and dedicated to the purpose of a multi-racial society and the two-party system of government. Her political stability is assured, something that must be considered a rare and valuable asset in the West Indian world.

At the time of the Cuban missile crisis, Jamaica's first Prime Minister, Sir Alexander Bustamante, was the first politician in the western hemisphere to throw his support solidly behind the United States. He flatly rejected the creed of "better red than dead", which had become popular in the Caribbean area at that time. His stand was a courageous one, considering the proximity of Cuba to Jamaica, and it should be remembered by Americans with gratitude.

The present Prime Minister, Hugh Lawson Shearer, is a man of great imagination and responsibility. He has taken the motto of Jamaica, "Out of Many, One People", with commendable seriousness, and has conscientiously included representatives of all the significant ethnic groups in his Government. He has also had the courage to speak candidly to his people about the necessity of hard work and the desirability of keeping the population growth at a reasonable level. Both of these programmes are potentially unpopular politically, but are necessary for Jamaica's development as an important and contributing element in the free world.

The opposition leader, Norman Washington Manly, is equally determined to maintain the two-party system. He has manfully resisted the temptations of demagoguery, and has been a most useful and constructive political leader. His splendid legal training has made him a most effective parliamentarian.

Naturally, as a businessman with long experience in Jamaica, I have numerous suggestions for the development of my country. I put one forward at this point as a "trial balloon" for the consideration of Jamaica's leaders.

It is absolutely necessary for Jamaica to attract foreign residents and foreign capital, if we are to achieve our full potential. At present, there is no Estate Duty Law for either foreign or local residents. This is a good thing, but I would suggest some further refinements which, I feel, would be most helpful to the economy. For example, I would make the Income Tax Law inapplicable to all foreign residents whose income is more than £5,000 a year, or who possess more than £25,000 capital.

I am quite aware that this is the absolute reverse of the income tax philosophy in almost every other country in the world, but such a system as I propose would provide incentives for foreign *entrepreneurs*. There is a great need for housing in Jamaica, and with such a tax inducement, foreign builders would be encouraged to reclaim the low-lying lands near the sea, as well as the other swampy and non-arable land, for development tracts.

Tourism can be increased greatly by imaginative action. A full-scale, progressive programme should be worked out to sell the beauties of Jamaica to Europe and the United States, with the hope of attracting an immigration wave of reasonably solvent permanent residents. Salesmen should be trained and dispatched on this mission throughout the free world.

210

A special effort should be made to inform the housewives of the free world about Jamaica's attractions. For instance, if they emigrate there, they can forget about doing household chores. Competent domestic help may be hired for as little as $20 a week. A good, modern two-bedroom house, located near the sea, and right next door to all kinds of recreational facilities, can be purchased for $12,000. Beautiful modern apartments, with access to swimming pools, golf courses, tennis courts, and so on, can be purchased, free-hold, for $10,000.

The income tax inducement could make life on our beautiful island most attractive to retired persons of means. What the Government would lose in taxes would be more than offset by the increase in land value taxes, by duty on imported goods, and by the stimulation these new settlers would provide for the economy. Every new family would employ from one to three persons. The newcomers would also have money for investment and for the purchase of goods in the local mercantile establishments.

The suggestion has, I think, considerable merit and it could lead to the repeal of income tax laws for Jamaicans as well as for foreigners.

There is one further thing to be said about Jamaica, and it concerns racial matters. The population of Jamaica is 90 percent negro and, under present conditions, too much emphasis is placed on colour. In Government offices it is difficult for non-negroes to find employment. In commercial institutions, and especially the banks, negroes are discriminated against and are seldom hired or promoted.

This is a pity. In Jamaica we do not have all that much talent that so much of it can be ignored and rejected because of racial prejudice. Every person who has something to contribute to the political, social and economic life of the country should be encouraged, regardless of the pigmentation of his skin. Racial prejudice is a luxury few nations can afford, but Jamaica can afford it less than most others.

In August, of 1962, when Jamaica was awarded her independence, the feeling of friendship with America was at full flood. The first U.S. Ambassador to Jamaica, William C. Doherty, was an inspirational choice for this delicate position. He was the first representative of organized labour in the States ever to be proffered an ambassadorial post, and he filled it with great wisdom and style. He was deeply loved by the entire Jamaican nation.

Since his retirement, some Jamaicans have become impatient because the United States has not emptied out her purse sufficiently to their taste. They choose to resent the fact that America sends her money in greater profusion to lands of doubtful loyalty and doubtful friendship, than she does to lands which are demonstrably her friends. Jamaicans have begun to think they are being taken too much for granted.

There is some point to the argument. Personally, I feel the U.S.A should be considerably more generous than she has been to a friendly country so strategically placed as Jamaica is, and that she should take up the slack by being less generous to nations which have not deserved her friendship. But, the fact remains, the United States has been reasonably generous to Jamaica and shows every intention of continuing her generosity. The money she is spending is her own and, surely, she has the right to spend it in the way she thinks best.

And, without the support, protection and friendship of the U.S.A., Jamaica would be a simple target for almost any sort of outside aggression.

Jamaica is useful to America and could be more useful than she is, but America is absolutely essential to Jamaica. All Jamaicans should remember this.

Jamaica, in short, is a paradise on earth, which has a long way to go before she realizes her full potential in the community of western nations. She has the leadership, in both her major political parties, to create a magnificent future for herself. It is up to the people of Jamaica to exhibit the discipline and the industriousness necessary for the fulfillment of her dreams.

XI
RUSSIA

Let us begin with a quotation:

"There are at the present time, two great nations in the world —the Russians and the Americans. The American relies upon personal interest to accomplish his ends and gives free scope to the unguided exertions and common sense of the people. The Russian centres all authority of society in a single arm. The principal instrument of the former is freedom; of the latter, servitude. Their starting point is different, and their courses are not the same; yet each of them seems marked by the will of Heaven to sway the destinies of half the globe."

In the last third of the twentieth century, this seems an intelligent, but rather commonplace analysis. However, the words were not written in the present era. They were written by Alexis de Tocqueville, in 1835.

There never has been a more prescient historical writer than de Tocqueville, but in this passage he outdoes himself. It has an air of divine inspiration about it. In 1835, the United States, under President Andrew Jackson was a small but vigorous new nation groping its way towards its ultimate destiny in the west. Russia, with the reactionary Nicholas I as Czar, was a massive world power but generally considered backward, vulnerable and hopeless. To most competent observers, de Tocqueville's prophecy was pure moonshine. England and France were the great powers in the West; China was the great power in the East. There was no indication that this condition was likely to change for many centuries to come. But the condition did change, and de Tocqueville, as usual, was proved to be absolutely correct.

Russian history is a horror story. Except for a few short periods, the Russian people have never known anything but tyranny and absolutist rule. Even some of her most "enlightened" Czars were savages; some of them certifiably insane.

Peter I, called "The Great", who became Czar in 1682, at the age of 10 and reigned until 1725, has often been characterized by sentimentalists as a progressive ruler. In some ways, he was. But he also liked to take his exercise by substituting for the public executioner and personally decapitating his convicted subjects. On one occasion he accounted for 125 in one day. When the boyars refused to cut off their beards because Peter thought they would look more modern without them, the Czar ordered thousands of them buried alive. (When the royal cupboard grew comparatively bare, he permitted the surviving boyars to retain their beards if they paid a substantial tax for the privilege. This has been considered a proof of Peter's progressiveness.) On one occasion. while travelling in Sweden, the King of that country showed the young Czar a new device for executing prisoners after the most exquisite torture. The King apologized for the fact that he had no prisoners at the moment convicted of capital offenses, so he could not demonstrate the qualities of his dreadful machine. "Think nothing of it," Peter replied, "take one of my retinue." So a healthy and innocent young man was selected at random and slowly put to death, and a splendid time was enjoyed by all. Excepting, of course, the victim.

Yet Peter was one of the best of an extremely bad lot. Catherine (also, for some reason or other, called "The Great"), who ruled Russia for 34 years, dying in 1796, had the unpleasant habit of killing off her numerous lovers as soon as she grew tired of them, lest they prove indiscreet about the pleasures of the royal bed. The female spider had much in common with her. Ivan IV, who reigned as the first Czar of all the Russias (1547-1584), richly deserved the title of "The Terrible". He

214

indulged himself in mass murders, but he still had time and taste for little individual efforts. He beat his own son and heir to death. When two architects (Barna and Postnik) built, at his order, the great Cathedral of St. Basil, in Moscow, Ivan was so delighted that he ordered the architects eyes, arms and tongues removed so they could never again build an edifice of such beauty. He had the reputation of being a difficult boss.

Life in Russia, under all the Czars, was, in short, precarious, nasty and cheap unless one had the good fortune to be born into one of the upper strata of society. Even so, the chances of violent death were higher than in any other nation in the world. The peasants were treated with far more brutality in Russia than were dumb beasts in other lands.

I mention these things because the Revolution of 1917 did very little to change this aspect of Russian life. National characteristics do not change. After 50 years of Communist rule, life in Russia is still precarious, nasty and cheap.

Events need not have turned out the way they did. Unfortunately, the rest of the world muffed the opportunity, in 1917, of bringing Russia happily and constructively into the 20th century.

Czar Nicholas II the last Czar of all the Russias was, in some ways, well meaning, but he was also the complete autocrat, a reactionary with very limited mental capacity. When Russia's participation in World War I turned out to be an unmitigated disaster, the country was blockaded and famine stalked the countryside. Revolution broke out almost by spontaneous combustion, the Army revolted and the Czar abdicated in favor of a provisional government (March, 1917) of which Alexander Kerensky became the head.

This was a comparatively bloodless revolution, contrived by none and enjoyed by all. It was the most popular revolution in history.

There was nothing Communist about the revolt. Kerensky, an honourable and brilliant man, was a socialist, but not a Marxist. The future Bolshevik leaders were all out of the country: Lenin in Switzerland, Stalin in Siberia, Trotzky in the United States. But Kerensky and his provisional government planned to continue the war effort against Germany, so the Germans did everything possible to overthrow him, including arranging for the return of the exiled Communist leaders, who were pledged to stop the war against Germany.

Kerensky who, miraculously, is still alive in New York City, claims that if the United States and other European nations had given his regime at that time one-tenth the assistance they gave the Soviets during World War II, Russia would be a democracy today, and World War II would never have happened. He may be right, but it was politically impossible for any Western nation to behave at that point in the way they behaved 25 years later.

The Kerensky government announced a program of civil liberties and legal equality for all citizens. They promised land distribution to the peasants and sweeping economic reforms. They also decreed that there would be freedom of the press, trial by jury and due process of law in every respect.

Kerensky tried to organize all democratic elements in Russia behind his government and to arrange for credits from his western allies so as to provide for the immediate necessities of the populace. He also urged the disorganized army to regroup for a further effort against Germany.

All this was completely opposite to what the Bolsheviks wanted. The Bolsheviks were not at all interested in the welfare of the people; they were interested in power. They organized their efforts to block every program of the Kerensky government.

The Bolsheviks demanded an immediate end to the war. (That's what they had been hired by the Germans to accomplish.) They also made political capital out of the fact that the Government didn't distribute the land to the peasants immediately. Kerensky wanted to wait until the harvest was in, and then to effect an orderly and just redistribution. This made good sense but was not dramatic enough, or violent enough, for Bolshevik tastes.

216

On November 6, 1917 the "Red Guards"—a military revolutionary committee organized by the Bolsheviks—seized the Winter Palace, arrested and/or executed all the members of the Provisional Government they could find, and took over. Kerensky escaped. By revolutionary decree a Council of People's Commissars was set up, with Lenin at the head, and with Trotzky and Stalin in prominent positions.

The Kerensky Government had ordered a general election for November 25, at which a Constituent Assembly was to be chosen. The Bolsheviks permitted the election to take place, but were vastly displeased by the results. The Communists polled only 9 million out of the 36 million votes cast and won only 225 seats as opposed to 420 for the moderates.

This was the only free election ever held in Russia in its entire history. The Communists took one look at the results and vowed never to let anything like that happen, ever again.

When the Constituent Assembly tried to meet, the Red Guards drove them off at bayonet point. The Council of People's Commissars then began a reign of terror aimed at stamping out all vestiges of democracy inside Russia.

The Bolsheviks set up a secret police organization more ruthless and far more efficient than anything devised by the Czars. The leaders of the new regime were completely doctrinaire in their approach, organizing the entire society along collectivist lines. They nationalized the banks and factories, prohibited private trade, took over the distribution of food and clothing. The people starved. By 1921 it was estimated that fourteen *million* Russians died in three years either through starvation or through civil strife.

The figure, in fact, would have been many times higher if that great American humanitarian and political conservative, Herbert Hoover, did not organize a relief mission to Russia which brought food and the necessities of life to a nation ravaged by famine. It is ironic that Mr Hoover was later to become one of the foremost targets of Communist savagery when he had the misfortune to be elected President of the United States on the eve of the Great Depression.

Another ironic footnote to the Revolution was the fate of the Russian labour unions. When he was struggling for power, Lenin called the unions the "classrooms of the revolution" and made great use of them in organizing discontent against the Czar throughout the major metropolitan centres. The labour unions were indispensable to him.

But, once the Revolution was accomplished, Lenin moved to suppress the labour unions and made them instruments of the State. The unions henceforth would be involved primarily in increasing the production of the individual worker and not in protecting his rights. They would be useful in organizing pro-Government demonstrations among the members and in collecting Party dues. And that was all.

The right to strike was strictly forbidden. In fifty years, there has been only one major strike in Russia. This occurred in 1921 among the sailors at the seaport city of Kronstadt. The sailors wanted their money; they wanted decent working conditions and reasonable hours of work. They also demanded the right of free speech, as well as the liberation of peasants being held as political prisoners. They were mowed down by machine guns, a dreadful massacre of unarmed men. There has never been a strike in Russia since that time. Somehow the workers got the message.

In Russia, labour is not even permitted to be critical of management and the managers are *ex officio* government officials.

It is curious, in view of this dismal record, that one finds so much Communism in the trade union movement in Europe today, particularly in England, France and Italy. One would think that the cold-blooded subversion of all the ideals of the trade union movement would have turned all working men irrevocably against Communism, but that has not been the case. The trade union movement in the United States is far more sophisticated than that in Europe. The American Federation of Labor-Congress of Industrial Organizations (AFL-CIO) has done a

218

remarkable job of fighting Communism at home and abroad, at every level. They have poured millions upon millions of dollars into a global effort and have done a better job than the American Government has done, at a people-to-people level, and a far better job than American management has done. Organized labour in Europe is still naive about Communism and far too tolerant of it.

When the great Communist experiment began to fall on its collectivist face in Russia in 1921, massive unrest and revolt began to proliferate throught the country. Peasants and workers revolted and were shot down for their trouble. Lenin, an intellectual himself, decided to make the intellectuals the scapegoats and started a blood bath among the *intelligentsia*. Many of Russia's best brains, who had supported the principle of the revolution and helped make it possible, were blown out during this period of terror.

Another cause of unrest at this point was the development of the Comintern. It became a major source of resentment and trouble throughout the entire world.

The Comintern, or Third Communist International, was organized in 1919 to foment trouble and rebellion, and develop propaganda in other nations. Its rather grandiose program was "immediate world revolution". At its birth, Lenin shouted: "Communism and capitalism cannot live in peace. In the end, one or the other will triumph!" (The Comintern was abolished in 1943 to placate Russia's allies in World War II. However, its principles of world subversion still persist.)

Many Russian Communists objected to the Comintern programme, pointing out that it would be wiser to make Communism a success first in Russia before trying to export the doctrine elsewhere. When it became increasingly obvious that Communism was not working out well in Russia, the carping of these realists became embarrassing to the regime. So the realists were purged as counter-revolutionaries. The Comintern has been a major reason for distrust and dislike of Soviet Russia throughout the world, ever since its inception.

At the same time, and with a perfectly straight face, Lenin declared (1921) a "New Economic Policy" which was, in effect, a reversion to some of the practices of capitalism. A State bank was created and the financial system was revised to accord more with capitalist procedures. Some foreign owners were permitted, once again, to operate their own plants. Some farms were restored to private enterprise. A certain degree of trade with capitalist nations was allowed.

This retreat from Communism proved to be a tonic for Russia. She began to make economic progress *in direct proportion to the amount of capitalistic practice she permitted within her borders.* Industrial and agricultural production reached the same level it had enjoyed in the Czarist days. This was, indeed, a remarkably low level, but it was considerably higher than the Communists had been able to achieve through the application of their classical doctrine. There were two years of comparative progress and peace in Russia. Famine was abated. The purges stopped. A certain amount of personal freedom was permitted.

The doctrinaire Communists were annoyed by this turn of events, but there was no denying that things *were* better because of the accommodation with capitalist practices.

On January 21, 1924 Vladimir Ilyich Ulyanov Lenin died, at the age of 53. The circumstances of his death were mysterious and there has always been a strong suspicion that he was poisoned.

The death exposed one of the great weaknesses of the Communist system: the lack of any provision for an orderly succession in the seats of power. There was, of course, no hereditary succession as in the Czarist days, and no apparatus for elections, as in democratic countries. An intense power struggle began among the members of the hierarchy, which was considerably complicated by Trotzky's insistence that Stalin had murdered Lenin. The struggle was finally brought to an end in 1928 when the Politburo denounced Trotzky as a deviationist and expelled him from the Party and the country. Stalin assumed the leadership of the State and eventually had one of his agents axe

Trotzky to death in Mexico City. It was a shocking and bloody murder of an old man who was no longer dangerous to the regime.

Stalin announced the first Five Year Plan and sought, and received, considerable assistance from the capitalist countries, including the United States. An all-out effort was made to achieve industrial competence equal to that of the free world.

Although some progress was made, Stalin committed the classic error of collectivizing the farms again. The more successful farmers, particularly in the Ukraine, resisted. They were killed or shipped off to Siberia. (More than ten million persons disappeared from the Ukraine in this period. Another five million disappeared from Byelorussia.) In 1931 and 1932 famine once again marched through the land.

Some of the programmes of the Stalin regime were incredibly stupid. The nomads in Soviet Central Asia, who understood very little about Communism, and cared less, were rounded up and forced to work on collectivized farms. Their herds of livestock were abandoned and left to die on the steppes. This caused an acute shortage of meat throughout Russia which has not, even to this day, been alleviated. The herds were never replenished.

Stalin followed the traditional practice of Russian dictators in troubled times by creating sanguinary diversions. In 1934 alone there were almost a million executions, either formal or informal, including 98 of the 139 members of the ruling central committee and 1,108 of the 1,966 members of the Party Congress. When this orgy of assassination failed to produce the desired results, Stalin turned on his military leaders whom he believed to be plotting a *coup d'etat*. The best men in the Army corps of officers were killed. The purge had dire results in 1941 when Hitler attacked Russia and the Russians, because they were badly led, suffered almost ruinous reverses.

The free world trembled in the summer of 1939, when Stalin formed a partnership with Hitler, causing Communists throughout the West to denounce and try to sabotage the Allied war effort. The partnership lasted only two years, but Russia profited mightily through it. She seized half of Poland, deliberately and cold-bloodedly murdering wholesale the members of the "officer class" in the Polish Army. She stole a considerable portion of Finland (after an embarrassingly hard struggle) all of Lithuania, Latvia and Estonia, and large slices of Rumania and Czechoslovakia.

Then, on June 22, 1941, Hitler inexplicably threw away whatever chance he had of winning World War II by attacking his Russian partner. (Communists throughout the West immediately shifted gears and overnight began to applaud and support the Allied war effort.)

Although the United States was not officially in the war as yet (Pearl Harbor was five months away) President Franklin Delano Roosevelt and his government determined to mount an enormous program of assistance to Soviet Russia. More than $11 billion worth of U.S. military equipment was handed over to the Red Army under lend-lease. The programme made the difference between victory and defeat on the Eastern front. Without American tanks, trucks and guns the Red Army would have been immobilized and chewed up by the German offensive. The Russians, of course, have never acknowledged this enormous contribution to Russian survival. They have even used the *materiel* against the United States.

When the war was over, Stalin kept all the territory he had stolen during the lucrative two years as Hitler's partner. He also took East Prussia for good measure. Always the opportunist, he declared war on Japan just six days before the surrender and, for his pains, (which were minimal) he was rewarded with almost all the territory Russia had lost in her war with Japan in 1904. He also walked into North Korea, Manchuria and Outer Mongolia.

In retrospect, it is amazing that the United States and England permitted Russia to get away with all this. Stalin at the bargaining table was belligerent and immovable. Franklin Delano Roosevelt was a dying man, incapable of standing up to Soviet intransigence. The allies were exhausted, mentally, physi-

222

cally, economically. It was far easier to yield than to resist, so they yielded.

Russia had promised to permit free elections in the countries she had "liberated". Of course, no free elections were ever held. Instead, Russia sent highly-trained officials of the Comintern into each captured nation to set up a subservient Communist government. She has refused to let her captive satellites leave her field of gravity.

It should be pointed out that no nation in the world—not even Russia herself—has ever voluntarily adopted Communism as a way of life. When the 1917 elections in Russia turned out unfavourably for the Communists, the Red Guards ignored the wishes of the people and seized power anyway. The satellite nations which Russia now took over were all highly nationalistic and had enjoyed a far higher standard of living than did Russia. None of them wanted to be part of the Communist apparatus, but they had no choice in the matter. Each country was turned into a weapon against the United States, which had emerged from the war as the other dominant power in the free world.

This juxtaposition set the stage for what Churchill called "the cold war", and which Stalin called "the cold peace", the bitter struggle between the forces of freedom and tyranny which has burdened the world for the past twenty years.

To call the struggle "cold" is to employ a euphemism. There have been major wars in Korea and Viet Nam; minor wars in Greece, the Middle East and Malaya; violence in Africa, the Philippines, India and elsewhere; insurrections in Cuba, Hungary, the Dominican Republic and Guatemala. There have been more than 200,000 U. S. casualties in these "cold" war engagements, including 45,000 killed. The United States taxpayer has been forced to pay out more than $500 billion (over and above normal military expenditures) in twenty years to stave off the Communist aggression.

It is awesome to think of what this money could have accomplished if it had been spent on constructive peaceful programmes such as the elimination of disease, poverty and ignorance throughout the world.

In the post war years Stalin became even more neurotic. He believed every man's hand was against him, and he reacted in the same savage way that all Russian tyrants have reacted. He conducted the traditional blood-letting. Hundreds of thousands were killed. Approximately 14 *million* people were sent to slave camps. Holy Russia became once again an *abattoir*.

Then, on March 5, 1953, Stalin died. Once again, the circumstances were suspicious and poison the rumored instrument. The usual struggle for power was re-enacted and Nikita Khrushchev eventually emerged as the strong man of Russia. Soon after assuming power, in 1956, Khrushchev startled the world by delivering a speech to the 20th Party Congress denouncing Stalin as a tyrant and a mass murderer of millions of innocent citizens.

This rejection of Stalinist terrorism gave hope to the captive satellite nations. Revolts broke out in Czechoslovakia, East Germany and, especially, in Hungary. While the rest of the world stood by helplessly and made disparaging sounds (but not too loudly lest they give offense) Khrushchev put down the revolts with appalling viciousness. Stalin would have been proud of him.

But the bold anti-Stalinist speech of 1956 continued to give Khrushchev trouble. It led Red China to denounce him as a traitor to Marxist principles and precipitated the break between the two major Communist nations of the world, which, at times, still threatens to develop into a major war. This, in turn, contributed to the bloodless downfall of Khrushchev in 1964 and the succession of the two rather colourless "organization men", Alexei Kosygin, who is now head of the Russian government, and Leonid Brezhnev, who leads the Communist Party. The new regime does not flaunt its differences with the free world as flamboyantly as did Khrushchev, or as menacingly as did Stalin, but the old Communist hostility and imperviousness to reasonable negotiation is still there in undiminished supply. The cold war shows no signs of thawing.

We have reviewed the fifty years of the Russian Communist experience. The history has been brutal and savage, but impressive, in a barbaric way. But what, exactly, has been accomplished during these fifty years?

Russia has become a mighty military and industrial power, second only to the United States. In 1913, before World War I, she was ranked fifth among the nations, behind Germany, Great Britain, France and the United States. Today she ranks second. She has increased her industrial output 5,000 per cent. She stands second in the world in industrial and military power and is capable of running neck and neck with the United States in the race for outer space. In fifty years she has leaped from the *troika* to the stars. This is an incredible achievement.

But the cost of this achievement has been enormous in human freedom, human happiness, human lives. In some ways the ordinary Russian citizen, especially outside the large cities, is worse off than he was under the Czars.

Industrialization was forced through by collectivizing the farms, killing off or transporting to slave camps millions of reluctant farmers, compelling citizens to work in factories at slave wages. Machinery was imported from abroad and paid for by grain which the hungry populace needed. Materialistic progress has been achieved by transforming Russia into an enormous and ruthless police state in which every man goes to bed in fear and wakes up in apprehension. Nowhere else in the world do the police have such complete power over human life.

In 1913 Russia grew enough food to provide for her people, though the methods of distribution were so poor that all sections of the population were not provided for adequately at all times. Nevertheless, Czarist Russia was an important exporter of grain. After 50 years Soviet Russia cannot grow enough food to feed her people. She must import grain from the West.

Since 1913 the per acre yield of grain has risen by less than 50 per cent, an insignificant increase in view of the improvements that have been made elsewhere. The per acre yield in Russia is only one-third of the yield in the United States.

The United States, with far less land and far fewer people than Russia, produces several times the amount of food Russia produces.

Soviet Russia concentrated on heavy industry in order to build a war machine, but she has done this to the exclusion of almost everything else. She is woefully deficient in the field of plastics and the development of petro-chemical synthetics; she has done very little in the area of light weight, high strength metals; she has accomplished surprisingly little on her own in the miniaturization of instruments or in automation or electronics. As for computers? The common adding machine in Russia today is the ancient Chinese abacus. I doubt that there are three computers operating in Russia today outside of the military and space fiields, and these would be foreign made.

The Soviets have shamefully neglected housing in favor of heavy industry. Most Russians live under conditions that would be considered sub-standard in Appalachia, U.S.A. or in Mexico, and certainly below acceptable norms in North Wales or the East End of London. The average Russian still has only one pair of pants to his name and one pair of shoes. He is ill-fed, ill-housed and ill-clothed.

But his Government makes lovely bombs and beautiful planes and a few of his compatriots are privileged to explore the twisted enigmas in the outer reaches of the universe.

The Communist revolutionaries promised the Russian people they would give them a standard of living far higher than that of any other people in the world. The overall standard of living is far lower than the accepted standards in the western world, and is scarcely, if at all, higher than it was in 1913.

In a revealing speech to the 23rd Part Congress recently Leonid Brezhnev promised that under the *next* Five Year Plan the wages of office and factory workers would be increased to the equivalent of $126 a month and that the work week would be reduced from 5½ days to 5 days. There is hardly a capitalist country in the world where the worker does not do a great deal better than he does in the promised paradise of the proletariat.

The Bolsheviks promised the people a classless society in which the State would eventually, in the classic phrase, "wither away" and become virtually unnecessary in the management of their affairs. The exact opposite has happened. The State has grown enormously into a tyrannical monster that dictates almost every move the average citizen makes. Communism, like socialism, creates its own class structure which is just as rigid, just as unfair, and just as intolerant, as the social structure under Louis XIV of France or Czar Nicholas II.

The solemn truth of the matter is that Communism is a failure as a system under which an economy can be operated in the modern world. Communism simply cannot compete with the free market system. It cannot compete with systems which offer solid incentives for superior performance. Eventually Russia will find it necessary to seek some kind of accommodation with the European Common Market and, once she does that, Communism, in its classic sense, will be dead.

There is no immediate prospect of this, unfortunately, because of the peculiar and maddening *doctrinaire* obstinacy of the Communist hierarchy. They are incapable of making admissions of error. They feel that if they admit classical Communist doctrine to be wrong in even a minor detail, this will lead to the dissolution of the entire system—and the preservation of the system and the regime that administers it come far ahead of such considerations as the welfare of the common man. The common man does not count; the State is everything.

The leaders of the Communist State are not ignorant. They are not uninformed. They *know*, by this time, that the collectivization of agriculture does not work. (Lenin admitted that, by indirection, in 1921.) But they cannot bring themselves to bring this disastrous experiment to an end. They *know* that in every thriving economy the development of consumer-goods is the key to the growth process, but they do not dare admit the truth for fear that such an admission would weaken the basic fabric of the Communist system. Self-preservation and self-perpetuation in office supersede all other considerations. This kind of ideological blindness can continue only in a closed society where political opposition, even of the mildest sort, is not tolerated and where the exchange of political ideas is violently discouraged, and where freedom of the press is unthinkable.

The Union of Soviet Socialist Republics, to give Russia her formal name, covers an area of 8,649,489 square miles. This is well over twice the size of the United States, and about one-sixth of the earth's surface. Its population is over 230 million, or a little more than 30 million more than the U.S.

However, shortly after World War II, these statistics, impressive as they are, indicated only a portion of Russia's real strength. She controlled, absolutely, a vast empire consisting of 14 nations, including more than a billion persons and 13.6 million square miles. Her empire covered more than one-fourth of the earth's surface and one-third of the world's population.

Since this high-tide of the Communist revolution there has been a gradual recession, and one by one the Communist nations of the world have broken off from Moscow and have sought to work out their own way of Communist life.

Yugoslavia began the run on the Moscow bank when it defied Stalin and broke away. It is still a Communist country, but it has very little to do with either Moscow or Peiping.

Red China was the major defector, breaking away when Moscow rejected Stalinism and abandoned the wild-eyed opposition to the western world which had been for so many years a trademark of "classical" Communism. China, with little to lose, wants a thermonuclear war. Russia, with far more to lose, does not, as yet, want one.

Little, insignificant Albania, curiously enough, also broke with Russia and chose to string along with Red China. Communications between the two countries are, understandably, difficult to maintain. They are hardly worth the trouble.

North Viet Nam is caught between the two Communist powers and veers according to the way the wind is blowing at the particular moment. It could never be accounted a Commu-

228

nist success any way. Communism merely filled the vacuum left by French colonial failure.

North Korea does its best to keep neutral. It cannot be subservient to Moscow with China sitting massively on her doorstep. North Korea also was originally a Communist acquisition because of colonial failure.

Cuba depends on Russian aid but is equally close to Red China. She refuses to take orders from either side. Her international stance is irresponsible and reflects Chinese attitudes more than it does Russian.

Rumania has broken away and tries to remain neutral.

Hungary is subjugated by a Russian occupation force, but basically hates Moscow and Peiping, and wants to be part of the West.

The Mongolian Republic, never a strong link with the Moscow chain, is wavering constantly and is kept in the Soviet orbit only with great difficulty.

Bulgaria, Czechoslovakia and Poland are still Russian satellites but they exhibit spasms of independence which would have been unthinkable when the Moscow tide was running at its strongest. They can no longer be depended upon for instant subservience.

Only East Germany remains totally loyal. She has no choice. Russian troops occupy her soil. Russian trade keeps her meager economy going. She has no chance for successful opposition to Russian desires, even in the smallest degree, and goes meekly along with the situation.

In the years immediately after Worly War II it looked as if Russian Communism really were the wave of the future. Its impulse seemed irresistible. Then the wave receded and the fortunes of the world conspiracy dimmed perceptibly.

The emergent and fundamentally naive African nations have been assiduously courted by the Communists but show little inclination to exchange their freedom for monetary and technological aid. India has seemed wishy-washy on fundamental international issues concerning Western freedom and Eastern slavery, but domestically she has been firm in her resistance to Communism within her own borders. Even the highly irresponsible Arabian states have shown no inclination to embrace Communism as a national policy. The sheikhs are not adverse to accepting Russian money, Russian arms and Russian technicians, but they see no future in forswearing the profit motive in their personal affairs On reflection, the very thought of a Communist sheikh is absurd, almost an oxymoron. They love profit as much as they love the Prophet.

Part of the credit for the failure of Russian influence to advance, or even to hold its own, since the end of the war can be given to the lavish U.S. foreign aid programme. The programme has been extremely expensive to the American people, and much of the money has been dribbled away in feckless nonsense, but the proof of the pudding is in the eating, and Communism, once considered irresistible, has been, at least temporarily, stopped and forced to retreat. The money of the taxpayers of the U.S. has not been spent with complete foolishness, and some of it has been spent with remarkable effect.

The real success of the Russian diplomacy in the post war world has been its ability to get other people to fight its battles. The United States has not been so persuasive. No Russian soldiers have fought and died in Korea or Viet Nam. Russia has cheered her satellites on and thrown them some bones in the form of armaments and supplies, but no men. The U.S. has had little success in persuading her allies—even those whose liberties she is fighting to preserve—to engage in the fighting. The Viet Namese war is being fought to check the Communist advance in Asia, and if it were not being fought the Communist conspiracy would spread unchecked through Australia, New Zealand, the Philippines and everywhere else in that vast area. But, for the most part, the countries most affected and most threatened are content to view the whole affair as an American war and to give the U.S. only minimal support. Even the South Viet Namese want to concentrate on the keeping of peace in their own provinces and leave the dangerous work to the Yanks. Sometimes it looks as if the imprisoned princess of the medieval tale were spitting in the eye of St. George and cheering on the dragon that is bent on her destruction.

This leads to a puzzling point: what is there about Communism which creates a certain degree of attraction among otherwise intelligent people?

Certainly, from a domestic point of view, Communism has proved a failure. After 50 years of complete power, the system has produced wonders in the military field and in heavy industry, but very little, if anything, in the way of improving the lot of her citizens. Everywhere Communism has been tried as an economic system, it has failed. The dreams of the revolutionaries have turned to nightmares. Communism has not lived up to a single promise put forth in the early and formative days of the revolution.

It is doubtful that Russia could ever have survived as a nation, or Communism as a system, without continued aid from despised capitalistic sources. Her financial record is deplorable.

In 1917, when the Revolution proved to be successful, the Bolsheviks repudiated all debts and claims against the Czarist regime, and confiscated all property owned by foreigners. Russia was then the most heavily indebted nation in the world. Her national debt was around $20 billion.

In 1923 and 1924, when Russia was literally starving to death, the American Relief Administration, under Herbert Hoover, distributed more than $63 million in food to the wretched people. This had an enormous effect on Russia's prestige throughout the world and made her survival possible.

During the first Five-Year Plan, beginning in 1928, America trained Russian engineers in U.S. schools and factories, and sent teams of experts to Russia to build the enormous industrial complexes which are now referred to by Moscow as "glorious examples of Socialist building". These complexes include the famous Dnieper Dam and hydroelectric plant; the largest steel works in the country; the largest motor-vehicle plant; the largest tractor factory, and others.

231

As we have seen, immediately after World War II Russia received more than $11 billion in Lend Lease aid. This was in addition to half a million trucks; 2,000 locomotives and 3 million tons of petroleum products. This has never been repaid.

Moreover, Russia systematically looted every country she occupied. She shipped whole factories and plants back to Russia. Although she was engaged in "war" against Japan for only six days, she stole a billion dollars worth of industrial equipment from that country and sent it back home.

Not content with that, the Russians asked the U.S., after peace was declared, for a $6 billion reconstruction loan. U.S. Secretary of the Treasury, Henry Morgenthau, actually advised President Roosevelt to increase the loan to $10 billion. The negotiations eventually fell through, so the United States made a flat contribution of $2.7 billion for Russian rehabilitation. Other capitalist countries added another billion dollars to the kitty. This helped rebuild Russia's war machine.

In 1964, Canada sold the Russians $500 million worth of wheat to help stave off another nationwide famine. In the previous year, the United States authorized the sale of $250 million worth of wheat and flour for the same reason. The collectivization of agriculture was showing its customary inability to produce and the people, once more, were hungry.

As these words are being written Russia is once again making the rounds of the capitalist capitals seeking loans and technical aid in order to modernize her industry and bolster her failing agriculture!

The truth of the matter is that Communism cannot even feed its own people. There cannot be a more basic failure than that.

How can people still believe in it?

Even more puzzling, how can intelligent people believe it can be fruitful to negotiate with Communism, make treaties or arrive at mutually beneficial international accommodations? The Communist world has been in moral bankruptcy for years.

It is estimated that since the Revolution of 1917, Soviet Russia has entered into 169 major international treaties, and has

232

violated every one of them. Lenin, as a matter of fact, made it a part of Communist doctrine that international agreements were to be considered only as a means of permitting Russia to gain a breathing period, and were to be broken, like eggs, whenever Russia's self-interest seemed to require it.

The Soviet Government is officially godless. It does not operate under a code of ethics like those which motivate and moderate the nations of the free world. They have no intention of keeping their word unless it suits Russia's purpose to keep it.

How can a western nation hope to do business with any nation governed without moral principles?

In Viet Nam in 1966 Communist soldiers were captured with documents on their persons, telling them that even if a cease-fire were to be declared, to pay no attention to it but to push on resolutely, taking advantage of the relaxation of American vigilance. This, in a nutshell, epitomizes the Russian approach to any agreement.

But, despite the fact that these grievous shortcomings are well-known to thinking persons in every land, the Communist world conspiracy has never lacked for fervent apostles in every land under the sun.

Men and women by the thousands have ruined their lives in a free society, and even thrown their lives away, in order to be of service to the slave society. A Communist spy ring handed over atomic secrets to Moscow in 1949 and made it possible for the Russians to build an atomic bomb at least 10 years before any reasonable expectation. Spies, *agents provocuteurs,* saboteurs and assassins are constantly at work for the Communist cause in every corner of the earth.

Despite the fact that it so obviously does not work, Communism has been able to produce its own martyrs to an extent paralleled in history only by Christianity. (Of course, it can be argued that Christianity doesn't work, either.)

The Communist conspiracy has perpetrated throughout the world a monstrous fraud, so gigantic in scale that few people have thought of challenging it. They have spread the propaganda

233

for half a century that they were determined to build upon this earth a classless society of world-wide scope in which all peoples will be equal in a utopian Communist world government. She never had such an intention. The society she has built is even more class conscious than was the world of the Czars. She has never shown the slightest intention of treating her satellites as equals. The function of the satellites is to pour their treasure and their produce into an overall effort to make Russia great, and to pour their young men into Communist-inspired wars. The Russian propagandists delight in demagoguing about "American colonialism", an obvious bit of nonsense, while they themselves follow the most arrant and brutal colonial policy ever known to man.

Persecution of the Jews has been a Communist policy in Russia, just as it was under Hitler's Nazi regime. The Russians haven't gone as far as creating gas ovens, but they have filled Siberia with Jewish victims who die more slowly, and perhaps less mercifully, than did the murdered people of Auschwitz. The Jews have made a convenient whipping boy on which to blame Communist failures, but the cause of the persecution goes deeper than that. The Jews are *international* by nature. Most of them cannot be, and can never be, totally *Russian* in their thinking or in their loyalties, any more than they can be totally French, or totally British or totally American. Therefore Russia suppresses them. One would think that Communism would welcome and encourage people with international leanings, if it were truly interested in creating an international society. But it isn't interested in this. It is interested only in building an omnipotent Russian society. Internationalists are an embarrassment inside Russia, though the Communists encourage them outside Russia. Anything that vitiates nationalism abroad indirectly strengthens Russia's own imperialistic aims.

In view of the foregoing, it is amazing to find so many Jews in countries outside Russia, still practising, defending and working for Communism. A surprising number of convicted Communist spies and traitors have been Jewish.

234

The agitation throughout the world against the U.S. effort in Viet Nam is a case very much in point. In every country, and in particular in the United States itself, misguided souls are making heroes of the Viet Cong and the North Viet Namese and painting the United States troops as imperialist monsters. People who are presumed to be intelligent are swallowing and disseminating Communist propaganda without question, and refusing to believe anything emanating from official sources in the United States. Never does one hear these agitators express dismay or concern about the hundreds of thousands of atrocities the Communist Viet Namese have perpetrated against their non-Communist fellow countrymen. Never does one hear a word of sorrow for the innocent babies slaughtered by Communist guerillas who have wiped out entire families, and even entire villages. All the sorrow is reserved for a handful of Communist non-combatants who have been killed. One can feel sorrow for the victims of any war, but compassion, if it is genuine, should be universal and not confined only to just one class of victims.

Certainly no one argues for a moment that capitalism is a perfect economic system. It is, after all, a human product and is therefore flawed. It has its faults and its injustices, but far fewer of them than does Communism.

The Russian leaders have seemed to realize this over the years. That is one reason why they discourage Russians from travelling in western lands. If Russians could compare the two systems, they would be extremely impatient of Communism!

A certain type of human being who fails to achieve what he thinks is his due under the capitalistic system, turns away from it in blind rage and frustration and embraces Communism uncritically, unquestioningly. He never stops to consider that under Communism he will never in all the world achieve what he thinks is his due. Communism is his means of striking back against a world he never made, of lashing out at the Establishment which has denied him the recognition he thinks he should have received.

It is a mean and degraded reaction but, I suppose, a very human one. The puzzling thing is that it should be so widespread. It is most disturbing to find so many men and women who are so disappointed in finding capitalism short of perfection that they are willing to devote their lives to an economic and social theory that is so demonstrably more imperfect.

The imperfections of Communism would not be so disturbing to us if the Russians were not so insistent upon exporting those imperfections and making them universal. No one in the free world would seriously object if the Russian leaders insisted upon their own wrong-headed theories, but restricted their application to their own people. The greatest trouble in our beleaguered world is Russia's dialectic insistence upon the false logic of the Comintern principle: that the Capitalistic world is her natural enemy, and that Marxist practice must be imposed, by force of arms, by treachery, by stealth, by deceit and subversion upon every nation on the earth.

Ironically enough, Communism in Russia would be dead today if the capitalistic nations had not periodically come to the aid of the Russian government and people and bailed them out with money, material and technical assistance. Russia has accepted these gifts without thanks, and once she has found her feet again, she has continued the same old game of subversion and treachery.

After fifty years, at long last, the patience and gullibility of the West are wearing thin. Western nations, particularly the United States, have in the past been moved by philanthropic instincts, to come to the aid of the Russian people. The Capitalists are far more interested in the welfare of the Russian people than is the Russian government, which considers its subjects not as precious human souls, but as mere bullets in a worldwide ideological warfare.

Some theologians maintain that the Devil roams the world seeking the destruction of souls, hoping passionately to make them as degraded as he is himself. Soviet Russia can be viewed as an extension of the theologians' devil. She will apparently

236

never be satisfied until all peoples everywhere are as degraded and as miserable as those who live under her own iron, sterile hand.

There are indications that the Russian Communist influence is abating throughout the world. Orthodox Communist Parties in the West are suffering from attrition. After fifty years Communism is beginning to show its age. To the young rebels of the West, it is old hat. The new breed of rebels doesn't approve of capitalism, but they seem to view Communism with equal derision and disfavor, and reject out of hand the dull, grey, monolithic, regimented imitation of life which Communism is trying to impose on humankind. The young rebel of today is inclined to be anarchistic. He considers Communism as a rather more dreary "establishment" ideology, interesting only in that any seeming espousal of its principles irritates his elders so grievously.

The new generation of western youthful rebels is suspicious of anyone older than thirty years of age. Communist society is so hierarchial in its structure that there are virtually no young leaders. The leaders, almost always, are middle-aged men and women who have come up "through the chairs" and have survived the machinations of their rivals. Such leaders have little charm for the young rebels of today.

Communism's attraction for the young rebel has been diminished, in short, because it has achieved a certain amount of spurious success through force of arms. With the young, success, limited as it has been, has been Communism's ruin. With the new breed of rebel, nothing succeeds like failure. It is only when Communism's bankruptcy becomes apparent, as in Viet Nam, that the young western rebel is moved to evince localized sympathy.

This is not said in an effort to induce complacency. Far from it. The Russian propagandists are no doubt struggling with the problem of making their ideology more attractive to the new generation.

And, despite the recent recession of Russian Communism's influence beyond its own borders, the desire to subjugate the rest of the world remains undiminished among the leaders of the Russian State. If Russia, for example, were ever to win the battle for the moon, and control of outer space, she would be able to dominate the earth completely, and force her will upon all nations through sheer terror.

Then, all peoples would starve as her people have starved, and there would be no more capitalistic nations to rush to her aid in times of disaster.

XII

THE UNITED STATES
OF AMERICA

THE UNITED STATES is the youngest of all the major nations of the world, but it is by far the oldest of all the current democracies.

As a young nation America has unparalleled vigor, unparalleled enthusiasm, unparalleled philanthropic instincts, but also unparalleled *naiveté,* in her dealing with other nations. As a country in which democracy has been an extraordinary success, she has been consistently overly-enthusiastic about spreading her concept of government into other parts of the world which often are not temperamentally or ethnically equipped to make a success of democracy.

Constantijn Huygens, the Dutch savant, once said to his *patron,* William of Orange, late in the 17th Century:

"Every country has its own needs and its own ways of doing things, and it is foolish to try to foist a foreign system onto it. He who can gather figs and olives in the fields of the Low Countries can bring the Italian mode of living among us."

It is just as difficult to export the American way of life to other countries as it was to export the Italian ways of life to the Netherlands 300 years ago.

American salesmanship, or missionary zeal (which is the obverse side of the same coin) has caused resentment in many parts of the world in the past, and is still causing resentment today. It causes more resentment through its successes than it does through its failures.

The average American, including those in the very highest places of her government, instinctively feels that if all nations could behave as his nation behaves, then most of the troubles of the world would blow away. He fails to see that the particular form of Republican government which the Founding Fathers devised for his own country was, and is, unique, and uniquely suitable for his fellow countrymen. There is no evidence whatsoever to substantiate the assertion that the North American brand of democracy would work any better in Latin lands, in Oriental lands, or in nations that are predominantly Slavic, Scandinavian, Gallic, Teutonic or, especially, African, than Christianity has worked. It is a specialized form of government suitable for a special kind of people, and is not particularly exportable. I have a suspicion that, like many light wines, American-style democracy does not travel very well.

As we have observed, the United States came into the Big Power game late, and rather reluctantly. She could have become a major international power any time after her settlement of the Civil War, but she held back and let the British enforce their own *Pax Anglicana* everywhere except in the western hemisphere. In 1913, when Woodrow Wilson became President, and when Europe was obviously trembling on the precipice of total world war, he appointed William Jennings Bryan, a pacifist, an isolationist and an obvious incompetent in international matters, as his Secretary of State. It was not until two years later that the United States began to realize, slowly and painfully, that her ultimate prosperity and survival at that point in history depended upon her involvement in the world outside her borders.

In her search for her "manifest destiny", America had spasms of international aggression just like any other nation of the time. She bullied Mexico in the approved 19th Century manner and took from her Texas and other sections of the Southwest, as well as California. In the last years of the 19th Century she entered a

240

needless war with Spain and, through it, acquired the Philippines and Cuba. Unlike other "imperialistic" nations, she almost immediately showed embarrassment at her possessions and had very little idea of what to do with them.

Hot-headed Cuban Communists and Philippine patriots scream about American imperialism, secure in the knowledge that their followers know nothing about the facts of the American occupation. Some exploitation went on, it is true, but not nearly to the same extent as that which went on in British colonies, or, especially, in French, German, Dutch, Portuguese or Spanish colonies. And, unlike other colonial nations, America got rid of her "colonies" as fast as she decently could, without coercion or threats of secession, or fear of international disapproval. Indeed, it may be argued that she granted independence to Cuba and the Philippines too hastily. Neither nation has shown much talent for self-government since it became a sovereign state.

Unlike all other nations in recorded history, the United States has been remarkably benevolent toward those whom she has conquered. She has been unique in her generosity toward the vanquished, often treating defeated nations with more consideration than she has treated her allies. Whenever she has won a war, the yeast of the old Christian conscience has gone to work and the American Government has tried to work as a social worker among its former enemies.

The most obvious blots on the record of American benevolence toward defeated enemies concern her treatment of those within her own borders. Despite the intentions of the martyred Abraham Lincoln and of his successor in the Presidency, Andrew Johnson, the radical Republicans of post-Civil War days behaved with great vindictiveness against the South during the days of "Reconstruction". And, of course, the American treatment of the vanquished Red Indian, has been worse than shameful. If any other nation in the world (Russia excepted) were treating a defeated nation as callously as America, to this day, is treating the red men from whom she stole her land in the first

241

place, resolutions would be pouring out of the Congress like a Niagara, sanctions would be proposed, and irresistible pressures would be applied.

I mention these *lacunae* in the ethical pattern of America lest anyone think that I am blind to the faults of this great and beneficent nation. America has her faults, like every other nation, and some of them are grievous, but, on balance, I feel she has fewer faults than any other country in the world, and she has unique virtues which cause her to tower over other nations to an extent unprecedented in recent recorded history.

Certainly the economic development of the United States has been unparalleled. The fledgling nation declared its independence from the England of King George III in 1776, but it cannot be said that it became a nation until 1789, a bare 178 years ago.

In the eighteenth century, European observers gave the new nation little chance for survival. The distances were so great, the communications so primitive, the population so scattered that dissensions, regional jealousies and general lack of interest in the isolated central government would certainly combine to tear the youthful country apart. In addition, the United States had adopted a radical, republican form of government unlike any other in previous history. Europe smiled indulgently and waited for the young nation to come apart at the seams and eventually crawl, gratefully and penitently, back into the womb of the Mother Country.

Of course, nothing like this happened. The United States prospered, survived the most harrowing internal turmoils and grew to the point where she was decisive in the first World War in saving old Mother Europe from ruin, and in World War II in saving her from slavery. She then went on to save Europe from starvation and total degradation.

Today this nation of heterogeneous races and widely divergent heritages stands astride the world like a benevolent, if somewhat clumsy Colossus. She has more than 190 million people living on 3,615,211 square miles of territory. She leads the world in every area of meaningful production. She has achieved the highest standard of living in the history of mankind. In 1965, her production workers averaged, in wages, $2.63 an hour, a sum that would be considered princely in any other nation of the world. Her workmen eat and live and save better than do executives in many other nations of the world.

The postal volume is one of the most accurate of all barometers of the health of a nation's economy. The annual postal volume in the United States is approximately 80 billion pieces, more than the volume of all the other nations in the world put together. The volume increases by 3 billion pieces a year. This annual increase is greater than the total volume of many European nations.

There is only one dark cloud on the horizon of this remarkable nation. Because she has attempted to carry out an impossible mission of acting as policeman and benefactor for the entire world, and at the same time to perfect a social program on the domestic front on a scale unapproached by any other country in history, her gold reserves have dwindled dramatically. In 1959, the gold reserves of the U.S. were worth $17.9 billion, or 44% of the world total. Five years later, the gold reserves had dropped to $14.1 billion, or only 33% of the world total. This is certainly an indication that the United States, as great and as powerful as she is, has bitten off more than even she can chew and must begin to become more selective in her national and international goals if she is to survive her own beneficence. The gold reserves are still dropping to the consternation of her dependent nations.

The truth of the matter is that, despite her wealth and her resources, the United States is in trouble.

The trouble is not insoluble, but it is potentially serious, and it stems from America's almost limitless idealism and her unquenchable donative instinct.

America has plunged into the international power business with the enthusiasm that has characterized her activities in every other field, from industry to missionary activities, to sports. She has adopted the role of world policeman with the vigour of a hyperthyroid games mistress, blowing her whistle and explaining the rules to people who have been playing the game, albeit with relative inefficiency, since before she was born.

She has adopted the role of Lady Bountiful, much to her credit, scattering her benevolence with an open hand to friend and foe alike, to the impoverishment of her domestic programmes. But perhaps in her eagerness to get things done, she has neglected the ceremonies of subservience which older nations demand of their benefactors.

She has unselfishly undertaken to protect the sovereignty of little nations, like South Korea and South Viet Nam, when the other large nations preferred to turn their backs. Instead of instilling confidence and hope throughout the civilized, western world, she has engendered hatred and suspicion of her motives. She has also given rise to unrest within her own borders through her support of unpopular causes in distant lands.

What boots it if the Americans win South Viet Nam and lose Detroit?

As rich as the United States is, it does not have enough money to accomplish its international *and* its national goals. There is not so much money in all the world. If she is going to succeed she must curb her impulsive eleemosynary activities in the international field, and concentrate on creating a paradise within her own borders before trying to make that paradise universal.

The Russian critics of the Soviet Revolution held the same sensible view and were exterminated as counter-revolutionists. In the United States the State Department's doctrinaire internationalists depend upon the word rather than upon the sword. Their spokesmen label such opponents as "isolationists" or "reactionaries", and the Washington press corps picks up the refrain. The mild oppositionist eventually finds himself labeled and libeled forever after as a small-brained, small-souled parochial nonentity. When international affairs are discussed in Washington, Truth is mute and sits in the Visitors' Gallery.

As 1967 nears its end, let us consider where the United States stands.

A stupid and unnecessary war has been temporarily concluded in the Middle East. The Arabs hate the United States and blame their defeat on her "intervention", a palpable lie promulgated by the Cairo radio which is the illegitimate father of many lies, but is still believed by those who want to believe falsehood. And yet the Israelis, of all people, excoriate the United States because she did *not* play a more active part in supporting her war.

In their irritation, the Israelis cold-bloodedly and without warning attacked an American communications ship, causing great damage and killing 34 American young men. Jewish pressure in the United States reduced official indignation to a minimum. It was a case of the State Department (but not the Defense Department, which was overruled) saying "Boys will be boys! Too bad about those youngsters being killed, but that's the way the bagel crumbles." If the attack had been made by Arab forces, of course, the reaction would have been quite different and quite violent. The demands for blood and retribution would have rent the skies and the cry throughout America would have been "On to Cairo!"

The Soviets, who help nobody but themselves, sit by, chuckling at the American ineptitude. The Russian Ambassador to France was quoted recently in *Le Nouvel Observateur* as follows:

"The diplomatic and political battle we are going to wage at the side of the Arabs . . . will be very hard. We will blackmail the Americans with respect to their oil interests and their shipping in the Suez Canal. . . We will lead an incessant propaganda campaign among the young generations of Arabs against the cowards, the opportunists and the collaborators of the Anglo-Americans. . ."

In other words, the Russians are playing their own game of inspiring unreasoned hatred against the United States, without committing a single soldier to the effort.

The Arabs are inefficient and disorganized and badly-led, but they outnumber the Israelis by 15 to 1 and they fully intend to return to the battle as soon as they regroup their forces. When they do so, it is hoped that the United States will remember that the Israelis dislike Americans as much as the Arabs do, and will recall the brutal sneak attack on the U.S. communications ship, and the 34 American sailors murdered, before she embarks on any painful adventure in a totally unrewarding theatre of war.

In Europe, matters are even worse. The dominant but distressingly paranoid European figure, Charles de Gaulle, has evidently declared a personal war on both the U.S. and Britain. He has insanely decided that these two former allies, and the saviours of the country he now rules, are his real enemy, while Russia is his friend. He has even tried to arrange for French oil interests to be given the right to appropriate Anglo-American holdings in Arab nations. This would amount to outright theft, since the French did absolutely nothing to develop the oil fields and, if the Americans and, to a lesser extent, the British, had not explored and produced, these oil fields would still be sterile desert lands. If the Arabs ever were to accede to this French pressure, the United States would be justified in breaking off diplomatic relations with France. But, of course, it won't.

De Gaulle has ruptured NATO and has impoverished the German-American alliance. He is rallying the rest of the world against the British and the Americans. So crazy and reprehensible has this old man become that he violated all traditions of hospitality in Canada in July 1967, by inciting the French-Canadian citizens of Quebec to revolt against their own Government. To Canada's great credit, Prime Minister Lester Pearson politely maneuvered him out of the country.

The American effort in Viet Nam is a noble effort to preserve the integrity of a small embattled nation against Communist aggression. It is also a long-term attempt to halt a Communist sweep across the entire South Pacific, which would engulf Australia, New Zealand, Japan, the Philippines, South Korea, Laos and other nations important to the future of the free world.

America stands almost alone in this massive and unselfish effort. She has more than 300,000 young men engaged in this dirty little war. South Viet Nam, with a population of 17 million, has only 700,000 troops, and most of them are in non-combat areas. America gets precious little help from the nations she is striving to preserve and, indeed is much criticized for her efforts.

One would think that the small nations of the world would take heart in the fact that here is the most powerful country in the world spending her treasure and the flower of her youth to preserve the freedom of a little nation which could never be of any real importance to her welfare. One would think that the other small nations of the world would be encouraged by this example and support the American ideal in the belief that if they ever would be threatened, America would come to their aid, also. But no, the small nations who *should* be impressed and grateful, are the most spiteful and the first to scream imprecations at American imperialism!

What in God's name is imperialistic about America's activity in South Viet Nam? What can she *possibly* gain except the right of self-determination for the South Viet Namese people? She has nothing to gain except the preservation of her honour as the protector of the freedom of the weak, and she has a great, great deal to lose.

In her many years of power the United States could have seized many territories which would have enriched her, and she scrupulously has refrained from doing so. What could she possibly want *now* with an impoverished, unproductive little hell hole like South Viet Nam?

The American effort in Viet Nam is the most totally unselfish national military effort in my own memory, and, I am sure, there is none more unselfish in the history of humankind. Yet, it has been widely and maliciously misinterpreted everywhere in the free world, and even by a noisy minority in America itself.

It would serve the rest of the free world right if America were to pull up stakes and leave Viet Nam for the Russian Communists and the Chinese Communists to fight over, perhaps to the death. It would be rough on the South Viet Namese, of course, and it would be rough on the rest of Asia but it would give these carping and unco-operative nations their very just deserts.

Certainly, I feel, the United States should either win the war or abandon it. Without recourse to nuclear devices, the U.S. could win the war in Viet Nam in six weeks by bombing North Viet Namese military targets wherever they are found, and by destroying the harbour at Haiphong. She has refrained from doing so mostly through humanitarian reasons, preferring to sacrifice her own soldiers rather than kill North Viet Namese civilians. This is ethically admirable, of course, but it is practically foolish. The U.S. could end it all in a short while and then concentrate on spending her money on her own domestic programmes, from the war on poverty to the development of a modern postal system and an adequate ground transportation system. She could concentrate on purifying her polluted air and waters, and on raising the standard of living of her own people.

But, if she did this, she would incur the criticism of lesser nations who are willing to do almost nothing either for their own citizens or for their international neighbors. And, the adolescent instincts of the United States rebel at this prospect. She must be *loved* by all, or she suffers. She cares greatly about how others feel about her instead of capitalizing on her strength, and making others care greatly about how she feels about them.

How much better it would be if the United States would recede from her position of wet-nurse and banker for the world for a while, and make the other nations come to her as suppliants. She would earn respect, save herself billions of dollars in wasted money, and accomplish a great deal more for her own people.

It is quite understandable that Americans might tell me, a Chinese Jamaican, that it is none of my business how she spends her money, how she dissipates her funds, how she distributes her largesse. Basically, they are right. It *is* none of my business how Americans spend their own money, except—and a very large *except* it is—that the United States has assumed the role of leader of the free world and has insisted upon certain prerogatives as a result of that assumption of leadership. I, a Jamaicain, am a member of the free world. Therefore I have a stake in the role of leadership that America has insisted on assuming. I am passionately devoted to the cause of individual freedom and America is the only hope in all the world for its ultimate preservation.

The United States has done much with her expenditure of money abroad, but her enthusiasm and haste and sentimentality have made the expenditure far less effective than it should be. The indiscriminating generosity has produced envy, hatred, suspicion and raw antagonism everywhere where the people's dollars have been poured out.

At home, despite its affluence and incredible prosperity, America has serious troubles of her own. Her waters are polluted mainly because of her industrial complex, to such an extent that by the year 2,000 there will not be enough fresh water to sustain the population, unless there is a major breakthrough, technologically and politically, which would clean up the rivers and the lakes, and build enough dams of the right size and type to preserve the integrity of her waters, and enough desalination plants to utilize sea water significantly.

In most urban areas, America is running out of breathable air. In such an affluent society, the automobile has become king, and the exhaust pipes of the eight-cylinder monsters are vomiting death into the atmosphere. The affluent society is becoming the effluent society. It cannot even take care of its own garbage and trash. The fumes from garbage dumps are poisoning the air of countless communities and the government has no idea how to take care of the problem without visiting upon the citizenry more and more of the same.

And, with all its richness, America is experiencing an armed rebellion by certain activist elements among its negro minority which threatens to split the nation. Great cities like Detroit (which has for 25 years been a model of fairness toward minority groups) are being burned almost to the ground by mindless illiterates spurred on by conscience-less *agents provoca-*

teurs who are (in all probability) financed and instructed by the Communist conspiracy.

After more than twenty years of trying, urgently and sincerely trying, the United States of America is in a mess, both at home and abroad. With all her money and power she cannot keep peace in the world, keep peace within her own borders, and still develop to optimum strength her own economy.

Grateful as I am to America for her unprecedented generosity toward less fortunate peoples, I must, as a businessman, suggest strongly that she take care of first things first. In other words, she should concentrate for a while on putting her own neglected house in order before rearranging the furniture in other houses. If America were to collapse, financially, politically or militarily, the rest of the free world would collapse with her and the ruin of the West would be universal. It is imperative for the preservation of world freedom that America should concentrate on shoring up her own foundations instead of trying to shore up the foundations of distant nations which have doubtful intentions and impeachable ideals.

The domestic tranquility of the United States has recently been shattered by a shocking series of race riots in which savage mobs of negroes have brutalized whole sections of great cities. The riots, which in some cities, such as Detroit and Newark, approached total civil war, were put down with remarkable restraint. If the American police were half as brutal as the negro agitators say they are, the casualties would have numbered in the tens of thousands. If such an outburst were to occur in Soviet Russia, the corpses of the rioters would have been piled along the gutters in cords, like firewood.

The negro has cause to be resentful of the history of his race in the United States. Slavery, the "peculiar institution" of the Southern States, was a shocking episode in the development of the nation. It went on far too long. It brutalized its victims and degraded those who indulged in the trade.

Slavery was officially outlawed more than 100 years ago. Unsavoury vestiges of the practice persisted in some areas of the deep South and, if given the chance, would persist to this day.

But, in recent years, the white people of America have bent over backwards to make amends. They have poured out their money and employed their most fertile brains in a massive effort to help the negro help himself. There are still some areas of the sociological pattern of the States in which the negro has cause to feel resentment, but they are not nearly serious enough to have caused the violence which has plagued the great cities in the past few years. Those who rioted represented a minority of the total negro community and they included, by and large, the ruffian element who cannot, or will not, be helped by any programme of education or training.

Every nation on earth has a history of persecuting its recognizable minorities, and the United States is no exception. When the Chinese first came to the West Coast, to help build the western section of the transcontinental railroad, they were abused and insulted because they were regarded as cheap competitive labor. Riots occurred in San Francisco and injustices were perpetrated, but the Chinese remained and endured and, eventually prospered. They earned the respect of the community, and some of San Francisco's most treasured citizens are Chinese. The city even has a Chinese postmaster.

The Irish also had their troubles. Nativist thugs and Protestant bigots persecuted them for their religion, burned down convents and churches, stoned priests and nuns to death. The Irish fought back and overcame their tormentors. They ended up seizing, through lawful methods, political control of the communities in which they were so widely abused.

The Italians, the Poles and the Latin Americans have all, in varying degrees, had cause for serious complaint at their treatment but endured and lived to see better days.

None of these minority groups was given anything like the help that the negro has been given. Their assimilation took place long before the day of billion-dollar social programs. They helped themselves and they helped each other and they carved their niche in American life the hard way.

251

Over the years, negro leadership has been deficient. The negro press, which could have been an enormous force for good, has been shoddy, destructive and often venal. Talented negroes who have made a success in the white man's world—doctors, lawyers, scientists, merchants—have shown more inclination to maintain their fingerhold in the white society than they have to go back and work among and help their own people.

The negro population of the United States—roughly 13 percent of the whole—has suffered mightily from this power vacuum at the top. Into the vacuum have rushed the loud-mouthed irresponsible firebrands, the professional agitators, the Communist *agents provocateurs*, the demagogues who preach hatred, rapine, murder and black power.

Even those leaders who began their careers as responsible men, like Nobel Prize winner Martin Luther King, have shown alarming tendencies toward extremism when they felt they were losing their influence among their followers. The most reponsible and moderate of all negro leaders, Roy Wilkins, of the National Association for the Advancement of Colored People, has been shunted aside and ignored by the wave of hysteria that has engulfed the noisiest elements in the negro community.

It is my opinion that the American political leadership has been far too indulgent toward this irresponsible negro leadership. It is unfair to the responsible negroes, who make up the vast majority of the community, and are injured by the excesses of the firebrand minority. If a white demagogue were to make the same kind of anti-negro inflammatory speeches that the black demagogues make against the whites he would be pounced upon by the Federal authorities and led away to durance vile. The white power structure lets the negro agitator get away with it, and the negroes regard this as proof of the white man's weakness. Thus far, "whitey's" restraint has merely encouraged the negro demagogue to even more criminal excesses.

Some of the indulgence toward the negro has been caused by a feeling of guilt and compassion among American leaders, but far too much of it has been inspired by the crassest kind of

252

political considerations. Millions of negroes have migrated northward from the deep South and have clustered in the big northern cities. In many of these cities they now hold the balance of political power, especially as white urban dwellers have foolishly moved out of the cities, abandoning them to negroes rather than running the "risk" of living next to them. More than any other segment of the American populace, negroes vote as a bloc, pretty much the way their leaders tell them to vote. Since control of the big city vote is essential to the success of the Democratic Party in America, the negro has been courted by Democratic politicians to an almost painful degree. More than 90% of the negro voters in America are Democrats.

I would not dream of setting myself up as an expert in American politics, but it does seem to me that this gambit of over-indulging the wrong kind of negro has backfired. The population of America is still 87% non-negro, and the non-negro is showing ample evidence of the fact that he is sick and tired of being threatened and bullied by an irresponsible minority among the negroes. They demand more aggressive protection from their political leaders and, if they do not get it, they will make their anger known at the polls.

Ironically enough, the Democrats seem to get little or no thanks from the new breed of negro leader. Lyndon Johnson, for either compassionate or political reasons, has tried to do more for the negro than any other President in American history, with the exception of Abraham Lincoln. Yet, in Detroit, in New York, in Newark, in Atlanta, in San Francisco and in scores of other American cities, negro demagogues have called him the vilest of names while their supporters cheered themselves hoarse.

In Washington, D.C. recently, less than a mile away from the White House, a negro firebrand, out on bail that morning on charges of inciting a riot, illuminated his hour of freedom by calling Lyndon Johnson, a "mad, wild dog" and an "outlaw" and urged his cheering audience to burn down the city and shoot their white "oppressors". The police shrugged their shoulders

253

and contented themselves merely with keeping reasonable order among the natives.

It could well be that in the 1968 elections the negro will desert the Democratic Party either by boycotting the elections entirely, or by forming a splinter party of their own. It should be remembered that the only negro U.S. Senator, and the first member of his race to be elected to the Senate since reconstruction days, is the brilliant and outstanding Edward Brooke, a Republican who is eminently reasonable on racial matters. The new breed of negro leaders level violent verbal attacks upon any member of their race who makes a success in the white world. All such successful negroes are labeled as "Uncle Toms."

The negro unrest in the United States has got out of hand, and will continue out of hand, unless stern counter-measures are undertaken. No nation should be subjected to the kind of disorder that has paralyzed and terrorized the cities of America, the most powerful nation in the world, in recent years. It is obvious that these riots have been well-planned and have been synchronized by central planners, probably agents of the Communist conspiracy. Riots must be put down with sufficient severity to discourage their occurrence elsewhere, and the principals responsible for them should be hunted down and punished expeditiously and severely, through due process of law. The Federal Government must make it clear to the irresponsible elements that it will stand no more nonsense from black or white citizens.

During the past 10 years the Federal Government has spent approximately $300 billion on programmes to benefit the poor, the unemployed, the ignorant, the ill. Most of that money has been spent on the negro population, but the more the money has been spent, the more the rioting grew. Detroit has received $100 million in six years for its urban renewal program—building better living quarters for the poor, and especially for the negroes —and this is where the riots were worst.

Too many negroes have been told by their demagogues that they "deserve" everything their hearts desire and there is no need for them to work to earn the luxuries of life. One of the leaders of the Detroit riot said that the widespread looting was planned and encouraged so that "his people" could steal and take away items which they could not afford to buy, such as colour television sets! He regarded it as inherently right for the negroes to do this. It did not seem important to him that millions of white and negro Americans, hard working and responsible, cannot afford colour television sets, but have no intention of breaking windows and stealing them out of stores.

For too long negro demagogues have been telling the most volatile and least responsible elements of their people that all their troubles are caused by imaginary injustices perpetrated by the white men. Most of the injustices never existed but, no matter!, it gives the ne'er do well an excuse for his inherent inadequacy and a "justification" for committing wholesale theft.

This kind of gravely reprehensible teaching must be counteracted. The young negro is being told that he "deserves" executive jobs with executive salaries, without having had the education necessary for such advancement, or without having the sense of responsibility which must accompany executive position.

America, to a great extent, is in danger of being spoiled by its own success. Her technological advances have made life remarkably easy for many of her citizens, and, as a result, fewer and fewer Americans are willing to work hard to achieve an improved standard of living. Too many Americans of every ethnic strain are mesmerized by the "easy way" to gain success. This is apparent in almost every field of endeavour.

Work is indispensable to the individual and to the nation. Man needs it, not only for his economic and artistic success but for the preservation of his personal integrity. America's success, the most astonishing success of any nation on the face of the world, was built on a prodigious national talent for hard work. If she throws away this priceless heritage upon the altar of limitless welfare programmes, limitless give-away schemes, limitless plans for withering away incentives, she will lose her positon of dominance among the countries of the world and become once

255

again a second class nation. She could even become a vanquished nation.

Americans must realize that there is not—and never was—any such thing as a free lunch. Everything we get in life must be earned and paid for in one way or another. Nothing, *but nothing,* is given us free of charge.

The negro, especially, must learn this truth.

The vast majority of negroes in America are decent, hard working, middle class people who have made their way in the white man's world, often against stupefying odds. They know that conditions are far, far better than they were when they were young. They are proud of what they have achieved through hard work and intelligence, and they resent the mindless violence and unreasoning uproar caused by the least intelligent element of their race.

The riots in 1966 and 1967 took place in *negro* sections of American cities. The negroes burned up their own homes and the homes of their more affluent negro neighbors. The riots were a protest, but were masochistic in their effect. They did harm only to the negro communities and to certain white merchants who did business in those negro communities. The white man was not severely injured by the riots, the negro was. The white man will be hurt by having to direct his tax money to the reconstruction of the burned-out areas. The negro must find a place to live, a place to buy food, a place to work, a place to eat. He is the real sufferer from the intemperance of his own people. What sense is there in that?

The demagogues who preach the doctrine of total war against the white man, usually issue their preachments from localities far removed from where the shooting is likely to take place. They are ideological hit-and-run artists more interested in stirring up strife than in participating in it. They have done an immense amount of harm to the middle class negro, and have exploited the lowest classes of negro to a point where they have, under the power of emotional stimuli occasionally become less than human in their brutality and viciousness.

256

The fact of the matter is the United States is in trouble because she has undertaken an impossible mission. With the typical vigor and impatience that have characterized her entire history, she has tried to do everything on a global scale and on the domestic scene, all at once. She has shown little talent for selectivity in choosing her goals. She has often seemed unable to distinguish between goals of total significance, and goals of secondary or even doubtful significance.

She has shown immaturity in her eagerness to do good wherever good can be done. She has also shown an expensive and unwise tendency to over-react to international situations of relatively minor importance.

This tendency to over-reaction comes from inexperience. The United States is new at the international power business. She has a lot to learn. She is inclined to consider as incipient catastrophes incidents which other, more experienced nations would regard as merely routine.

The average American in his private affairs is a pragmatist, but he is also suspicious and impatient of long drawn-out solutions. He is a go-getter and he wants to see results, fast. This quality serves him well in the commercial world, but it is not necessarily an advantage in the world of international affairs where quick solutions are not often available and, when they are available, are inclined to be dangerous.

The foreign aid program of the United States has been less of a success than it should have been because it has been conducted on an emotional crisis-basis, almost on a year-to-year basis, without an overall plan and without even well-defined goals. American leaders talk more about the necessity of "stopping Communism in its tracks" than they talk about the need for building up the social and economic structures of the lands that they help. The only permanent way to stop Communism is to make certain of the social and economic development of those lands most susceptible to Communist doctrines.

Certainly the United States has been unwise in its haste to combat Communism by giving massive military aid to impover-

257

ished countries which need butter more than they need guns. This short-sighted panic-button type of operation has had some grim results, as in 1965 when Pakistan and India started warring with each other, each side employing American-manufactured tanks. The ironic result was that Soviet Russia, presumably the target for the military build-up in both countries, had the pleasure of acting as mediator, and brought about the peace.

As great and strong as America is, it is not omnipotent. Lots of things are going to happen in the world which America does not want or like to happen, and Americans must get used to this fact. The future turn of events in Latin America, Cuba, Europe and the Middle East will be determined by the people and their leaders in those countries and not by politicians and bureaucrats in Washington, D.C. Washington may influence events by creating favourable conditions in other nations, but it cannot expect to make final determinations.

America occupies a position of power and influence in the world unparalleled in all history. She has used that power and influence with unprecedented generosity, though her wisdom has not always matched her magnanimity.

But now she must learn to exercise restraint on her own almost limitless energies. She must learn to practise a greater selectivity, to choose her major goals and concentrate only on what is most worthwhile.

She has permitted unscrupulous leaders of small nations to blackmail her into almost foolish open-handedness with the threat that unless large sums of money are forthcoming, the leaders will seek help and comfort from Soviet Russia. American leadership takes such threats with far too much seriousness, and Soviet Russia is increasingly less eager to engage in the game of buying dubious and expensive friendships. Soviet Russia demands a strict *quid pro quo* when she assists another nation, and she selects her goals with great care and forethought. The United States must learn to do likewise, or she will find herself in dangerous economic straits, and with little return for her extravagant philanthropies.

258

This is not to say that America should turn completely inward and revert to isolationism. This would be impossible, no matter what the ultra-conservatives may say. She lost her international virginity in World War II and, like all virginity, it is unreclaimable.

But, having lost her virginity, America should not continue to cling so tenaciously to her innocence! She should not insist that she can exorcise all the devils and democratize every corner of the earth, and concentrate more on how to live at peace within a world full of diversity and among nations less idealistic than she.

Ronald Steel, in his fine book, *Pax Americana* argues that intervention in the affairs of other nations is a fact of major power relationships, but it should be subordinated to "clear and attainable purposes". Otherwise, he says, "It is likely to become an end in itself, dragging the nation down a path it never intended to follow, toward a goal it may find repugnant."

The United States, in short, has abandoned pragmatism in its approach to world affairs, and has embraced certain idealistic abstractions. It has permitted its sense of mission to obscure its sense of national interest. This, as Mr. Steel points out, is trapping the nation into new involvements in order to reinforce old involvements which have become less and less useful to it.

Certainly, if I were President of the United States and were seeking "clear and attainable purposes" I would seriously consider abandoning all, or almost all, the eleemosynary adventures of the United States in Europe, Africa and Asia and concentrate on making a paradise on earth in the western hemisphere, i.e. in the United States, in the West Indies, and in all of Latin America. The United States has done more than enough for Europe, and has received little thanks for it. She has put Europe back on her feet. Now she should let Europe walk by herself. She has also done more than enough for Africa and should move away from that unrewarding continent. If Soviet Russia chooses to pour aid into emerging African countries, what of it? The effort will only weaken Russia without significantly strengthening Africa. It is my guess that if America were to stop involving herself in

African affairs, Russia would soon be happy to abandon the effort also.

The money that is now being spent so freely in other continents could be spent much more satisfactorily on the American continent, raising the standards of living to unprecedented and undreamed-of-heights, abolishing ignorance and poverty, driving disease to the wall, creating new industries and developing new skills, elevating personal incomes.

It has always been surprising to me, an outsider, that America should go meekly along with lesser nations who demand loans without any strings attached. This, in my opinion, is madness. The American people have every right to insist upon knowing to what uses their money will be put, and to make certain that it goes to those for whom it is intended and is not appropriated by the politicians.

Latin America is the sleeping giant of the modern world, and its proprietors, both in the State and the Church, are quite content to let it sleep. The southern half of the western hemisphere has almost limitless untapped natural resources and an almost limitless potential for wealth. If the United States would concentrate its aid programmes in this area, making certain that the money and the technical assistance are used for the betterment of the masses and not for the enrichment of the already rich oligarchs, she could make Mexico and Central and South America as well as the Caribbean nations, significant factors in world affairs.

And, if some nations insist that supervision of the spending of U.S. funds amounts to an intolerable interference with their internal affairs, then it would seem a simple matter to withdraw offers of assistance and spend the money elsewhere. The recalcitrant nations would soon be begging for aid—on American terms.

I have always thought the Monroe Doctrine an admirable document, and I feel it should be unwrapped, dusted off, re-defined and reactivated. The best security the U.S.A. can obtain is through building up the strength and the friendship of her neighbours, and by keeping hostile foreign elements at bay.

This is a policy that the rest of the world would understand, since it would be based on enlightened self-interest. It would be far less costly than the present scatter-gun dispersal of funds in every corner of the earth, and it would earn respect and a certain amount of healthy apprehension throughout the rest of the world.

The United States State Department is a peculiar institution. Partially because of the dominance of Rhodes Scholars in policy making positions, its programmes have been aimed at Europe and at traditional centers of European colonial power, while the needs of Latin America have been sadly neglected. She has given Latin America lip-service through such programmes as the Kennedy-inspired Alliance for Freedom, but, comparatively, very little solid assistance. The money and the technical assistance have flown to the glamour-spots of the world, while Latin America has been taken for granted. Intelligent Latin-Americans, quite naturally, resent this and are inclined to become less and less sympathetic with North American goals.

There is a curious sidelight, incidently, to the history of the Rhodes Scholarships. When he was still an undergraduate at Oriel College, Oxford, Cecil Rhodes composed his first will, leaving his money "to and for the establishment, promotion and development of a Secret Society, the true aim and object whereof shall be the extension of British rule throughout the world . . . the ultimate recovery of the United States of America as an integral part of the British Empire. . ." Age and experience tempered his opinions considerably, but not entirely. There are times when the Rhodes Scholars in the State Department act as if this original will were still in effect and they were, in truth, members of a Secret Society dedicated to the spread and perpetuation of British rule throughout the world.

The great need for U.S. foreign aid is in Latin America. Most Latin American nations today are natural targets for Communist propaganda. The average native knows nothing about Marxist

261

principles or any of the fine points of Communist doctrine, but if the agitators preach land reform to them, they understand and enthusiastically applaud. In a nation like Chile, for instance, more than 90 percent of the arable land is owned by less than 10 percent of the people. It is obviously simple to gain sympathy for a program of land reform in such a situation as this.

In little El Salvador, the Church authorities were forbidden by the ruling families, to build and operate schools for the education of the peasants. Education, it was argued, would only give the peasants "ideas" and would make them dissatisfied with their pitifully low wages.

Many rich Latin Americans maintain extensive Swiss bank accounts and keep some travelling bags packed so they can make a quick getaway in case of a serious uprising of the masses. They have no real interest in their country or in their countrymen who are so very much less fortunate than they, except for purposes of exploitation. It would never occur to them to try to attack the causes of the dissatisfaction of the poor and to seek to raise their level of living, or improve their standards of education. When trouble strikes they can be expected to skip the country hastily and live abroad as rich expatriates to spend the rest of their days bemoaning the ingratitude of the common people who were so rude to them.

The United States, for her own good and for the good of all humanity, should concentrate on improving the social and economic conditions of Latin America, despite the hostility and objections of the oligarchs. If she does not concentrate her efforts in this direction, she will awake one day to find Latin America a Communist empire with an anti-American posture similar to that of Castro's Cuba. A situation such as this would represent a very real and present danger to American safety, prosperity and even its sovereignty. *It could be avoided by an intelligent concentration of effort now!*

And of course the United States should concentrate to a much greater extent on building up the economy of the Caribbean nations that are her true friends.

Naturally enough, such a plan, if it were to be successful, would necessitate an early cessation of hostilities in Viet Nam. Even the United States is not rich enough to spend $40 billion a year on this embarrassing little war and still expect to keep progressive domestic programs operating and, in addition, to pour aid and treasure into every indigent, semi-indigent and non-indigent corner of the world.

It is perfectly absurd that the United States should demean herself by wrestling around in the mud with a third class power, with her right hand tied behind her back. She could well take a page out of the book of the Israelis: hit hard and decisively and swiftly, and let world opinion make the best of it that it can.

I see no reason why the United States should be so overpoweringly sensitive to the opinions of the rest of the world. Russia shows no such sensitivity, and appeals to world opinion only when she sees an opportunity to embarrass the U.S.A. She uses the United Nations as a *maison de convenance,* with the ineffable Secretary-General, U Thant, as the ever-pliable Madam.

U Thant makes a great show of being an impartial and objective man of peace, but he has never found it in his heart to utter a serious word in criticism of the U.S.S.R., or a serious word in support of the U.S.A.

The United Nations serves a purpose, no doubt, in that it sometimes keeps entangled nations talking instead of shooting, but the United States takes it far too seriously. The U.N. is very much like one of those ridiculous fraternal organizations in which the whole purpose of being seems to be the enrichment and enactment of its rituals. It has proved itself just as inept and powerless in serious situations as did the late and unlamented League of Nations.

The rules by which the U.N. governs its affairs preclude any reasonable solution of its problems. It may be theoretically very fine and democratic to give such nations as Gambia, Tanzania and Upper Volta a vote equal in effect to the vote of the United States or of Russia, but it is a practical absurdity. The delegations from many of the new nations consist of young, inexperienced, uninformed, and sometimes venal, persons who should be in school instead of trying to participate in serious discussions conducted by grown-up nations. It is as if the Vatican were to decide that the cause of ecumenism could best be served by conducting dialogues with the African Castor Oil Dead Church, or the Bed Bug Church, mentioned earlier, with the same seriousness as that with which she conducts dialogues with Methodists, Lutherans and Episcopalians.

The United States should treat the United Nations like the interesting debating society it is, with politeness, but with no great seriousness. She should insist on all participating members paying their dues, instead of footing most of the bill herself. And she should allow herself to be ruled by the decisions of the U.N. only when it suits her purpose to be so ruled.

It should be clear from what I have said that I am pro-American. I am, whole-heartedly. I wish all Americans loved their own country as much as I do. If I were an American I would be so proud of my country that I would be eager to do battle with anyone who dared to denigrate her. I quite understand that it is "square" to be pro-American in these parlous days. It is unspeakable in Europe; it is hardly respectable in Latin America. Beyond the Iron Curtain it is a political offense, and in the United States itself it is almost a matter of embarrassment.

Americans are such critics of their own country, and of their own way of life, that they forget that they constitute the greatest and most productive nation in all the world, capable of developing the greatest degree of happiness among their own conglomerate people. Alone among all peoples, the Americans seem intent on seeing the beam in their own eyes, and only the mote in the eyes of others.

America is the only major country in the world where a man, even a foreigner, can start with nothing and through hard work and honest means make something important of himself. This is still true, of course, in some of the developing countries which will be the giants of tomorrow, like Canada and Australia, but nowhere is it as true as it is in the United States.

And yet, among most Americans, patriotism has become "corny" and brings an embarrassed blush to their cheeks. Americans have had the cultural "superiority" of other lands drummed into them for so many generations; they have been treated condescendingly by Englishmen and Europeans for so many years, that they have almost instinctively accepted the fact that they really are culturally inferior to the products of older naions. In theatre, in music, the dance, painting, *haute couture* and many other allied areas American opinion-makers subserviently crook their knee and make obeisance to all cultures but their own.

In the early 19th Century the brilliant and witty Sydney Smith asked contemptuously: "Who reads an American book?" It would have been far better for England, and for France and for the rest of Europe if more people on that side of the Atlantic did read American books at that time. Some excellent books were being written and they revealed national yearnings and aspirations which, if better understood by Europeans, could have helped to shape the course of future events in a more intelligent pattern. (De Tocqueville *did* read American books and was impressed by them. He saw the greatness in the skull and in the bone structure of the nation; most Europeans then and now content themselves with examining only the skin.)

The same complacency in Europe predominates today. American books and plays are admired only if they are bitterly critical of American *mores* and American political institutions. The same is true of American painting and sculpture. If an American playwright with the genius of Shakespeare were to write a great pro-American play, it would be torn to shreds by critics on both sides of the Atlantic.

It is true that American culture derives from the culture of older lands, and once was dependent on these cultures, but this is no longer a fact, and in most of the arts, America today is far

265

more culturally alive and creative than the whole continents of Europe and Asia combined.

Many Europeans are aware of this condition and are jealous of it. Too many Americans are not aware of it at all, and still look slavishly to Europe for the approval they do not need.

I would like to make an observation in another field which, if not allied to the arts, is allied closely to the development of civilization: viticulture.

California produces some wines which are equal to all but the very best of the wines of France, and superior to most of the run of the vineyard, adulterated drivel that France exports at fancy prices to the United States. There are no *Romanée Contés* produced in California, of course and none of the *Montrachet,* but there is very little of these noble products produced in France, either—and precious little of the best is allowed to cross the Atlantic ocean. The average French imported red Burgundy of Bordeaux is inferior to the California products of the Inglenook and Louis Martini vineyards in California; and very few French white wines can touch the excellence of those of the Wente Brothers. The Korbel people in California make champagne equal in quality to all but the very best French product. And there are some small, experimental wineries on the west coast which are producing vintages which would be respected anywhere in the world.

But, outside of California itself, Americans are so bemused by the European cachet that they pay three times as much for a European wine of inferior quality than they would pay for a superior California wine.

I mention this only as an example of how Americans are hesitant to take pride in certain of their own products, and how they are inclined to accept uncritically the poorest products of Mother Europe. They lack faith in their own greatness.

This same unsureness of their own excellence has invaded almost every aspect of American life, and especially the arena of world politics. Never before in history has a nation exhibited such enormous muscle, and never before has a nation been so apologetic for flexing that muscle.

After World War II American power poured over the earth. American arms protected the entire West from Soviet agression. American money saved whole continents from starvation. The United States which had for so long hesitated on the brink between isolationism and internationalism, had suddenly become ubiquitous and omnipotent. It was instant empire.

And what an empire! She never combined her power with authority, her strength with power. The nations whom she saved cursed her because she had the power and the will to save them. This made little difference. She persisted in her salvatory efforts.

The envious intransigence of the rest of the world has turned most of America's international dreams into dust.

In Europe, a silly, super-annuated General has wrecked the North Atlantic Treaty Organization and rendered it almost useless.

The "special arrangement" with Great Britain has withered away until it has degenerated into little more than an amiable exchange of platitudes.

The *Pax Americana* in the Far East has blown up in her face, so much so that she is burdened with a hideous war which has caused the rest of the world to vilify her.

All the attempts of the U.S.A. to aid Latin America have been derided because the Latins feel they are too little and too late. They have brought about riots, insults, animosities.

Most of America's troubles with the rest of the world stem from her efforts to be fair to everyone. This has not set well with nations which have sought to be treated with unfair partiality, or who wish to have their competitors unfairly discriminated against. America has made herself incomprehensible to the rest of the world by applying moral principles to her international postures. Her impeccable motives make a strange contrast to the age-old policy of Great Britain: "No lasting friends; no lasting enemies; only interests." The policies of America in the world have their faults, but they are vastly preferable to the bloodless, amoral cynicism of older, fading lands.

Europeans become furious when they consider what they call the "Americanization" of their countrymen. This attitude is stupefying. Nobody is forcing American products on them. It just so happens that America produces most of the things in the world that make life simpler, easier and more enjoyable, and she sells them at attractive prices.

It is unrealistic to expect middle-class European housewives to continue to wash their family clothes by hand when an American washing machine can do it better and with far less effort. It is stupid to expect English households to rely on iceless "coolers" for the preservation of their food-stuffs, or to expect Englishmen to continue to drink their whisky and their beer warm, when American refrigerators are available. It is not to be expected that Europeans in search of a non-alcoholic drink should insist upon the disgustingly sweet fruit "squashes" manufactured in their own lands, when Coca Cola is being offered at competitive prices.

What Europe needs is more Americanization, not less. She needs to adopt the American talent for hard work and for bold planning. She needs a massive injection of American morality in dealing with other peoples. She needs an enormous transfusion of America's red blood and vigour to counteract the cancer of her own decadence. She needs more of America's courage and more of her restraint and patience in the face of insult. She needs a great deal of America's forward look, and far less of her own dependence on a fading past.

There is no reason for Americans to feel apologetic about their role in world affairs. They should feel proud. They have a right to be prouder than the citizens of any other nation on the face of the earth.

Every American should feel eight feet tall in the presence of others. He should feel impervious to the envy of those who have not their heart and vigor, and have not the will or the capability for assuming gigantic responsibilities and for undertaking gigantic tasks.

And, above all, Americans should take stock of their resources and reassess their goals and determine to distribute their largesse only to those who are deserving of it. They should mix with their unparalleled generosity a strong element of enlightened self-interest.

Whether Europe and Asia like it or not, the entire future of the world depends upon the maintenance of America's strength. It is necessary for the freedom of the human race that this enormous strength not be dissipated in unworthy causes.

XIII
L'ENVOI

MOTH: Is not l'envoy a *salve?*

ARMADO: No, page: it is an epilogue or discourse, to make plain
Some obscure precedence that hath tofore been sain.

Shakespeare: Love's Labour's Lost III/i

IT SHOULD BE CLEAR to anyone who has read thus far in this book, that I, Patrick Chung, detest Communism, and all it stands for. I have tried to express my repugnance in moderate terms, as a kind of running theme throughout the various Chapters, without becoming too strident on the subject. To me, the deficiencies and the constant failures of Communism are so apparent that it is an insult to the intelligence to belabour the point.

But, unfortunately, too many nations of the free world, and particularly that keystone of the free world, the United States of America, have exhibited a disturbing ambivalence toward Soviet Russia. They have opposed the international conspiracy only sporadically when Russian aggression has become overtly dangerous to world freedom but, when the heat has subsided, they have flirted with the Soviets in the vain and deluded hope that the Kremlin will change its baleful purpose.

The western world has always had a deep-seated distrust of Russia. "They of Muscovy ben devyls", the ancient chronicler

271

said, and he knew whereof he spoke. When the decadent rule of the Czars was overthrown, and the Communists inherited the land, the militant attitudes of the new regime threw the western world into a panic. In the United States and elsewhere, vigilante groups took violent action against any individual, or any group of individuals who were suspected of having a Communist taint.

Then, during the 1920's, when it became apparent that the experiment was not working out, and when Russians were starving because of the inefficiency of their government, world opinion changed. As long as they were demonstrably inefficient and helpless, the Russians were sentimentally embraced by the capitalistic world. The U.S.A. sent millions upon millions of dollars worth of aid, which saved lives and also permitted the conspiracy to survive.

During the Great Depression, when so many people lost faith in the capitalistic system, Communism became almost respectable in even the most exalted circles. American Communists were able to infiltrate high positions in the Government (even in the U. S. Treasury and State Departments), and were honoured guests at the White House.

A brief reaction set in during the late 1930's when Stalin teamed up with Hitler and the victory of totalitarianism over freedom in World War II seemed almost a certainty.

Then came the break between the two dictators. Russia overnight became our ally, and in England and the U.S.A., the vicious and unprincipled Stalin became "Uncle Joe", the smiling, benevolent, although somewhat difficult, leader of a valiant people.

The war ended, and the Russian bear showed its fangs and claws. The heartless depradations of undefended nations mentioned earlier took place, and the free world once again began to clutch its heart in fear. Through almost incredible carelessness and treachery within the free world (particularly in Great Britain), Russia was enabled to unlock the secrets of atomic power with a purloined key, and thus threaten the freedom, and even the very existence, of the West.

Now the pendulum is swinging back again. Communist China has shown herself to be so insanely and irresponsibly hostile toward the West, that Russia, by comparison, seems reasonably respectable. There is widespread talk about Russia once more being our ally against the common foe, Red China.

Nobody has yet called Kosygin "Uncle Aleksei", but this is only because (1) he is not a particularly charismatic personality, and, (2) nobody can pronounce his name that well. But certainly after the "summit meeting" at Glassboro, a small town in New Jersey, Americans, in their wishful thinking, became almost unbearably sentimental about the Russians and indulged in absurd hopes for a permanent peaceful arrangement between the free world and the slave world.

I find this vacillation immature and disturbing. It leads me to believe that despite all that has been written and said about the Communist conspiracy, too few people in the free world really understand it or appreciate its enormity.

Americans, particularly, are hopelessly optimistic. They are inclined to be generous and decent in their own reactions and foolishly believe that everyone else will behave in the same high-minded way. We Chinese have been around a great deal longer, and, for better or for worse, we have learned the arts of skepticism. We learned these arts in a very demanding school, the school of survival against enormous odds.

So, I would like to state a few home truths about Soviet Russia and the Communist Conspiracy.

(1) *The Russian claim that Communism aims at a world revolution designed for the betterment of all mankind is a propaganda lie.*

In every country in the world members of the Communist Parties have stood shoulder to shoulder and sung the *"Internationale"*:

" 'Tis the final conflict
Let each stand in his place
The International shall be the human race."

273

Poor deluded souls, they have accepted this falsehood as gospel! They have repeated it so often they have lost the ability to question it critically.

The truth is that Communism, as practised by the Kremlin, is totally *nationalistic*. It is a *Russian* conspiracy designed to benefit, not the world, but Russia, and Russia alone.

Every land that Russia has invaded and turned into a Communist satellite has been denuded of its riches, stripped of its industrial potential, robbed of its agricultural produce, and everything of value has been shipped back to Russia. Everything has been done to enrich Russia and impoverish her satellites.

This has hapened in Hungary, Czechoslovakia, East Germany and everywhere else the hammer and sickle dominate. There has been no question of "partnership" with Russia in a stateless, international world; the satellite nations have become helpless captives chained to the wheels of the Russian chariot.

Communism has never been willingly accepted by any population in any nation in the world, not even in Russia. There is not a nation in the Communist orbit that would not shake the dust of Communism off its shoes if only it had the strengh and the power to do so (or the shoes!). There is not a satellite nation in the world in which Communism is not imposed upon the people through force of arms.

Those who know Communism best detest it the most. Communism is popular only among fuzzy-minded minorities in western nations who have never been subjected to it, who never have had to live under it, and who remain impervious to reason or to factual information.

Communist agents encourage internationalism in other countries because this can weaken their resistance to Communism. The Communist leaders would never tolerate any internationalism within Russia itself. For this reason Jews are persecuted and Catholics have been eliminated, because their loyalties are suspected of being supranational.

(2) *There is no hope of ever entering into a meaningful*

treaty with Soviet Russia. Peaceful co-existence can never be achieved through negotiation.

When Adolf Hitler was first threatening the world, few people could be bothered to read *Mein Kampf*. Those who did read it, refused to believe it. It was far more comfortable *not* to believe it. So, Hitler followed the program laid out in *Mein Kampf*, chapter by chapter, almost page by page, and each move he made caught the rest of the world by surprise.

We are in danger of falling into the same trap in regard to Soviet Russia. Few of us have taken the trouble to read the pronouncements of the Communist leaders. And those of us who have taken the trouble find it more comfortable not to believe them.

This is insane. The Communist leaders, when they are talking Communist doctrine, mean precisely what they say, just as Hitler meant precisely what he said. The Communist leaders, whenever circumstances have permitted, have followed their doctrinal pronouncements almost slavishly.

Here is a sampler of Communist doctrinal pronouncements for the reader to ponder.

Trotzky (1914):

"The time for fireside politics is over. We are now in the phase of permanent revolution. It will go on, without interruption, until one side or the other is lying conquered on the ground."

Lenin (1920):

"Promises are like pie-crusts, made to be broken . . . Treaties are like egg-shells, made to be broken."

Radio Moscow (August 20, 1950):

"From the point of view of Communist morality, only those acts are moral which contribute to the building up of a new Communist society."

Khrushchev (1959):

"Communism will sooner or later rule the world. We live in the epoch of revolution."

275

George Dimitrov, Secretary General of the Communist International, to its Seventh Congress:

"We are sometimes accused of departing from our Communist principles. What stupidity! What blindness! We should not be Marxists and Leninist revolutionaries, not disciples of Marx, Engels, Lenin and Stalin, if we were not capable of completely altering our tactics and mode of action as circumstances may dictate. But all the ins and outs of our tactics are directed to a single end—the world revolution."

Khrushchev (1957):

"The Communists will destroy capitalism, not with nuclear weapons but through the spread of the ideology. We are as sure of this as we are sure the sun will rise tomorrow. *All we have to do is grease our ideology with butter.*"

Khrushchev (1959):

"We shall never forego our ideological principles. We are waging and shall wage an implacable struggle for the Marxist-Leninist ideology, for the triumph of the ideals of Communism."

Lenin (1921):

"First we shall take Eastern Europe, then the masses of Asia, then we shall encircle the United States, which will be the last bastion of capitalism. We will not have to attack. It will fall like an over-ripe fruit into our hands."

(Note: *Lenin did not even contemplate a peaceful victory, and his use of the first person possessive makes it quite clear that he was dreaming of a Russian-dominated world in which all other nations would be captives.*

Khrushchev (1956):

"We will bury you!"

Lenin (1919):

"It is necessary to resort to all sorts of stratagems, manoeuvres, illegal methods, to evasion and subterfuge, only so as to get into trade unions, to remain in them and carry on Communist work in them at all costs."

Molotov (1946):

"We are not fighting America *as yet*. But once we have deprived her of her markets, crisis will follow and cause confusion. After we have taken her markets in Europe, expelled her from Asia and elsewhere, she will have no market where she can dump her merchandise. She will curtail her production and then will follow unemployment. Our opportunity to square accounts with America will be at hand."

(Note: *This was immediately after World War II, in which Russia and America were beloved allies. The idea of "squaring accounts" is a sublimely ungrateful one, since America had twice saved Russia from almost total starvation, and had just recently saved her, through gifts and "loans" of money and material from being destroyed by Nazi Germany. It has never occurred to the Kremlin to "square accounts" by paying back to America the billions of dollars it owes her.*)

Lenin (1921):

"Communism and Capitalism cannot live in peace. In the end, one or the other will triumph."

Krushchev (1956):

"But, of course, we must realize that we cannot co-exist eternally. One of us must go to his grave. The Western powers don't want to go to their graves, either. So, what must be done? We must *push* them into their graves."

Manuilsky (1931):

"War to the hilt between Communism and Capitalism is inevitable. Today, of course, we are not strong enough to attack. Our time will come in twenty to thirty years. The bourgeoisie will have to be put to sleep, so we will begin by launching the most spectacular peace movement on record . . . The Capitalist countries, stupid and decadent, will rejoice to co-operate in their own destruction. They will leap at an-

277

other chance to be friends. As soon as their guard is down we shall smash them with our clenched fist . . ."

(Note: *The German attack upon Russia in World War II upset this timetable, but the same techniques are being used today.*)

These selections are gathered from an almost endless list. The important thing is that these are *ex cathedra* statements, statements of policy, and the policy has not changed one iota in fifty years. When Communists are talking policy, particularly when speaking to other Communists, there is never any talk of peaceful co-existence with the capitalist world, never any suggestion that the lion and the lamb may one day lie down in harmony together. The party line has been rigid and immutable: total victory over capitalism and freedom, with no concessions, no mercy, no adjustments, no conciliations.

Peaceful co-existence must be bi-lateral if it is to have any meaning. If the western world were to attempt co-existence on a uni-lateral plane, it would be overrun by Russian military brutality within two years.

When the free world talks about co-existence, it is speaking a different language than that which the Communists speak. There is almost no semantic accommodation between the two ideologies. When the Communists speak about "co-existence", they mean taking over all the real estate they can lay their hands on, using every means available, short of a nuclear war.

When they talk of peace, they mean the peace of the grave.

It is obvious that it is impossible to negotiate with a power that has no intention of operating in good faith. The quotations I have listed, and there are thousands of similar quotations available, indicate quite clearly that in the Communist decalogue, good faith is a grievous sin if Russian interests can be better served by bad faith.

How can there be co-existence when the Communists, by their own words, repeated endlessly over the past 50 years, insist that they are sworn to fight until Russia rules the world? How can there be co-existence when Russia interprets that word as meaning that she can spread her poison throughout the earth, subverting States and enslaving peoples, while denying the admission of even the most unavarnished truth within the meridians where she claims dominion?

An when we talk about co-existence, we must talk about trade. Every nation, and every individual, who trades with Communist Russia is helping to dig a grave for western democracy.

Lenin, Stalin, and Khrushchev have all predicted that capitalist greed could not resist the temptation of trading with Communist Russia, and this weakness would lead to the destruction of the western world. As Lenin said: "When the capitalist world starts to trade with us—on that day they will begin to finance their own destruction." Too many western nations are eager to gain ephemeral material profits even at the cost of endangering the ideological security of the entire world.

In our complex world, every commodity is part of the *materiel* of war. Russia has made no bones whatsoever about the fact that she is at war with us, irrevocably and permanently. It is madness to trade with her and supply her with the sinews which can give her the strength to destroy us.

Russia has broken every treaty she has made with capitalistic nations. Why should anyone believe that she will mend her ways and keep the most important of all treaties, which would create world peace, which she is ideologically committed to violate?

The world has grown so small that co-existence is equivalent to sharing the master bedroom together. There may be twin beds, but, still, a mutual amity must exist if the arrangement is to be viable. But, twin beds or no, who will share the master bedroom if one of the partners secretes a loaded revolver under the pillow and intends to use it as soon as the other falls asleep?

(3) *Red China is not the real enemy; Red Russia is.*

The western world has become more and more tolerant of Russian excesses because of even more extravagant Chinese excesses. This has led to a feeling that maybe Russia is all right, after all, the lesser of two evils, and that she may one day become our partner in an effort to subdue Red China.

This is nonsensical thinking. Red China is an abomination, but she is an inherently inefficient abomination. Her ideology is almost manically hostile, but there is precious little she can do about making it operative.

Certainly, Red China has the bomb, although the efficiency of her atomic capability is still suspect. She does not have the means of transporting the bomb where it can do the most harm, unless Russia gives her the means to do so.

As I have said earlier (Chapter II), China would lose a great deal of her uncompromising hostility and learn a great deal more about the rest of the world if she were permitted to join the United Nations. But, even lacking the civilizing effect that the United Nations might have upon Red China's leaders, there is no way that common sense and competence can be infused into her present leadership.

When anti-Communist Chinese left the mainland for Taiwan, most of the national competence left with them. The mainland Chinese may make all the hostile noises they want, but they still lack the competence to transport their hostility to where it can do the most damage. They have no air force, no navy, and no missiles.

Russia is now in the position of playing the free world (and particularly the United States) against Red China. Russia is quite content to supply the bullets, if Red China will fire them. If she can instigate an exhausting struggle between China and the rest of the world, she can then emerge, unscathed and un- wearied, much as America emerged after the end of World War II.

It is up to the free world to see that no *rapprochement* takes place between the two Communist powers. The present split must remain permanent. Surely this is not beyond the powers of di- plomacy backed by military persuasiveness?

It has aften come into my mind that it would be extremely wholesome if the United States were to get rid of the obligation of housing the United Nations in New York City.

280

The U.N. has become so overloaded with little, quarrelsome, inconvenient nations that it is quickly losing its ability to act as a responsible and meaningful agency. But that's a little beside the point. I, personally, would like to see the U.N. situated in Russia, where the delegates can see at first hand the drab, grey, lifeless existence that people live under Communism. When delegates talk in the sumptuous freedom of New York, they discuss Communism as a kind of theoretical abstraction. Most of the delegates from uncommitted nations know nothing about Communism at first hand, and lack practical experience of its deadening effect upon the human mind and the human heart, as well as the immortal soul. If they had a little personal experience of living in the prison camp environment that Communism imposes upon all who live under its jurisdiction, they would be far less tolerant of the ideology and of those nations that profess it.

At least the attempt should be made. It is most unlikely that Russia would permit such a move, because she does not want the embarrassment of a peaceable invasion by hordes of diplomats, who would be virtually uncontrollable by law, within her borders. It could be that such an invasion would impose upon Russia a necessity of liberalizing the deadening restrictions which are part and parcel of her everyday life and that would be intolerable.

If the United Nations were to set up shop in Moscow, the delegates, quite naturally, would want the courtesy of being permitted to roam at random, talking to whomever they pleased, visiting wherever the spirit listeth, just as they do in the United States. Russia would be in a dilemma. If the delegates were permitted this freedom (even perhaps to visit Siberia) they would learn the truth about Russian Communism. This would be inadmissible. If she refused to grant the delegates personal freedom while in Russia, this would be a dead giveaway, and would arouse the hostility of uncommitted delegations.

Russia may be able to fool small, selective groups of travellers who are guests within her borders for a short time, about the true facts of her closed society but she could never hide the truth

281

from national delegations stationed there on a more or less permanent basis.

Admitted, this plan would have been risky when the U.N. showed promise of meaning something in the world drive for peace, but now that it has degenerated into a rather ineffectual debating society (on a distressingly low intellectual level), the risk is almost non-existent.

The question is academic. Russia would never accept the challenge of being the permanent host to the U.N. But it would be most illuminating to review her excuses for not accepting such an honour, when proffered.

I cannot reiterate too vigorously the need to remember the soul-less, godless performance of Russia over the past fifty years. She has used every outbreak of "peace" as an interim in which she can regather her strength and marshal her forces for another outbreak of hostility in another direction. She has never willingly relinquished a square inch of territory she has inhabited; she has mouthed messages of peace for foreign consumption without ever applying such noble doctrines to herself; she has never freely released a single human being she has enslaved.

Democratic nations loathe war and will accept almost any fantasy to forestall it. The Comunist hierarchy does not feel the same way about war at all. They have contempt for human beings and consider them merely as shells in the ideological bombardment; they have nothing of the almost holy concern for human lives that the Christian-centered nations of the free world have in such abundance. They consider the Christians concern for human life as sentimental nonsense. Life is so much less desirable in the areas of Soviet slavery that it seems less worthy of preservation. Within the Communist hierarchy, of course, the struggle for world power is merely a gruesome chess game. The paunchy, middle-aged thugs in the Kremlin have no intention of ever hearing a shot fired in anger, and they are well insulated against the cries of agony which their relentless policies initiate, even if such cries were capable of moving them to a modicum of compassion.

282

The most oppressed and deprived person in Great Britain or America is better fed, better clothed, better housed, better treated, and enjoys far greater security than the average peasant living under the Russian Communist system. When hot-headed revolutionaries among dissident and dissatisfied groups in the western democracies claim otherwise, they are either lying or they are supremely deluded. If they are lying then they are trying to use the masses as a stepping-stone toward their own aggrandizement within the Communist Party. It is difficult to think of a more heartless practice of delusion. If only the masses would realize that these heartless demagogues are Judas Goats, leading them to their destruction! The provokers of riot, murder and pillage in the metropolitan centers of America, for example, will go to any length to avoid the contagion of reason and peace. Such a contagion would ruin them and destroy their ephemeral influence. The only way they can retain their place in the sun of disorder is to make certain that chaos remains a way of life.

During the 1930's the United States suffered the traumatic shock of a dark depression, which followed on the heels of almost unprecedented affluence. For the first time in American history the citizens of that country—almost one-third of them—went hungry and had great difficulty in keeping their families from starvation. This was before the time of massive Federal relief programmes, poverty programmes, rehabilitation programmes, food stamp programmes, and so forth. People were desperate and, above all, hungry.

But, during those years there was no example of undisciplined mobs ransacking and looting grocery stores, butcher shops and dairies in the search of something as basic as food.

During the past two years America has been plagued by widespread and dangerous rioting in its greatest cities. Mobs stormed into thousands of stores and cleaned the shelves of their merchandise. But, what were the articles they were seeking? Food? Milk? Clothing? Don't be "square". They were looting the stores of liquor, of narcotic drugs, and, (God save the mark!), of colour television sets!

283

Does there not seem to be signs of serious moral deterioration here?

When the operative word in a civilization becomes "gimme" then that civilization is on the materialistic skids and is on its way to oblivion.

And this brings me to the final points of this discourse with you.

At every hand today we hear men say that western civilization is on the way out, and that it will be given the *coup de grace* by World War III. For this reason they argue that it is better to be Red than dead.

In all humility, I would like to suggest that those who make this claim have no experience of either condition on which to base their opinion. I would also suggest that a craven pusillanimity before Communist aggression would also result in the end of western civilization, and on far less honourable terms.

Why do civilizations come into being? Why do they decline?

The process is never a swift one. It is never an instant evolution.

A civilization is, in essence, a body of ideas. It grows, like the chambered nautilus, bit by bit, chamber by chamber, and it deteriorates the same way. Historians are mad for dates, and they like to place convenient labels on the comings and goings of cultures and civilizations, empires and nations. But, while the outward manifestations of a given civilization may be destroyed in a single catastrophic battle on a given day in history, the process of deterioration leading up to the final catastrophe can always be found to have been continuing for a long while before the ultimate blow.

I happen to be far more interested in Man than I am in men. I am totally dedicated to the proposition that nothing but the individual exists, and that in the individual nothing exists but the individual. It is my firm belief that God made every man, in essence, a king and then left it up to each individual to prove himself. In an age of almost epidemic unbelief, I am unfashion-

284

able enough to know in my heart that the soul is the only reality, and that all else is chimerical.

This philosophy has been the very heart of western civilization. It reduced Government to the position of being the servant, not the master, of mankind. It cleansed mankind of its ancient, crippling fetishes. It excited man's sense of adventure and sent him pioneering into new worlds, on earth, in the skies, in the mind, in the heart.

It is, of course, the very antithesis of the philosophy promulgated by the leaders of Communism. Yet, to me, it is much more native to the human spirit than is the brutish philosophy of the slave State.

Unfortunately, there is evidence that western man is losing faith in his own philosophy. Leaders of thought in the western world are inclined to sneer at the concept of natural rights traceable only to God, because they deny the existence of a God. They argue that men are more important than Man, that the group is more important than the individual, that "society", acting through the State, is an entity in itself, independent of, and superior to its component parts. The individual, they claim, is a means, not an end.

Too many, far too many, of our spiritual, intellectual and political leaders today are merely blind tools of a ruinous development they do not understand. They have made a god of science and, through this, have enthroned materialism in a spurious kingdom of the mind. Science is very fine and essential to our progress and our survival, but without guidance by the spirit it does not create order out of chaos, it does just the opposite.

Materialism is corrosive to the spirit, and without the spirit there is no will. Materialism corrupts, and absolute materialism corrupts absolutely. The corrupt man is defenceless, for there is no reason for him to defend himself.

The more that this heretical doctrine of materialism spreads and is accepted, the more the chambers of our intricate and wonderful civilization deteriorate and disappear. If our world, as we know it, is destroyed by World War III (if there is such a catastrophe) it will be because we have liquidated the strength of our civilization through the moral and spiritual attrition that is taking place today. If our civilization cannot survive a war, it will be because there was nothing left of it to survive before the war took place.

The key to our civilization is the primacy of the individual. War is by nature an anti-social, anti-civilized, though sometimes necessary, condition. It reduces human beings to automatons; it discourages individualistic thought; it imposes herd living. Up until now, these impositions have been only temporary; our civilization has survived them and has recovered from them. If our civilization cannot survive or recover from the cataclysm of another war, no matter how universal it might be, it will be because its strength and reason for being have been sapped beforehand.

Even in the face of severe discouragement we must hold high the value of personal, human dignity. We must insist, in every way we can, every day we live, on Man's rightful place in the universe.

A war under the horrible conditions which man's inventiveness has made possible, would destroy most of the physical manifestations of our heritage. Our great buildings, our books, our music, and even the rituals of our religions might be obliterated. But some individuals and some things would escape and it is essential that among these persons it will still be remembered that once upon this earth there was a civilization built upon the primacy of the person, the faith of man in his God, and in himself, and that the elements of such a civilization must be reinstituted. War is to be avoided if at at all possible, but there are some things worse than war and slavery is one of them. Slavery of the soul is worse than death.

For those who cry "Better Red than Dead", the physical accoutrements of civilization are of paramount importance, and must be preserved even at the expense of the death of the spirit.

As for me, Patrick W. Chung, give me the spirit every time. It is the only reality, and it must be preserved even at the expense of everything else upon this earth. For the spirit is the only element upon earth that comes from God. All else merely comes from man himself.